AL-QAIDA, THE TRIBES, AND THE GOVERNMENT

Lessons and Prospects for Iraq's Unstable Triangle

NORMAN CIGAR

MIDDLE EAST STUDIES OCCASIONAL PAPERS

NUMBER TWO | SEPTEMBER 2011

Published by Books Express Publishing
Copyright © Books Express, 2012
ISBN 978-1-78039-667-5

Books Express publications are available from all good retail and online booksellers. For publishing proposals and direct ordering please contact us at: info@books-express.com

DEDICATION

This study is dedicated to my lovely daughter Mariam.

Acknowledgments

The author would like to express his gratitude to Ms. Stephanie Kramer and Ms. Andrea Connell for their expert help with editing and to Mr. Robert Kocher for layout and design. This study was prepared as part of the Minerva Research Initiative.

Executive Summary

Dealing with tribal systems has posed a continuing challenge to Al-Qaida as it operates in the Middle East and Africa, where a tribal environment is still an integral part of society in many of the countries. How Al-Qaida views and manages the tribal system within its individual areas of operation in many cases can mean the difference between success and failure, and the jihadist movement cannot ignore this issue, which has been a major factor affecting its prospects, especially in Iraq. This study examines Al-Qaida's experience dealing with the tribes in Iraq in terms of a triangular relationship involving the Sunni tribes, Al-Qaida, and the government (or the United States as the governing authority in the initial stages), with latter two entities often competing for the allegiance of the tribes.

As part of its anti-American insurgency in the Sunni areas, Al-Qaida's policy errors, characterized by an arrogant and uncompromising approach to tribal economic, social, and cultural interests, as well as the alienation of the existing tribal leadership, engendered considerable popular discontent and contributed to an eventual shifting of tribal alliances to the United States. The ensuing establishment of the Sahwa (Awakening) tribal forces and the combined campaign with U.S. and Iraqi government forces resulted in a major setback for Al-Qaida, both in terms of casualties and the abandonment of Al-Qaida by local allies. However, Al-Qaida was able to reassess and modify its policy, especially after the death of its field commander, Abu Musab Al-Zarqawi, in June 2006. Al-Qaida's new approach was characterized by an easing in of the implementation of strict Islamic practices, a reduced reliance on foreign personnel in leadership positions, a greater willingness to work with tribal leaders and to accept neutral tribes, and a more focused targeting to avoid collateral damage.

At the same time, growing friction developed between the heavily Shia Iraqi government and security establishment on the one hand, and the Sahwa and its Sunni tribal base on the other, especially after the transfer of security responsibility to the Iraqi government. Differences over late pay, alleged government harassment, and complaints of the government's failure to absorb Sahwa personnel into the security services and ministries as part of the planned demobilization of the Sahwa, have contributed to considerable friction between the tribes and the government, as well as to a weakening of the Sahwa. Al-Qaida has been able to exploit this new dynamic, resulting in a modest but disconcerting revival in its fortunes and contributing to continuing instability.

Al-Qaida's resurgence, despite its limitations, presents a continuing security challenge in Iraq, and the tribal factor remains a significant element in the security equation. To be sure, barring a disintegration of the current Iraqi government, it is highly unlikely that Al-Qaida would be able to seize control of any significant area, much less of the country, as the Iraqi state structure and the security apparatus have become sufficiently rooted and powerful to deal with such a threat. Rather, the greatest danger that Al-Qaida presents—as long as it can rely on sufficient support in the Sunni community and in particular among the Sunni tribes—resides in its ability to create chronic security problems. These problems could negatively affect stability and an already difficult economic situation and hinder national integration by heightening tensions between the Sunni community on the one hand, and the central government and the non-Sunni communities on the other.

Among the conclusions of the study are that Iraq's Sunni tribes remain an important element in the country's political life and in the security equation and will continue to be the major arena for Al-Qaida's recruitment efforts and operations. As such, it will be necessary for the Iraqi government to craft realistic and effective policies that will address the Sunni tribes in order to undercut tribal support for Al-Qaida if the latter is to be defeated decisively.

Second, as the Iraqi case shows, local resentment of Al-Qaida's cadres as foreigners can negatively impact the latter's effectiveness. Psychological operations and the crafting of inducements intended to highlight the gap between the local societal leaderships and populations and Al-Qaida's "foreign" character can be effective.

Third, despite its past failures with Iraq's tribes, Al-Qaida is an adaptive organization and has exhibited the ability to learn from experience. It has modified its approach at least sufficiently to place it in a position to try to take advantage of an evolving political situation and the emerging critical vulnerabilities that the situation presents.

Fourth, supporting proxy local forces in a counterinsurgency has consequences. The use of Iraq's tribes may have been a reasonable or even an unavoidable option at a particular juncture in time for an outside power in dealing with an insurgency. However, the encouragement of such local forces may lay the groundwork for longer-term consequences with which a local government will have to deal eventually, challenging the development of an emerging government's authority and possibly heightening the likelihood of future violence in the absence of effective demobilization strategies.

Fifth, it is possible, and vital, to shape Al-Qaida's operational environment, and deliberate actions by other players can make this environment either more benign or more difficult for the latter organization, which can make the difference between success or failure in the fight against Al-Qaida. Iraq's Sunni tribes, in a sense, are still an asset to be won over, wholly or in part, by either Al-Qaida or the government, and the results may hinge on an effective national political and economic integration of the Sunni community into the country's political system.

Sixth, an outside power's ability to shape the domestic social and political environment may be limited. While an external player such as the United States can advise and encourage both the Iraqi government and the Sunni tribal leadership, the effectiveness of such outside influence on shaping the domestic environment in which Al-Qaida operates may be limited—and increasingly so given the expected withdrawal of most of the U.S. military with a near-term horizon. Ultimately, the local players will have to bear the responsibility for finding a new power equilibrium between the Sunni tribes and the Iraqi government.

Contents

	Page
Introduction	xiii
Chapter 1: The Human Terrain: The Tribal Factor in Iraqi Society	1
Chapter 2: Al-Qaida Tackles the Tribes	5
Chapter 3: Al-Qaida Alienates the Tribes	9
Chapter 4: Mobilizing the Tribes Against Al-Qaida	23
Chapter 5: The U.S. Strategy Matures and the Awakening Develops	33
Chapter 6: The Shayks' Positions Assured	38
Chapter 7: The Tribal War Against Al-Qaida	44
Chapter 8: Al-Qaida Responds	48
Chapter 9: Al-Qaida Adapts	54
Chapter 10: The Tribes and the Iraqi Government: A Rocky Relationship	61
Chapter 11: The Evolving Tribal Environment	89
Chapter 12: Al-Qaida's Own Carrot-and-Stick Approach	100
Conclusions and Prospects	122
Notes	131
About the Author	207

Iraq and Vicinity

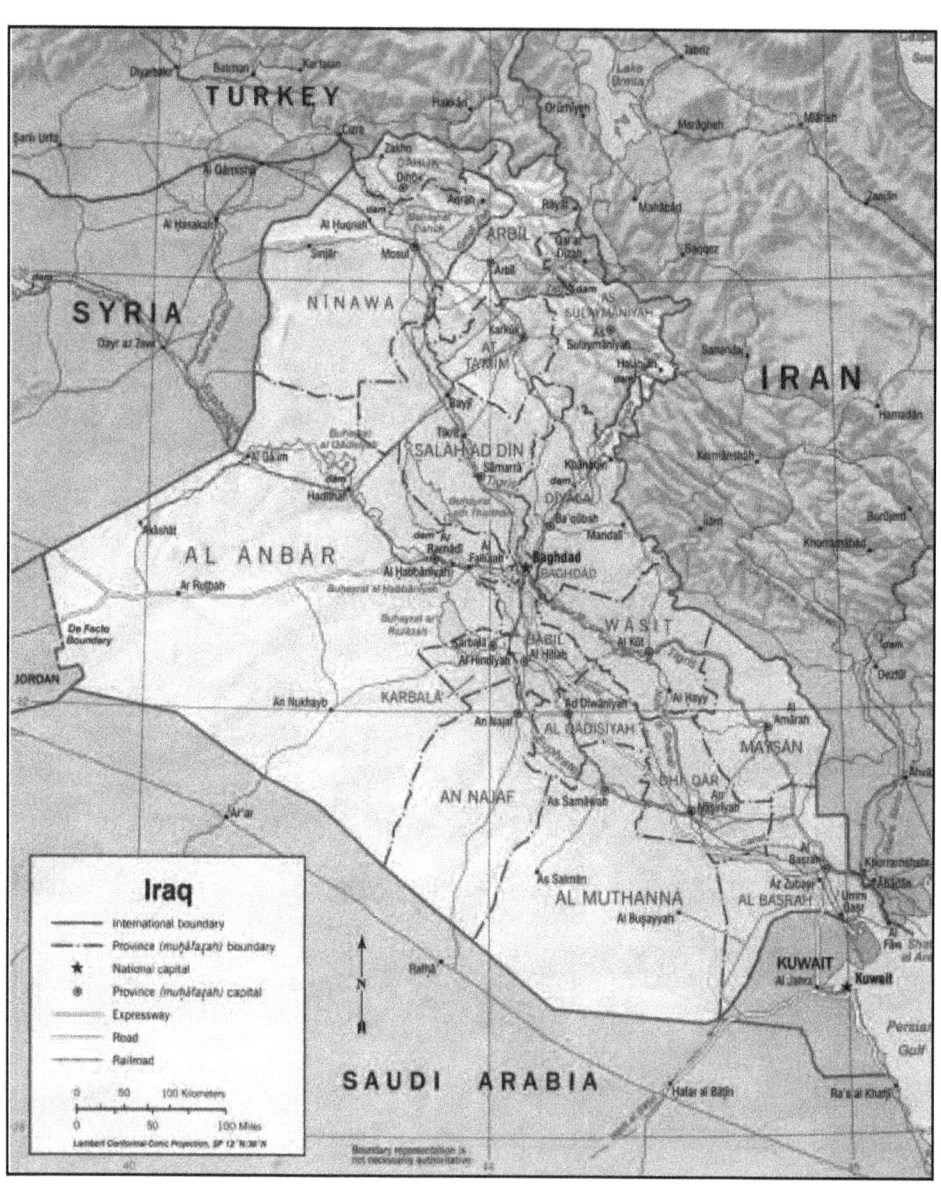

Iraq Majority Groups

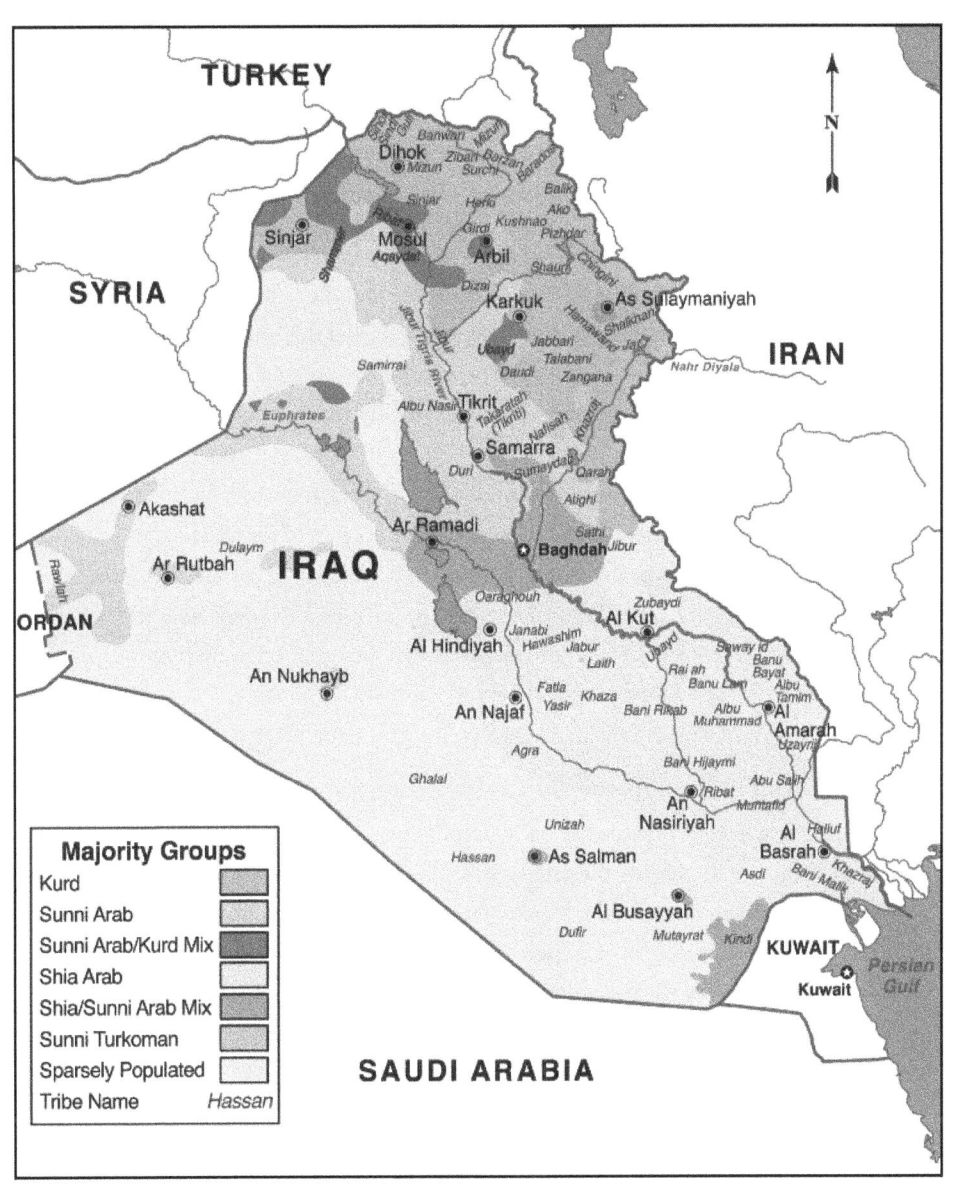

INTRODUCTION

Dealing with tribal systems has posed a continuing challenge to Al-Qaida as it operates in the Middle East and Africa, where a tribal environment is still an integral part of society in many of the countries. How Al-Qaida views and manages the tribal system within its individual areas of operation, in many cases, can mean the difference between success and failure. The jihadist movement cannot ignore this issue, which has been a major factor affecting its prospects, especially in Iraq.

Al-Qaida, in its campaign in post-Saddam Iraq, has had to deal with social realities as part of the human terrain that it has engaged, and the tribal sector represents the bulk of the rural and a sizeable portion even of the urban areas. Given the centrality of the tribes in the country's political and social life, Al-Qaida recognized that Iraq's Sunni tribes would be a critical factor in its overall strategy. However, interacting with the tribes has often proven frustrating and problematical for Al-Qaida and has necessitated adaptation and a rethinking of its basic assumptions and approach to the issue over time. The thesis of this study is that, after painful lessons on the ground, Al-Qaida has sought to learn and to adapt its universalist Islamic ideology to local social and political realities. The organization has progressively adopted a more pragmatic approach toward the tribal factor, although such an approach cannot completely escape its central ideological assumptions and limitations.

One can view Iraq's tribes as the basic population pool over which Al-Qaida and the government (whether the Iraqi government or, earlier, the U.S. governing authority) have competed. The tribes, however, are far from an inert actor. Rather, they are players with their own interests, objectives, and strategies, and a force that also interacts and seeks to manipulate the other actors, thus forming an unstable triangular relationship.

In many ways, at least at the operational level, Al-Qaida's experience with the tribes in Iraq has paralleled that of the United States, in terms of a process of analytical thinking and of adjusting to conditions on the ground. A key element in the United States' success in dealing with Al-Qaida in Iraq has been attributable to the ability of U.S. forces to establish a positive relationship with the Sunni tribes and, conversely, to Al-Qaida's inability to do so. However, this study will suggest that this situation, understandably, could not remain static, given such shifting factors as the handover from U.S. forces to the Iraqi government, efforts at adjustment by Al-Qaida, and intertribal and intersectarian dynamics on the ground—and that the evolving result has been a renewed opportunity for Al-Qaida to regain some of the lost ground and foment continuing instability in the country, despite the disarray that may result in the wake of Usama Bin Ladin's death in May 2011.

THE TERMS OF REFERENCE AND METHODOLOGY

Of necessity, an appreciation of Al-Qaida's policy requires a broad understanding of the operational environment, the "human terrain." Although the focus of this study is on Al-Qaida's policy in Iraq, one can only understand such policy toward the tribes within the context of a dynamic process of two—or more—wills or, as Carl von Clausewitz aptly characterized it in his classic work, as a wrestling match where opponents' behavior is to be understood by how they interact, thereby shaping each others' options and reactions.[1]

Indeed, the government and Al-Qaida can be said to be competing for the loyalty of (or at least acceptance by) the population, which in much of Iraq entails navigating through the tribal system as a basic unit of organization of the country's society. In effect, the equation has always involved at least three principal players (and several smaller ones), with the often-fragmented Sunni tribes, Al-Qaida, and the government interacting in volatile relationships intended to achieve often mutually exclusive objectives, in a process very often marked by violence and instability.

Although the "government" at present refers to the Iraqi government—or "state" in analytical terms—in an earlier phase, the "government" in Al-Anbar Province, as well as in other regions, was embodied on the ground by the United States in the absence of an effective organized Iraqi government presence. To a great extent, the relationship between Al-Qaida and the tribes can only be appreciated in light of the tribes' relationship with the government, and special attention must be devoted to that factor. The composition of these three principal players has varied over time due to the kaleidoscope of fluid alliances as elements of the tribal component have often shifted allegiances, and the need operate within this three-sided equation has proven challenging for all players.

This study will analyze Al-Qaida's approach to Iraq's tribes as part of its anti-American insurgency in the Sunni areas, and those factors that contributed to an eventual shifting of tribal alliances to the United States. It will then assess the subsequent period beginning with the turnover from U.S. control to that of the Iraqi government, and the developments that have characterized the evolving current situation as Al-Qaida seeks to adapt to conditions in which the Sunni tribes and the Iraqi government struggle to find a new power equilibrium.

To be sure, the very definition of "tribe" has frequently elicited academic debate, and tribes can vary greatly in size, social and political functions, power, origin, degree of cohesion, or longevity from country to country or within a single country. In the context of Iraq, this diversity of tribes over time has been evident, and tribes have at times been a factor to be reckoned with in the country's politics, especially so in terms of their relationship with the central government. In this study, the term "tribe" is intended as a unit of analysis such as is perceived and addressed by the players themselves, whether the latter are within or outside the tribal system.

The tribal leadership in Iraq is embodied in the person of the shaykh—whether of a tribal confederation (*qabila*), tribe (*ashira*), or clan (*fakhdh*)—and other members of shaykhly families and their top clients, often referred to as notables (*wujaha'*). The plural used here for *shaykh* is *shaykhs*, although in the Arabic it is *shuyukh* or, more rarely, *ashyakh*. The term *Al-Qaida* in this study, unless otherwise modified, refers to Al-Qaida in Iraq, even though the organization had started out, under its original leader Abu Musab Al-Zarqawi, as the Monotheism and Jihad Group (*Jamaat Al-Tawhid wa'l-Jihad*). When Al-Zarqawi had adhered to Usama Bin Ladin and his Mother Al-Qaida (*Al-Qaida Al-Umm*) in 2004, the Iraqi organization changed its name to Al-Qaida in Mesopotamia (*Al-Qaida fi Bilad Al-Rafidayn*). In October 2006, at Al-Qaida's initiative, the Islamic State of Iraq (*Dawlat Al-Iraq Al-Islamiya*) was proclaimed. This was an umbrella organization of jihadist groups, with the Al-Qaida entity, which supposedly retained its distinct identity—for all intents and purposes controlling and pretty much synonymous with the umbrella group

CHAPTER 1

THE HUMAN TERRAIN: THE TRIBAL FACTOR IN IRAQI SOCIETY

The system of tribes has ancient roots in the Middle East, and tribalism continued to be—albeit in a variety of ways and in a range of intensity—a social and political factor to be dealt with even after the advent of Islam. In Iraq, the importance of the tribal factor in society has waxed and waned over the years and has usually been influenced by the tribes' relationship with the government.

Successive Iraqi governments, following the 1958 Revolution, managed with considerable effect over the years in loosening tribal cohesion and in diminishing the traditional power of the tribal shaykhs and notables. Initiatives on land reform, the elimination of tribal quotas in elections, the imposition of civil and criminal law in place of traditional tribal law, and the discouragement of tribal names for entities and individuals, reinforced by education and information campaigns equating tribalism with backwardness and as counter to national and pan-Arab unity—had a significant impact on tribal cohesion, although tribal customs persisted in many cases. Such top-down measures were reinforced by major structural changes in society, such as economic development, enhanced communications, urbanization, and education.

However, after the Iran-Iraq War and the Gulf War, a weakened Saddam Husayn, seeking to maintain political control, staked his fortunes on "re-tribalization," reviving traditional tribal organizations and loyalties or creating new ones as a way of dividing potential opposition and building a loyal base of tribal notables. This entailed a proliferation of shaykhs and sub-shaykhs at all levels, presiding over tribal confederations, tribes, and clans. By distributing money, weapons, honors, and administrative posts to a widely expanded number of shaykhs, encouraging the reappearance of tribal law, and ensuring that tribal leadership would become the conduit for government benefits to the individual—especially in the countryside—Saddam brought about a revival of many of the structures and processes that had been in decline or had disappeared altogether since the 1958 Revolution.[1] In the course of this strategy, the social landscape was changed significantly, with the tribal factor once again a key—and perhaps the key in certain regions—element in Iraqi politics and society. As one shaykh observed, "Since the 1990s, tribal shaykhs are the ones who have made and stood up for laws, and the lack of incidents in itself is due to people's fear of the power of the tribes."[2]

By the time Saddam was removed, the tribal factor in local society had become entrenched, with the expectation at least that tribal influence could be used in helping to obtain income (whether through jobs, organized extortion outside the tribe, or by eliciting largesse from the government); by acting as a conduit to the government (for jobs, licenses, access to education, military careers, contracts); by providing protection (both from threats outside the tribe and as a buffer against government impositions); or with something as banal as bypassing housing regulations or ensuring that one does not fail university exams. Thus, tribal shaykhs could use their influence (*wasta*) to benefit their relatives and clients in everyday life, thereby augmenting their own power by increasing their beneficiaries' dependence on them.[3] As one Iraqi study concluded, there has been growing tribal influence on language and dress, and tribal customs are reported to have had a significant impact even in cities, with migration from the countryside in recent decades, reflecting greater tribal authority in society.[4] Likewise, customary tribal law also made noticeable inroads even into city life, especially among those recently arrived from the countryside.[5] In fact, even government officials, bureaucrats, and judges were reported to use tribal law as a rapid alternative and with the intent of avoiding public scandal.[6]

Indicative of their new image of self-importance and the instability of the situation, shaykhs nowadays have even been coining new honorific tribal leadership titles for themselves without the need for the central government to do so for them.[7]

Following the collapse of the Saddam regime in 2003, the influence of the tribes increased significantly for, as a senior tribal shaykh noted, "The tribes have always become stronger when the government is weak, and become weaker when the government is strong."[8] The disappearance of the Saddam regime also resulted in a vacuum of government which, especially in the rural Sunni areas, the tribes sought to fill, notably by providing security to their fellow tribesmen in a chaotic situation.[9] The shaykhs soon established on their own initiative the Shaykhs' Council (*Majlis Al-Shuyukh*), as a consultative and lobby organ, and member shaykhs exercised quasi-governmental authority, such as providing security and limiting looting, in the post-Saddam vacuum.[10]

The tribal system after 2003, however, was in a state of flux with the end of government controls. Saddam had promoted or created large numbers of shaykhs at various levels of tribal society, in many cases from newly minted shaykhly families, often bypassing traditional tribal leadership pools in favor of parvenus, who no doubt could be expected to be more pliant and loyal than others with an established power base and clientele within a tribe. His arbitrary promotion and support of specific shaykhs, however, reportedly had often led to tensions within a tribe over leadership issues, with favored shaykhs commonly known derisively as the "test tube," the "1990s," or the "palm tree and phosphorus" shaykhs, in reference to the distinguishing features of the Iraqi currency which they received from the government.[11] This artificially congealed leadership pattern left the situation ripe for rebalancing after 2003.[12]

Once the controlling hand of Saddam was removed, one could expect a certain degree of instability and violence as new power balances were worked out both within a tribe and among tribes, as rivals competed for power. For example, in the case of the shaykh of Saddam's own tribe, the Al-Nasiri, Saddam had replaced him with someone of his own choosing in the early 1990s. Shortly after Saddam's ouster, the current shaykh who had replaced Saddam's appointee noted enigmatically of the latter, "He is now dead. He was killed two months ago."[13]

Moreover, the frozen power balances characteristic of the Saddam era applied throughout the tribal hierarchies, not only to the leadership positions. With the fall of the regime, pent-up personal grievances toward fellow tribesmen blamed—justifiably or not—for aiding the previous government with executions, arrests, mutilations, or house demolitions resulted in the victims or their families demanding compensation from those they accused. Most often, such cases were resolved through tribal channels, with mediation based on customary law, which is perhaps understandable in the absence of alternative systems of justice.[14]

Old grudges and rifts between tribes, likewise, ran deep and were not forgotten easily. As Shaykh Manaf Ali Al-Nida, head of Saddam's tribe, which had been seen as enjoying a privileged position under the former regime, complained angrily, resentment against the entire tribe continued even years after the collapse of the previous regime. "Saddam was one of this tribe's sons and no one can deny that . . . but what do they want? Must this whole tribe die just because it gave birth to Saddam? We must not be prisoners of the past."[15]

Chapter 2

Al-Qaida Tackles the Tribes

It was in this dynamic human terrain that Al-Qaida needed to operate. During the initial phase of involvement in Iraq, Al-Qaida could point to a certain degree of success with the tribes, but at the same time its approach would sow the seeds of failure due to significant mistakes at the heart of its strategy.

Al-Qaida had very limited prior experience dealing with tribes on an extended and intensive basis. Certainly, this was the first campaign that involved an effort to transform local tribal society and to establish a permanent quasi-governmental presence. In Somalia, Al-Qaida personnel had acted largely as trainers and advisers with the tribes. In Afghanistan, Usama Bin Ladin had studiously avoided becoming enmeshed in the tribal system, viewing the country not as an operational area, but as a base for operations elsewhere.[1]

If there was one driving force that shaped Al-Qaida's policy at this stage, it was the latter's ideology which, for all its coherence, skewed its assessments, inclined it to select unrealistic objectives, and placed severe limits on its policy choices. To be sure, Al-Qaida recognized from the beginning the importance of the tribal factor in Iraq and that it would have to deal with the tribes, notwithstanding any ideological repugnance to intermediate loyalties competing with religion as the presumed basis of loyalty for all Muslims. How to navigate in a complex Iraqi society would become a key element of Al-Qaida's strategy in its struggle against U.S. forces.

In the case of Iraq, it is necessary to recognize the differences between Mother Al-Qaida, as it styles itself, centered on Usama Bin Ladin and his close associates, and the movement that had coalesced around Abu Musab Al-Zarqawi, the Jordanian-born jihadist leader who would eventually amalgamate his organization with that of Bin Ladin. The uneasy, and at times openly contentious, relationship, reflecting differing perspectives and exacerbated by a lack of unity of command, would only be modified under Al-Zarqawi's successors, although by that time Al-Qaida's relationship with the tribes would have suffered perhaps irreversible setbacks in some cases.

Usama Bin Ladin and the top leadership in Al-Qaida had long eyed Iraq as a future theater—not least because of its potential as a stepping stone to Palestine—but had had no assets with which to operate there. Moreover, Saddam's hostility to Al-Qaida precluded any activity in Iraq as long as he was in power, apart from marginal areas in the north not under his control. The collapse of the Saddam regime removed a key obstacle to Al-Qaida's presence, although its lack of local operatives would still have posed a problem. However, Al-Zarqawi's organization, Al-Tawhid wa'l-Jihad, composed heavily of Jordanians, Syrians, and Palestinians, was soon in place and operating, and able to attract recruits on a wide scale from other Arab countries.

Not surprisingly, Al-Qaida clearly saw the Sunni community as its natural constituency in Iraq. As Al-Zarqawi recognized, Al-Qaida's success or failure in Iraq would depend on the Sunni community and the tribes: "The rise of the Al-Qaida in Mesopotamia Organization was built on the shoulders of the Sunnis in Iraq, since the proportion of Iraqi Sunnis [in the organization] are almost 99 percent, with only 1 percent foreigners." He noted specifically that "it is thanks to the Sunni tribesmen that the Organization [i.e., Al-Qaida] owes its existence."[2] As one of Al-Zarqawi's lieutenants, Abu Jafar Al-Ansari, also remarked, "Everyone should know that the tribesmen of Al-Anbar are the backbone of the jihad."[3] In order to be successful, any jihadist movement would have had to make proper use of the "human terrain"—that is, to navigate effectively the tribal environment in which it operated.

Irrespective of any policy initiated by Al-Zarqawi, he would have found, as noted, a tribal society in effervescence resulting from the removal of the controls Saddam's regime had imposed, thereby presenting both a challenge and an opportunity that could not be ignored. Operating in such a complex and dynamic environment would not have been easy under any circumstance. Iraqi tribes are normally wary of and hostile to outsiders (unless the latter are seen as potential allies for the tribe or for factions within the tribe), and hostility to foreign Arabs would not only be generated by potential ideological differences. For example, some tribes were reported already to have treated foreign volunteers—whom Saddam had recruited prior to the 2003 War—badly, on purely xenophobic criteria.[4]

One would have assumed that Al-Zarqawi, himself a member of the Bani Hasan, one of the largest tribal confederations in Jordan, would have been attuned to the functioning of power in tribal societies, but his jihadist ideological framework apparently provided a greater degree of guidance to his dealing with Iraq's tribes than his own tribal experience. To be sure, as one Iraqi security source noted, at least in Diyala Province early on, Al-Qaida had been able to attract some tribal shaykhs, who had then become field commanders.[5] However, Al-Zarqawi and his organization appear to have also pursued a tribal policy relying in the long run on those elements most receptive to its message—youth and those dissatisfied with the status quo and seeking a change in the emerging power structure—while envisioning deep and unsettling changes in tribal society.

In many ways, judging from his subsequent actions, one might trace Al-Zarqawi's approach in this arena to a strand of thinking exemplified in a study by a respected Al-Qaida figure from Saudi Arabia, Abu Bakr Naji, author of *Idarat al-tawahhush*

[*Governing Anarchy*]. This study probably incorporated ideas that must have been circulating within Al-Qaida in some form even before they were committed to paper. Naji suggested that it would be pointless to try to convince tribes to abandon their tribal solidarity. Instead, Al-Qaida should seek to mobilize traditional tribal energies and power for its own purposes. Some leaders could be attracted by money, others by honorific but meaningless titles and positions. After Al-Qaida's members and the tribesmen had interacted for some time, some of the tribesmen would be attracted through faith and would then no longer follow their original leaders when issued orders that were contrary to religious law. This situation would then impel the tribesmen to join Al-Qaida and switch their obedience to Al-Qaida leaders. As Naji put it, "They will abandon the former commander [i.e., the tribal shaykh], even if they remain with him outwardly," recalling an event in Islamic history where a convert had been prepared to kill even his own father had Muhammad requested it.[6] In essence, what Naji was suggesting was that the traditional shaykhs ought to be bypassed in favor of recruiting their tribal followers behind the shaykhs' backs and that tribal loyalties be replaced by religious ones, thus putting Al-Qaida in control.

Al-Qaida's information campaign promoted an uncompromising stand, whereby tribesmen were to lay aside what were seen as archaic tribal, or any other nonreligious, loyalties in favor of that to Islam and, specifically, to Al-Qaida. As a young Al-Qaida commander stressed, "This tribal system is un-Islamic."[7] In that vein, Abu Anas Al-Shami, Al-Zarqawi's legal expert, had promoted a severe approach based on a rigid outlook of religious loyalty to the exclusion of family or tribal ties, and even members of one's family or tribe who opposed "Islam" (that is, Al-Qaida) were to be considered enemies to be fought and killed.[8]

Chapter 3

Al-Qaida Alienates the Tribes

Despite an apparent success on the ground, the process by which Al-Qaida established its position in the tribal areas involved a combination of errors, arrogance, and harshness which—in addition to the fact that its top leaders in Iraq were seen as outsiders—all contributed to potential problems for Al-Qaida with the tribes. In many ways, Al-Qaida's policy was key in contributing to the gradual turnaround that was to mature in the tribal areas by late 2006, when much of the tribal leadership in Al-Anbar Province formed an alliance with the de facto government—the U.S. forces on the ground—and were to turn against Al-Qaida. The reversal of alliances was the culmination of a plodding and unsure process fueled by a parallel resentment of the threat Al-Qaida posed to existing tribal leaders and escalating disenchantment at a popular level among tribesmen. These resentments were accompanied by the increasing realization not only that cooperation was eventually possible with U.S. forces but that they could also serve as a vehicle for tribal leaders to remove Al-Qaida's presence and solidify and expand their own power.

Challenging the Shaykhs' Power

Al-Qaida's blueprint for a social transformation was to present an across-the-board challenge to the shaykhs, as seen by the grievances against Al-Qaida that the shaykhs themselves stressed. At the same time, these issues of social transformation mandated by Al Qaida also affected ordinary tribesmen, even if at times only indirectly and not clearly at first. The power and influence of tribal shaykhs and notables traditionally stemmed from their ability to reward or punish subordinate tribesmen. Benefits to the individual could take the form of material ones as well as judiciary processes that were often quicker and less onerous than those provided by the government's legal system. In addition, shaykhs served as the defender of collective and individual security and honor. In return for such benefits, the individual would be expected to sacrifice some degree of personal autonomy, accept a measure of social and economic stratification, and support the tribal entity as a whole—and, specifically, the tribal leaders—even if only grudgingly. Such a relationship was dynamic and required a continuous mutual intersection of interests if the shaykhs were to retain the loyalty of their fellow tribesmen and if a tribe was to maintain its cohesion.

However, Al-Qaida was an activist force, bent on reordering the society in which it operated and imposing its own values and leadership, thereby unavoidably being bound to clash with the existing tribal power structures. For Iraq's Sunni tribes, freed from central control after Saddam's demise, Al-Qaida began to represent a new permanent government, all the more so after formally proclaiming an embryonic Islamic State of Iraq in October 2006. As such, Al-Qaida increasingly appeared to threaten the tribal shaykhs' autonomy and authority by its control over local economic activity and by its intrusive presence in all social interactions, the levers on which tribal shaykhs relied to effect their power.

A Social Confrontation. Significantly, Al-Qaida had unleashed a version of a class war within some tribes, with elements who were disgruntled or outside the traditional shaykhly strata seeing Al-Qaida's armed presence as an opportunity to reorder tribal power hierarchies. It is not surprising that there would be pre-existing tensions within such a hierarchical system as that within and among the Iraqi tribes. For example, conflict between large landowner shaykhs and small landowners and agricultural workers had long been common.1 The approach that Al-Zarqawi adopted meant that, although he was willing to work, at least temporarily, with those tribal leaders who were accommodating, at the same time those leaders were being challenged by ambitious elements with lower status from within their own tribes, who were encouraged by Al-Qaida. Disenfranchised elements probably saw an opportunity for social mobility and a chance to exact retribution against those who may have treated them with some disdain in the past.

Not surprisingly, many established and would-be shaykhs saw this new dynamic that Al-Qaida had encouraged as a direct threat to their own positions and prospects. In effect, one of the main grievances expressed by many shaykhs was that Al-Qaida, supported by such lower-class elements, would usurp the shaykhs' position of leadership in a tribe. Typically, Shaykh Ali Hatim, shaykh of the Dulaym confederation and a leader subsequently of the Al-Anbar Sahwa, was clear about his perception of those tribesmen who attacked the shaykhs:

> Who is it who attacked the tribal shaykhs? Riff-raff. That is, in every nation there are individuals who—pardon the expression—are low-lifes (*saqitin*) and who are so far gone they are not even worth criticizing. That is why Al-Qaida bought those [tribesmen] and raised them up to the rank of commander (*amir*) . . . a homeless man, wandering the streets, and now he has become an amir!! . . . As a result, he would be paid and told, "Kill this guy, kill that guy."[2]

According to Shaykh Ali Hatim, Al-Qaida "focused on people at the bottom of a tribe's hierarchy, who they recruited with money, either by enticement or by instigation, trying thus to recruit them so that it ended up controlling through them most of the tribes."[3] He identified this as the method by which a small number of Al-Qaida cadres (he estimated about one thousand) were able to control the province's tribes.⁴ Shaykh Ahmad Abu Risha, later head of the Iraq Sahwa Council, despite some apparent hyperbole, nevertheless reflected a similar concern when he maintained that

> Those who rebelled against the shaykhs were from the lowest strata, that is, not from among the elite strata . . . they were all just son of so-and-so or son of so-and-so. That is, their fathers were not prominent, and even their mothers were more prominent than their fathers. Those who rose up against the shaykhs . . . were highway robbers, killers, and criminals who made a living only by theft, looting, and collecting ransoms. It was [tribesmen] such as these who were Al-Qaida's members. They were not from the elite . . . they were from the lowest rungs and the worst people . . . such were the people who targeted the shaykhs and others like the latter.⁵

Al-Qaida, for its part, looked at itself with some pride because it made help available to the poor in the tribes.⁶

Moreover, the leadership of Mother Al-Qaida has long seen the youth as a special resource for the jihad and as the most likely sector of the population where it would find support.⁷ However, Al-Qaida's focus on the youth was also an irritant and seen as a threat by the tribal leadership in Iraq. For example, a senior security commander in Al-Anbar— and himself from a tribal shaykhly family—claimed that Al-Qaida "took all the kids and the people who lived in poverty or had low social standing, and they provided them with extraordinary support."⁸

The Economic Factor. In tangible terms, perhaps the most visible aspect of the threat to the shaykhs' power was in the economic sphere. The role of tribal shaykhs can be viewed as similar to that of labor union leaders at the local level in their heyday, when such union bosses might have held great power over individual union members' daily economic lives and even physical security, but whose influence and authority also depended on a general perception among the rank and file of the leaders' effectiveness in ensuring members' benefits.

Broadly speaking, with the stalling of the Al-Anbar economy after the collapse of the Saddam regime, contracts from the U.S. forces had become a necessary source of revenue for a shaykh's credibility with his fellow tribesmen. As one tribal shaykh recognized, "A sheik has no power without contracts.... If I do not provide for my people, they will not cooperate with me."[9] However, Al-Qaida's violence and destruction in Al-Anbar and its growing control over the local society had a negative impact on communications, fuel supplies, electricity, water, and educational facilities, and had crippled the local economy, not to speak of the precarious security situation, which militated against U.S. investment in large-scale projects and the tribes' ability to protect their vital economic interests. Even as late as 2007, only two of the four factories in Al-Anbar were operating (and those at only one-half of their capacity).[10]

Al-Qaida also seems to have sought to establish a monopoly over local sources of revenue, both as a source of financing the organization and as a lever of control over local tribal society. For example, Al-Qaida engineered a monopoly over critical fuel supplies in Al-Anbar.[11] It also benefited financially from such projects that were let out by the United States to local contractors, and was routinely shaking down contractors (often themselves tribal shaykhs) for a cut of the contract money.[12] Perhaps more distressing for some shaykhs was the fact that Al-Qaida also forced its way into the profitable smuggling and extortion on road traffic, traditionally a monopoly of certain tribes.[13]

This chokehold on the economy not only enabled Al-Qaida to maximize its own income but also undermined the shaykhs' all-important role of economic patron. As one shaykh noted of the early period, Al-Qaida representatives "were spending huge amounts of money, giving to the people."[14] Sunni tribal shaykhs found themselves increasingly unable to meet the economic expectations of their fellow tribesmen, with all the negative consequences that implied for their own authority, and with no help in sight from the nascent Iraqi government. For example, when a number of tribal shaykhs from Ninawa Province in 2006 tried to impress upon the governor that their followers were suffering from shortages of food, fuel, and services due to "evident neglect," all they got from the governor was praise and vague promises that "the implementation of the major projects to come" would solve the "temporary problems."[15]

In the case of Shaykh Abd Al-Sattar Abu Risha, who was eventually to become the most prominent U.S. ally in Al-Anbar, a struggle with Al-Qaida for control of the main supply route from Amman to Baghdad pitted Al-Qaida against his tribe, which traditionally had supplied most of the truck drivers on that road, as well as probably extorted tolls from and raided the traffic.[16] Al-Qaida had managed to establish at least partial control over the road, on which it could charge hefty tolls, as well as carry out kidnappings and killings. Along its western stretch, however, control remained contested with the Abu Risha tribe, but by early 2004 Al-Qaida had eliminated the then-leaders of the Abu Risha (including by killing Abd al-Sattar's father and younger brother, and kidnapping and presumably assassinating two other brothers). This turn of events induced Abd Al-Sattar to return from Jordan in 2006 and approach the United States to join the fight against Al-Qaida. Not surprisingly, among the first projects of the newly established Sahwa in Al-Anbar was securing the Amman-Baghdad road, accomplished by setting up numerous tribal checkpoints as part of an agreement negotiated with U.S. forces, thus opening the way to economic benefits to the tribe from the control of trade and from the U.S. aid that ensued from the new alliance.[17]

A CLASH OF CULTURES

Another level on which Al-Qaida clashed openly with the tribes was that of culture, as Al-Qaida's agenda often ran counter to tribal values. With the imposition of its own interpretation of Islam and the concrete social measures that entailed, Al-Qaida, at the same time, also challenged the shaykhs' power. For Al-Qaida, establishing a religiously based society was central and was an objective that brooked no compromise. Tribal society in Iraq was not especially religiously observant. As was probably typical, one Iraqi Al-Qaida member recalled that most in his tribe did not pray and were not particularly interested in religion.[18] Al-Zarqawi himself taxed the Iraqi Sunnis as being "ignorant on religious matters."[19] As such, tribal society was bound to feel a major disruptive change in the religious sphere with the entrenchment of Al-Qaida.

For example, a key tenet of Al-Qaida's ideology has been the introduction of sharia, or religious law, and the courts to enforce it, which Al-Qaida sees as an essential prerequisite for an Islamic society. One of the first steps Al-Qaida would take when it established control of an area was to appoint a legal official and would actively work to suppress tribal customs that it considered contrary to the sharia.[20] The sharia-based legal system which Al-Qaida promoted not only excluded tribal traditions but was often harsher than that based on customary tribal law, which, in many cases, was conducive to accommodating compromise through mediation and the possibility of monetary settlements even for major crimes.[21] Understandably, shaykhs were often annoyed by Al-Qaida's imposition of the sharia and the introduction of sharia courts, as that diminished their own role in administering customary tribal law and meant the transfer of that role to outsiders.[22] Tribal shaykhs strongly support customary tribal law and mediation, in no small part because it gives them influence as mediators and judges and thus allows them to play a key role in the tribesmen's daily lives.[23] For some shaykhs, that may even be the function for which they are best known.[24] In what was probably a characteristic incident, a member of Al-Qaida recalled that when a new sharia court in his tribe had judged that a sheep thief should have his hand cut off, the tribe's skaykh had tried to intercede and substitute payment as punishment, but the court, backed by armed mujahidin, had refused, thereby no doubt undermining the shaykh's prestige and authority.[25]

Tribal sources also complained that Al-Qaida had been overly harsh in its enforcement of regulations, considering anyone who helped the police in whatever manner, even in matters of law and order, to be "an agent of the occupation" and were dismayed that Al-Qaida had killed many tribesmen on that charge.[26] Moreover, the sharia courts appear to have alienated many rank-and-file tribesmen by their draconic rulings for even minor infractions of perceived un-Islamic behavior, such as smoking in public or shaving, and the use of beating and harsh punishments, such as killing a cigarette peddler in their anti-smoking campaign, or killing men for wearing jewelry after accusing them of being Shia, chopping off heads, extracting ransom for kidnapped family members, or killing even women.[27] Iraqis indicated as a case in point the sentence of execution by one of Al-Qaida's judges in Iraq—a twenty-one-year-old Saudi at that—of a shopkeeper just because he had been accused of selling food to "apostates."[28] One of Al-Qaida's *qadis* (judges) in Iraq, originally from one of the Gulf countries, reportedly had even ruled that somebody would either have to change his name or die, because no one was allowed to bear a name drawn from Muhammad's family.[29] Mother Al-Qaida seemed uncomfortable with such an uncompromising stand in Iraq, as an article in Mother Al-Qaida's "in-house" journal, *Talai Khurasan* (*The Khurasan Vanguards*), comparing Iraq and Afghanistan noted pointedly that the Taliban had been too harsh in their own application of the sharia, which came back to haunt them in popular support. According to the article, "The Taliban . . . committed mistakes and excesses in applying the sharia." As a result, the United States was able to claim it was liberating the people from that situation and "before joining the jihad many now hesitate" and ask themselves "should I fight so that the Taliban can rule me again?"[30]

What is more, it seems that these new sharia courts in Iraq were run most often by foreigners, who had the requisite expertise, or at least the zeal, thus further alienating tribesmen who were normally already wary of outsiders. Foreigners as sharia judges, for example, included a number of Saudi members of Al-Qaida whom the tribes eventually turned over to U.S. forces.[31] Abu Anas Al-Shami, Al-Zarqawi's legal adviser, was Jordanian. The chief Al-Qaida qadi in Iraq during the Al-Zarqawi period, in fact, was Abu Sulayman Al-Utaybi, a Saudi and someone who, to boot, was only in his twenties. According to one of his defenders, hostile propaganda circulating at the time ran along the lines of "How can you accept a young Saudi foreigner ... to rule on your lives, your women, and your property, and to order you around, you who are shaykhs of tribes?"[32]

A prominent defector from Al-Qaida to the Sahwa, Al-Mulla Nazhim Al-Jiburi, himself an ambitious cleric, also had run-ins with Al-Qaida's senior sharia officials in Iraq, and seemed to resent in particular that they were a Moroccan and a Saudi, as well as that, in his view, they were not well versed in the sharia.[33] No doubt hoping to address this sensitive issue, when Abu Umar Al-Baghdadi took charge after Al-Zarqawi's death, he removed the above-named young Saudi chief qadi from office, although according to an official Al-Qaida communiqué, the reason was based on anodyne "requirements of legal utility," and replaced him with a qadi from the Iraqi Jibur tribal confederation, Abu Ishaq Al-Jiburi.[34]

More generally, Al-Qaida seems to have attacked long-standing manifestations of folk religion that the tribesmen held dear, as it judged such values to be vestiges of a pre-Islamic period and incompatible with "pure" Islam. Al-Qaida often went out of its way to breach or suppress these traditions, such as the cult of saints as intercessors. For example, reflecting the puritanical reformist outlook of its origins, Al-Qaida leveled the saints' mausoleums at which the faithful would gather, reportedly engendering considerable popular resentment and alienating the tribesmen.[35] Al-Zarqawi likewise railed against the local celebrations of the Mulid,

Muhammad's birthday.[36] Among Al-Qaida's negative acts had also been its violation of local tribal traditions by introducing alien concepts such as the *baya* (or pledge of loyalty) to Al-Qaida, whereas the tribes maintained they had been familiar only with a baya to God or to the nation.[37] The fact that Al-Zarqawi himself reportedly chided tribesmen for making their womenfolk work in the fields instead of themselves may also have been a typical irritant on a sensitive issue.[38]

Even Al-Qaida's operational procedures often ignored cherished tribal customs. For example, from the early days, Al-Qaida often targeted funeral ceremonies for tribal shaykhs it had killed, no doubt seeing that as an additional lucrative target because of the expected gathering of a large number of significant figures. However, in Iraq's tribal society such funeral ceremonies are sacrosanct, constituting an opportunity for tribes to display their hospitality, generosity with food, and skill in poetry, and any breach in the form of an armed attack would be considered a grave humiliation to the entire tribe. Indeed, such symbolic traditions as postfuneral banquets are seen as so important a measure of honor in a tribe that even poor families will spend far beyond their means on such occasions, so much so that the authorities and tribal leaders would like to limit this ruinous tradition by persuasion, apparently with little success.[39]

Such tribal traditions are not merely guidelines of social etiquette but a symbolic part of the social fabric that establish and publicize the hierarchical power and social relationships within a tribe and between tribes. To trample blithely on such cherished conventions as Al-Qaida was wont to do represented not just a social gaffe but a threat to traditional social processes and institutions and, as such, could be viewed by tribesmen as a slur to their honor and was likely to engender widespread resentment. Iraqis came to conclude that Al-Qaida's objective was the imposition of its alien version of Islam by eliminating what it called pre-Islamic traditions and that it was willing to use even drastic means to do so. As Shaykh Ali Hatim put it, Al-Qaida's intent was to trample on the tribes' cherished values, that is, to "do away with social custom (*urf ijtimai*) . . . that was the real goal of cutting off heads."[40]

Al-Qaida's disregard for tribal norms thus posed a challenge to both shaykhs and ordinary tribesmen. Although less tangible than economic interests, elements of social values and honor are no less real in the life of a tribesman and can be integral factors in determining a shaykh's authority. If a shaykh is unable to defend his tribe's honor, he not only loses face but this can also call into question a shaykh's ability and willingness to protect fellow tribesmen— all key aspects of a shaykh's standing and legitimacy.

Tribal Sensitivity to Outsiders

Iraqis in general resented that Al-Qaida's leadership was often of foreign origin, and its opponents used that factor as an effective propaganda theme. As Shaykh Ali Hatim scoffed, Al-Qaida wanted to impose its own leadership—and implicitly replace the shaykhs as leaders—and intended for the tribes "to follow Al-Qaida like sheep," forcing people to follow outsiders whose names they allegedly did not even know, or as he called them, "somewhat daft people who came from abroad and a handful of scum from the tribes who want to come and rule the province."[41] A prominent tribal shaykh who had defected from Al-Qaida to join the newly established Sahwa later noted that Iraqi insurgent leaders often had considerable military training under the Saddam regime, whereas he ridiculed the foreign Al-Qaida commanders as being incompetent amateurs.[42] Likewise, a senior Sahwa commander in Diyala, Shaykh Muhammad Al-Mujammai, tended to blame the foreign Arabs for much of the extremism and the harshness with which Al-Qaida operated and claimed that even he had been kidnapped and forced to join Al-Qaida in 2005.[43]

The divergence in views on targeting, with the tribes accusing Al-Qaida of attacking local civilians rather than U.S. forces, had been a major area of dispute from early on, and was especially galling since foreigners in Al-Qaida were seen as indifferent to Iraqi casualties. Initially at least, some tribal leaders appeared to have been unconcerned about Al-Qaida's attacks on U.S. forces as long as the tribes were not harmed. As the Jiburi confederation's paramount shaykh noted, "We said to them, 'If you've come to resist the U.S. occupation, Iraq is an open field. You're free to do what you want but don't come here and kill our people.'"[44] The issue often came down to a resentment of foreigners coming to Iraq rather than a problem with fighting Americans or, as Shaykh Ali Hatim put it, "We are not against the honest resistance . . . but let everyone fight the jihad in his own country, in every country where there is an American embassy and where there is corruption and nightclubs. Let them fight the jihad in their own countries."[45] Ironically, one of Al-Zarqawi's assumptions before entering Iraq had been that his fighters, of largely Palestinian and Jordanian origin, would blend in easily because of the similar dialect and their appearance.[46]

Al-Qaida implicitly acknowledged the need to rebut such accusations of relying on outsiders, arguing sarcastically about the tribes' new-found U.S. allies, "as if the Americans were from the Dulaym tribes!" and asking rhetorically, "What if God's Prophet (God's prayers and salvation on him) had taken refuge in our country?"[47] As for the claim that the mujahidin were foreigners, Abu Umar Al-Baghdadi countered in disbelief that "you can see with your own eyes that they are your own sons and the sons of your sons."[48] Likening the withdrawal of tribal support for Al-Qaida to the *Ridda* (the tribal apostasy following Muhammad's death), Al-Baghdadi added that the killers of Sahwa leaders had come from within the tribes themselves and that, in the case of Abu Risha, pointed out that his killer had even been a relative rather than a foreigner.[49]

In a letter to Al-Zarqawi, Al-Qaida's number-two leader, Ayman Al-Zawahiri, had shown concern over this issue, as he asked whether non-Iraqis had indeed taken over the leadership of the mujahidin, "which can make some people sensitive." Clearly, Al-Zawahiri knew that to be the case, as he then asked, "What means can be used to change that [phenomenon], while still retaining cohesion in jihadi action and avoiding any turbulence?"[50] And, Al-Zawahiri asked Al-Zarqawi to provide a detailed account of that issue. Apparently, not much was done to address this issue as long as Al-Zarqawi was in charge but, very likely as way to respond to such criticisms, after his death, an Iraqi from one of the Al-Anbar tribes, Abu Umar Al-Baghdadi (real name Hazim Abd Al-Razzaq Al-Zawi), became at least the nominal head of the Al-Qaida-controlled Islamic State of Iraq umbrella organization. When Abu Umar Al-Baghdadi was killed in 2010, his successor, Abu Bakr Al-Baghdadi (real name Ibrahim Awwad Ibrahim Al-Samarra'i), was also Iraqi and tribal, as was the new deputy, Al-Nasir li-Din Allah Sulayman (real name Abu Abd Allah Al-Hasani Al-Qurayshi). When the Islamic State of Iraq announced a slate of ministers in April 2007, of the ten, eight were prominently identified by their tribal names, one was nontribal, and only one was a foreigner; in September 2009, of the nine new ministers, seven were prominently identified by their tribal names, one was nontribal, and one was a foreigner.

What may have been particularly galling to many tribesmen was that foreign Al-Qaida fighters, as well as lower-class local tribesmen who had joined Al-Qaida, would pressure tribesmen to give their daughters to them in marriage using the armed clout they could wield. As Al-Zarqawi had stressed, Islam was henceforth the only measure of relationships to be considered for, as he saw it, "an American Muslim is our dear brother, while an infidel Arab is our loathsome enemy, even if from the same womb as we."[51] Such unwelcome demands for marriage blatantly impinged on a family's and a tribe's honor, and often gave rise to local fury, especially since the marriages were somewhat irregular, as Al-Qaida did not recognize the legitimacy of local religious officials or courts and did not go through them for the formalities.[52] In one case, when an Iraqi gave his daughter in marriage to a foreign fighter, and the daughter reported that her new husband was not circumcised (and presumably therefore not a good Muslim), the father-in-law and other Iraqis had killed the hapless groom.[53] Marriage under pressure to outsiders violated tribal custom, since in Iraq, as in most tribal societies in the Middle East, male relatives ordinarily have the right to prevent a female cousin from marrying (*nahwa*), regardless of the woman's opinion.[54] Likewise, unions of those viewed as of lower lineage marrying women above their station would also have been seen as a contravention of acceptable social behavior.[55]

CHAPTER 4

MOBILIZING THE TRIBES AGAINST AL-QAIDA

AL-QAIDA'S HUBRIS AND CHANGING THE TRIBAL HUMAN TERRAIN

Al-Qaida's uncompromising attitude toward tribal shaykhs, as well as toward other resistance groups, presented even elements predisposed to oppose the United States with a stark and unwelcome choice of either submitting to Al-Qaida's leadership and strategy or stepping aside, with little flexibility.[1] During the initial phase, Al-Zarqawi opposed anyone who remained neutral.[2] Al-Qaida was sufficiently confident that it did not have to accept neutral tribes and targeted tribal shaykhs who were unwilling to cooperate.[3] Al-Qaida, from the first, had identified the shaykhs, as leaders of the tribe, as the strategic center of gravity in dealing with the tribes and had begun to target uncooperative shaykhs in Al-Anbar already in 2004. In an undated situation report from the field in Al-Anbar, probably addressed to Al-Zarqawi, the author—apparently a field commander—details the decision to target hostile shaykhs as the most effective way to control the province and prevent hostility to Al-Qaida. As the report concludes, "The best and only solution [to opposition in a tribe] is to cut off the head of the snake."[4]

In a patrimonial system, such as characterizes Iraq's tribes, a leader would concentrate power (decision making, contracts, negotiations, loyalties, and armed might) in himself and lead through a network of clients personally loyal to him, while limiting access to benefits by potential rivals. If a leader was eliminated, the effect could be disarray within a tribe, or at least a period of uncertainty as would-be successors competed to replace the previous leader and built up their own networks of patronage and allies. Paradoxically, with many of the traditional legitimate shaykhs out of the country and the struggles for leadership within some tribes already activated following the demise of the Saddam regime, a coterie of would-be shaykhs was often already on the scene, ready to fill the vacuum resulting from Al-Qaida's elimination of an existing shaykh. In the case of Abd Al-Sattar's death, it was perhaps fortunate that his brother, Ahmad, had already been playing an active political role alongside Abd Al-Sattar and was able to step into the latter's shoes in the Sahwa movement (to be discussed below) fairly smoothly.

To be sure, Mother Al-Qaida was worried about the direction events were taking in Iraq, reflecting complaints lodged even by members of Al-Zarqawi's own organization, and had been advising Al-Qaida's local leadership to follow a more moderate and flexible approach in general in dealing with the local society. The individual, identified only as "Atiya," and apparently close to Mother Al-Qaida's inner circles, spelled out the leadership's guidance in a letter to Al-Zarqawi, as he reminded the latter of the requirement to win popular support and of the need to "consult" even neutral elements of local society, such as "tribal chiefs" (*zuama' al-asha'ir*), and, indeed, of the need to "be solicitous of" the shaykhs.[5] So concerned was Mother Al-Qaida that the organization even sent its Iraqi-born field commander in Afghanistan, Abd Al-Hadi Al-Iraqi, to "work out the differences with Al-Zarqawi," and probably to report on or even eventually replace him.[6] However, the envoy was arrested on his way to Iraq, probably in Turkey.

Nevertheless, as the above Al-Qaida field report indicates, killing some shaykhs had often been effective in intimidating other shaykhs and, at first, had usually not elicited a significant response from the cowed and still disunited tribes. By the time the Sahwa was launched in 2006, Al-Qaida had already killed over fifty tribal shaykhs.[7] Some individuals were even said to have avoided the office of tribal shaykh because they feared they would be assassinated.[8] When Al-Zarqawi launched an attack against three hotels in Amman in November 2005, this could also have been interpreted as the prelude to attacks against the senior Iraqi shaykhs living in heretofore secure exile in such hotels abroad. For the time being, this tactic seemed to have had the desired effect of preventing a concerted effort against Al-Qaida by the tribes, and Al-Qaida felt sufficiently secure to demand and expect the loyalty of tribal shaykhs.

However, as the Al-Qaida field report also cautioned, since rural people still respected their shaykhs, tribes at some time could well react against Al-Qaida if their leaders were attacked. In some cases, the assassination of a shaykh did create a backlash against Al-Qaida, which often took the form of traditional tribal commitments to exact revenge. In the case of Shaykh Hikmat Mumtaz of the Albu Baz tribe in the Samarra area, according to an eyewitness to a meeting on this issue between the local Al-Qaida commander and Shaykh Hikmat in 2006, the latter had said, "You have kilometers of roads filled with American military convoys which you can attack, so why are you putting bombs in the city?"[9] Al-Qaida, not surprisingly, killed the increasingly uncooperative Shaykh Hikmat after he had met with the Iraqi defense minister. Thereupon, his tribesmen had ambushed a group of Al-Qaida personnel in revenge, sparking in turn an attack by Al-Qaida during the funeral of the shaykh.[10] Similarly, when Shaykh Abd Al-Sattar Abu Risha was killed in 2006, his fellow tribal shaykhs swore to "take their revenge" for his death.[11]

Tribal loyalties could trigger revenge against Al-Qaida even when the shaykh was not the victim. For example, the Albu Faraj tribe turned against Al-Qaida in retaliation for its killing of some policemen who happened to be from that tribe.[12] Likewise, when Al-Qaida attempted to kill the country's deputy prime minister, Salam Al-Zawbai, his tribe turned against Al-Qaida.[13] For some, in fact, the possibility of revenge against Al-Qaida was an even more important incentive in joining the Sahwa than money. As Shaykh Ali Hatim of the Dulaym confederation claimed, perhaps with a bit of exaggeration, "We don't want money . . . what we need is to be allowed to do what we know best, since we are looking for revenge, not for billions."[14] Even when revenge could not be exacted because of fear of Al-Qaida for such killings, resentment toward the organization was probably still generated.

Many shaykhs, and would-be shaykhs, were no doubt anxious to move against Al-Qaida, whose presence represented both a threat as well as an opportunity for rearranging the power system. At one juncture early on, perhaps the majority of shaykhs had gone abroad to safety and were opposed to the launching of an anti-Al-Qaida movement in part, one can assume, out of concern that new local tribal leaders on the ground would replace them in the process. As Shaykh Al-Hardan, one of the founding members of the Sahwa in Al-Anbar, remembers of the senior shaykhs in exile, "They accused us of trying to take over the tribes, trying to be sheikhs. They said, 'You are not the sheikhs. You cannot do this.'. . . They laughed at us."[15]

To be sure, alone, the tribes—or the insurgent groups that were often intertwined with the tribes—realistically were no match for Al-Qaida's organization, zeal, and ability to mass mobile forces from multiple locations against isolated tribes. In those cases where the tribes did confront Al-Qaida, such as the attempt to activate the Al-Anbar People's Council in 2005, Al-Qaida won out with its escalation dominance on the ground.[16]

Overcoming the tribes' understandable fear was a major hurdle in convincing the tribes to challenge Al-Qaida. When Shaykh Ali Hatim of the Dulaym, in 2005, had wanted to launch an attack against Al-Qaida, he observed that his tribesmen were afraid, as they were "intimidated by Al-Qaeda."[17] When, in 2006, he again tried to organize some shaykhs against Al-Qaida, he likewise found that "very few reacted positively, because they were fearful."[18] An initial obstacle was that so many tribesmen had joined Al-Qaida, and even Al-Hamidi Al-Jarba, a prospective leader of opposition to Al-Qaida in the Mosul area and a shaykh of the large Shammar confederation, was reluctant to begin the fight, arguing, "How can we fight them [i.e., Al-Qaida] now, since most of our sons are in their ranks?"[19]

Al-Qaida in Iraq became complacent about the situation. Despite all the resentment its policies had stirred up, by 2006, Al-Qaida could convince itself, with some justification, that it was successful in Iraq, both in terms of its control over tribal society and in its dealings with the United States, at least in the Sunni areas. Al-Qaida seemed dominant, having edged out its local competitors in the insurgency and, as one local source described the control that Al-Qaida's *amirs* (or commanders) had developed, "Each amir had too much authority—to kill, to steal, to do anything he liked. He had the authority and the people obeyed him."[20] Al-Qaida knew that some shaykhs were hostile, as Al-Zarqawi noted that he was aware that some tribal clans in Al-Anbar had contacted the Iraqi government with offers to cooperate in eliminating the mujahidin.[21] However, he probably felt that his methods and the prestige accrued from his apparent success against U.S. forces would be effective in preventing any significant uprising from the tribes.

Validation for Al-Zarqawi's confidence, indeed, came from having created what seemed to be an intractable insurgency problem for U.S. forces. His confidence also stemmed from the pessimism in U.S. policy-making and military circles as to the future of parts of Iraq, particularly for many of the Sunni tribal areas, as in Al-Anbar Province, where Al-Qaida appeared to be entrenched. Al-Qaida, indeed, often expressed its hubris that victory was imminent. For example, in an after-action report that Al-Zarqawi submitted to Bin Ladin in 2005, after boasting about his military successes, he had assured Bin Ladin that "thanks to God's kindness, we are on the verge of strangling [the enemy] for good, and if our plan proceeds as laid out ... its results will show anyone who has eyes something that will gladden all Muslims and sadden every infidel and hypocrite."[22]

AL-QAIDA AND THE TRIBES: THE QUEST FOR RELIGIOUS LEGITIMACY

Religion has been an unavoidable dimension in the relationship between Al-Qaida and the tribes, and the legitimacy that religion could provide has often been an element in the balance of power. Al-Qaida had a considerable advantage over the tribes in terms of built-in religious legitimacy, at least insofar as it portrayed itself as a universal religiously motivated movement and as scrupulously adherent to Islam's tenets, and would claim religious legitimacy for its policy.

For the tribal leadership, that meant finding an alternate source of religious legitimacy from the only other available source: the ulama', or clerics, of the local Sunni religious establishment. The latter has had an ambivalent relationship with Al-Qaida, progressing from support to an increasing degree of rivalry, as the entity sought to impose its specific religious interpretations and organization. In effect, Al-Qaida's desire to dominate the religious establishment, through such means as providing texts for local clerics to give as sermons, often alienated the clerics, as it did the tribal leadership, a situation made worse by the fact that those making demands were foreigners.[23] The issue of youth was also galling to the established Iraqi clerics in Al-Anbar and was a grievance against Al-Qaida or, as one alim noted bitterly, "They [i.e., Al-Qaida] forced the ulama' from the pulpits and put children in their place."[24]

As for the tribes, local clerics often seem to have come from the latter, including some from prominent tribal families, judging by their names, and local Sunni clerics often were willing to cooperate with the tribal shaykhs.[25] What the clerics could provide to the tribal leadership was religious legitimacy as a counterweight to the religious pronouncements that Al-Qaida dispensed in abundance, and tribal shaykhs sought to manipulate the local religious establishment to gain its collaboration. The tribal shaykhs probably viewed religious legitimacy not as important on a spiritual level as much as an asset to use to cement the loyalty of their fellow tribesmen and to justify their policies. In the early days, those tribal shaykhs who favored resistance against the United States cultivated the clerics, for example, when they invited them to a banquet in order to gain their public support for calling a jihad.[26] Again, as a leading tribal shaykh was preparing to launch the Sahwa movement against Al-Qaida in Al-Anbar, he was careful first to garner religious support: "The first people I tried to get were the religious clerics. . . . I exhorted them to Islamic principles. . . . Through the internet, we got a *fatwa* [i.e., religious opinion] to start the fight against terrorism."[27]

The counterlegitimacy that the local clerics provided the tribes was unexpectedly effective. In fact, Al-Qaida believed that this religious support—or what it termed "the deviant fatwas" and "the lavishing of religious legitimacy (*shariya*) for the Sunnis to volunteer in the apostate government apparatus and to support the Crusaders in the fight against the mujahidin"—had been an important factor in mobilizing forces that contributed to Al-Qaida's setbacks.[28] Predictably, Al-Qaida dealt harshly with local clerics who competed with or opposed it, reportedly killing some five hundred senior Sunni clerics.[29]

Local Islamist resistance groups, having closer ties to the tribes, were not opposed to customary tribal law (as was also true of the secular Bathist-oriented groups), which was a significant benefit to the shaykhs.[30] What was perhaps equally important to the tribal shaykhs was that the clerics—unlike Al-Qaida—in most cases did not have guns, and thus could not threaten the tribal shaykhs directly. The shaykhs, for their part, could generate sufficient muscle to cow clerics. Or, the tribal shaykhs could just push the clerics aside if needed, as occurred in at least one case, in 2003, when a number of Sunni tribal shaykhs actually chose one of their own number to give the *khutba*, or sermon, probably as a way of controlling directly what was to be said in the mosque.[31]

Not surprisingly, the tribal shaykhs would view any organized religious element that sought to compete for power—not only Al-Qaida—as a threat. For example, when the largely Baghdad-based Islamic Party (*Al-Hizb Al-Islami*) tried to vie with the tribal shaykhs by seeking to create its own armed units, recruiting from the same tribal manpower pools, Shaykh Mu'ayyad Al-Hamishi lashed out against the project on behalf of the tribal Sahwa organization. As a result, the Islamic Party was never able to establish much of a presence in the tribal areas.[32] In 2009, tribal shaykhs in charge of the Sahwa even threatened to use force against the rival Islamic Party for allegedly falsifying the results of local elections in Al-Anbar.[33] Relations between Al-Qaida and the competing Islamic Party—which was willing to cooperate with the Iraqi government and with the United States—have also been, as one would expect, very poor, and Al-Qaida targeted its leadership.

Serious differences also developed between Al-Qaida and some of the other religious organizations in Iraq, including the Association of Muslim Scholars (*Hay'at Al-Ulama Al-Muslimin*), the largest organization of Sunni clerics, over strategy and relations with neighboring Arab regimes, and especially over Al-Qaida's fomenting of a civil war rather than focusing its attacks on the Americans. Initially, the association had been sympathetic to Al-Qaida and had opposed the Sahwa initiative, urging tribesmen not to join what it called a trap for the tribes, who were being lured by offers of U.S. arms and money.[34] The association, however, has a more nationalistic hue and is less doctrinaire than Al-Qaida and eventually began to support the Sahwa project after it broke with Al-Qaida. However, by 2009, the association was reportedly again critical of the Sahwa, claiming the latter had itself used terrorist methods and had helped the occupation and once again called for resistance, albeit not in cooperation with Al-Qaida.[35] At the same time, the association tried to lure Sahwa fighters into a new militia that it wanted to set up, and which would target only Americans—a clear challenge to the tribal leadership in the Sahwa.[36]

Ultimately, Al-Qaida's inability to establish a monopoly over religious legitimacy would hamper its strategy, as tribal shaykhs could count on Sunni clerics to neutralize Al-Qaida's religious advantage. At the same time, however, the shaykhs have been careful to restrict all Iraqi Islamic organizations in order to prevent competition in the political field.

THE CHANGED ENVIRONMENT

It was only gradually, with the mounting popular discontent with Al-Qaida and the backing of religious legitimacy, that those shaykhs bent on challenging Al-Qaida realistically could even consider doing so, and only with a new ally: the United States. But, first, the shaykhs had needed an environment that was conducive to such a confrontation and a tribal population that would be willing to countenance cooperation even with the occupier in order to do battle with Al-Qaida. Shaykh Ali Hatim highlighted his sensitivity to the need for popular support, noting that he was initially reluctant to cooperate with the Americans "because we didn't want it to look like an American initiative, because people were opposed to that."[37] Shaykhs can operate effectively only when there is a consensus of support, albeit a consensus they can shape by means of a skillful use of material assets and a deft manipulation of emotions and social symbols. However, at least the prerequisites for such a mobilization had to be in place. Such a benign and malleable popular environment seems to have developed only over time, as the negative impact of Al-Qaida's policies began to be felt progressively at all levels of tribal society.

In effect, Al-Qaida, through its own policies toward the tribal population, provided the catalyst for a changed environment of popular discontent that the shaykhs could exploit, and that some of them did with considerable skill. One can argue that at least some shaykhs saw even the assassinations which Al-Qaida carried out as an opportunity, not only in opening up leadership positions as replacements for those killed, but also as a mobilizing issue to stoke popular anger and to build support for an anti-Al-Qaida policy, including engendering support across tribal lines. Such a public event as the assassination of a tribal leader—especially if carried out in a demeaning and hideous manner—could be exploited to crystallize existing generalized latent popular annoyance toward Al-Qaida and would become the catalyst for action. As one shaykh noted of the killing and decapitation of another shaykh, "We used that as a pretext to start the revolution. . . . We used his tribe under the pretext of vengeance. We elicited his tribe to help us."[38]

CHAPTER 5

THE U.S. STRATEGY MATURES AND THE AWAKENING DEVELOPS

THE MATURING OF U.S. STRATEGY AND CONVERGENCE WITH THE TRIBES

In parallel, there was an evolution in American policy toward a greater willingness to work with the tribes and non-Al-Qaida elements in the resistance, and this proved key in taking advantage of the changed tribal environment. Initially, the Coalition had been reluctant to cooperate with the Sunni tribes, at least on terms acceptable to the tribes. In a way, ideology trumped realpolitik in policy making as, at first, there was suspicion and an expectation of divergent interests on the American side, since the promotion of a modern democratic government seemed to contradict a simultaneous encouragement of the tribal dynamic. As a former U.S. military intelligence officer noted to a reporter, "we couldn't get the CPA [Coalition Provisional Authority] to move.... The standard answer we got from [CPA Head L. Paul] Bremer's people was that the tribes were a vestige of the past, that they have no place in the new democratic Iraq."[1]

As one shaykh later complained, support from the Coalition in 2004, for example, "was minimal—you could say nonexistent."[2] When a delegation representing some three hundred self-styled "genuine" shaykhs met with U.S. representatives in the early days of the occupation and sought to provide advice on greater U.S. flexibility in dealing with Iraqi tribes during security operations, the shaykhs were disappointed when they were ignored, and a senior shaykh claimed that Al-Qaida was able to exploit the continuing excesses that occurred during such operations.[3]

No doubt the fact that many of the Sunni tribes were seen as intertwined with the Bath Party and the former Iraqi army and security services, whose dissolution was official U.S. policy, reinforced such standoffishness on the American side.[4] Some tribal shaykhs, indeed, were involved with various insurgent groups either affiliated with, independent from, or opposed to Al-Qaida.[5] But, one could argue that the U.S. propensity to view all local inhabitants in the Sunni areas as potentially hostile early on had facilitated Al-Qaida's activity among the tribes. And, the sheer complexity of the local situation required some time for familiarization to determine who had influence, at times resulting in some false starts. For example, there were reports that U.S. forces were initially induced to spend money in deals with some fake shaykhs in return for their offer to set up what proved to be nonexistent tribal militias.[6]

It was only by late 2005 that U.S. forces gradually became more supportive of some tribes already fighting against Al-Qaida. Elements of what coalesced into a general U.S. policy had already proved successful, albeit implemented ad hoc and only on a localized scale. For example, according to one Army officer, after an agreement with a local shaykh in return for construction projects in 2005, within a few weeks "what had once been the most dangerous area in my zone became one of the safest."[7]

However, a strategic policy change from the American side was to emerge only in late 2006 as the unfavorable facts on the ground, with a seemingly intractable insurgency posing a serious challenge to a continued U.S. presence, were to catalyze a U.S. policy review leading to a revision in the counterinsurgency approach.[8] One of the salient elements of this revised approach was a greater willingness to engage the Sunni tribes as partners with the Coalition, initially in Al-Anbar and subsequently also in other Sunni areas. Local tribal leaders quickly became aware of the changed atmosphere. As Shaykh Wisam Al-Hardan observed, the United

States had mistrusted the reliability of the tribes at first, but now the U.S. commander in Al-Anbar "had switched his thinking 180 degrees."[9]

DEVELOPING THE AWAKENING

At the same time, as seen, attitudes within the tribes had also matured as a result of Al-Qaida's actions. The tribes had limited interest—or in some cases downright hostility—for the United States' original declared policy objectives of promoting democracy, a market economy, human rights, women's equality, and establishing relations with Israel. Where tribal and U.S. interests increasingly did come to intersect was in their mutual hostility to Al-Qaida. The coalescing of these two trajectories would result in a process, rather than a single event, that came to be known as the Awakening (*Sahwa*). Some of its elements had appeared in Al-Anbar by late 2005 and early 2006, but the emerging alliance had jelled formally only in September 2006, when a number of shaykhs willing to commit their tribes to cooperation with the United States in the fight against Al-Qaida went public. It was then that, thanks to the leadership of Shaykh Abd Al-Sattar Abu Risha, a number of shaykhs had met at his compound and, with U.S. guidance, in effect proclaimed open war on Al-Qaida.[10]

The influence of tribal leaders on the recruitment process for the police and the army was evident immediately. By November 2006, after agreements had been reached with tribal shaykhs, there were three thousand new recruits in the local police in Al-Anbar, representing a thirty-fold increase from May of that year. After Shaykh Abu Risha and his peers urged tribesmen to join the police, in Ramadi alone 4500 signed on.[11] Where earlier there had been barely a dozen recruits, by 2008 the police in the province numbered 24,000.[12]

Similarly, there was a rapid standing up of Sahwa militia units. While there were some urban nontribal Sahwa militias in Baghdad, the Sahwa organizations were overwhelmingly tribally based, and commanders of the Sahwa units were ordinarily tribal shaykhs or notables (terms such as Sahwa commanders and shaykhs are used interchangeably in this study). Iraqi sources highlighted the essentially tribal basis of this organization, often calling it the "Tribal Sahwa" (*al-sahwa al-asha'iriya*).[13]

Within a few months, there were initiatives to replicate the Al-Anbar experience in other areas, but with varying results, given the different and, in some ways more complex, local environment. In some provinces, the Sahwa was set up considerably later, as in the case of Diyala, where it took until October 2008 to do so formally. Nevertheless, by March 2008, the Sahwa nationwide already numbered 91,000 personnel. At the time of the complete handover of responsibility for the Sahwa from the United States to the Iraqi government in April 2009, the Sahwa could boast 118,000 personnel, grouped in over 130 Sahwa councils, or local organizations.

A concerted effort was made to weaken Al-Qaida by peeling away some of its segments, which included a conscious policy of recruiting fighters formerly serving with Al-Qaida into the Sahwa, as was the case in Diyala.[14] As part of this process, there was also an initiative to attract into the Sahwa independent insurgent groups as well as groups heretofore allied with Al-Qaida. Al-Qaida had been able to establish its preeminence in the insurgency, outmaneuvering other organizations that were often motivated more by nationalist or local objectives, as well as the religious parties that were also motivated by religious ideology but differed in outlook from Al-Qaida or were simply competitors for influence. This growing Al-Qaida preeminence not only had created resentment among such organizations but also made them increasingly amenable to working with U.S. forces.

Moreover, many of these resistance groups—and even the religiously oriented organizations—were themselves closely linked to the existing tribal power structures—whose members and even leaders came from the tribes—so that Al-Qaida's unwelcome competition within the insurgency also would automatically spill over into competition with tribal leaders. As the Sahwa's representative, Shaykh Thamir Al-Tamimi, noted in defense of the incorporation of some insurgent groups into the Sahwa, "There is no distinction between the [armed] factions and the tribes . . . the factions are sons of the tribes."[15] The rifts between Al-Qaida and other insurgent groups even before the evolution of the alliance with U.S. forces, in many cases, seem to have been caused by tribal factors, such as revenge for Al-Qaida's killing of fellow tribesmen.[16] One tribal shaykh in the Abu Ghraib area, for example, dealt with the insurgent groups by either persuading them to switch sides or by splitting them through appeals to lower-level cadres. The shaykh was proud that he had thereby succeeded in recruiting a significant number of former insurgents into the tribal Sahwa he was developing—and that was spreading throughout the countryside—before also standing up a similar force in Baghdad.[17]

CHAPTER 6

THE SHAYKHS' POSITIONS ASSURED

For the tribal shaykhs, the attractiveness of an alliance with the United States lay not only in negative terms of enabling them to repel Al-Qaida but also in its immediate positive elements. No doubt many shaykhs or would-be shaykhs increasingly saw that linking themselves with the Americans offered a realistic opportunity to acquire the assets that would enable them to maintain or advance their own positions. One Iraqi pundit, despite a degree of exaggeration, made the point that most tribal shaykhs are motivated not by principle or ideology, but by self-interest.[1] Even a leading tribal leader, Shaykh Hamid Al-Hayis, went so far as to claim that "some shaykhs in Al-Anbar speak with two different faces, and they follow whoever pays them the most, whatever his orientation, while some of them are hired out."[2] Attributing this characteristic to the Bath-era political culture, when Saddam would buy the shaykhs' loyalty, Al-Hayis continued, "Today, for $500, I can induce a number of them [i.e., shaykhs] to yell out their support and to dance."[3] While no doubt reflecting some of the bitterness of personal rivalries and jealousies, such views also captured the fragility and the reality of the interest-based calculations of tribal shaykhs. Realpolitik appears often to trump ideology for most tribal shaykhs, as one has the impression that they are not overly concerned by doctrinal or confessional issues as such. For example, there are confederations or tribes with both Sunni and Shia components, while shaykhs from Sunni and Shia tribes, seeing common tangible interests, have often continued to stay in touch.[4]

Whereas some small tribes had earlier sought to gain leverage against larger ones by allying with Al-Qaida, the option of an alliance with another outside player—in this case, U.S. forces—opened new possibilities to reconfigure the fluid power balance and counter Al-Qaida's unwelcome influence. In some tribes, strongmen (often themselves from lower rungs of a shaykhly family, and at times having an unsavory reputation) took advantage of the passivity or absence abroad of traditional shaykhs and sought to establish themselves as the on-the-ground shaykhs by using U.S. support.[5] As a case in point, the Abu Risha tribe, to become perhaps the most visible player in the development of the Sahwa in Al-Anbar, had not been one of the strongest tribes until its alliance with and support from the United States. Abu Risha himself had been only a second or third-tier shaykh in his own small tribe; however, he and others like him had been present on the ground—while more senior shaykhs were often to be found in safety in Jordan, Syria, or the Gulf states—and thus could take advantage of their presence in forming an alliance with U.S. forces.[6]

Once engaged, the United States could, and did, provide a range of tangible benefits that also affected the ordinary tribesmen's daily lives. There was aid in the form of clothing, food, and public services. What was perhaps key were contracts to build or refurbish military facilities, pumping stations, roads, schools, clinics, and utility services, thanks to which, as one shaykh noted, "we were able to put our people to work."[7] In one case, the U.S. military was even subsidizing a local factory in Al-Anbar.[8] Salaries for tribesmen serving in the Sahwa were an especially an important benefit. According to Shaykh Ali Hatim, in just one section of Baghdad, the United States was supposedly paying $52 million a month on salaries to the Sahwa.[9] Whether such figures were accurate or not, the impression was one of considerable amounts of money being transferred to the tribes.

Equally important was the generous U.S. military assistance to the Sahwa—as well as to the local police—in the form of arms, ammunition, body armor, fuel, equipment, training, vehicles, and salaries for cooperating shaykhs, allowing them to field an organized, more or less full-time military force under their control.[10] The U.S.-supported information operation was also a key element, and Al-Qaida seldom failed to mention the impact of the hostile "disinformation campaign" on local opinion. And, of course, participation by American and Iraqi forces under U.S. guidance in direct combat support of the Sahwa was a vital part of the assistance. The enhanced security environment that U.S. forces, in conjunction with the Sahwa and Iraqi forces, were able to establish made possible an upsurge in reconstruction work, and the amount of money that poured into Al-Anbar from both military and civilian sources was substantial in the local context. By May 2009, the value of completed and on-going projects in Al-Anbar alone totaled some $1.8 billion, quite apart from aid sourced by the U.S. military units' own operating budgets.[11]

Even when funneled indirectly through the Iraqi government, the assumption was that the United States was behind the largesse. Tribes, in fact, saw the United States as a convenient lever to use with the central government in order to motivate the latter to provide aid, no doubt irritating Baghdad and confirming the tribes' view of the paramount U.S. role.[12] Typically, while the U.S. forces were in control of the Sahwa, tribal shaykhs reportedly had lobbied the latter to support the entry of their sons and clients into the Iraqi army, which would also provide the shaykhs with increased leverage within the military and the government.[13] Thanks to the new relationship with the United States, tribal shaykhs could also intercede with the Iraqi government, often through U.S. authorities, to obtain the release of fellow tribesmen who had been detained by the thousands.[14]

What was perhaps especially important as an enabling factor was the personal security that U.S forces now provided to individual shaykhs, which addressed a key vulnerability that Al-Qaida had been able to target up to then. Earlier, as noted, by simply eliminating selected recalcitrant shaykhs, Al-Qaida had been generally successful in nipping tribal resistance movements in the bud. Now, on the contrary, U.S. forces even sat outside the Abu Risha compound and residence for almost a year.[15] Likewise, U.S. forces stood guard outside Shaykh Aifan Al-Isawi's home, while quick-reaction helicopter forces provided protection for Shaykh Ali Sulaiman Al-Dulaymi's convoy.[16] While not foolproof, the new personal security regime afforded sufficient protection to convince shaykhs they could challenge Al-Qaida. The enhanced security with the retrenchment of Al-Qaida's power also enabled shaykhs to once again implement tribal law under their jurisdiction, further enhancing their role within local society.[17]

The shaykhs could now claim credit for having lifted the burden of Al-Qaida's oppressive presence from their fellow tribesmen. At the same time, thanks to the relationship with the United States, shaykhs could strengthen their control over subordinates and clients in their tribes through the power of patronage and prestige that was now available. The influx of U.S. aid not only reflected positively on a shaykh as the tribe's representative and as the key to the tribe's relationship with the United States, but it also enabled shaykhs to benefit directly by acting as the conduit for much of the funding being infused into the local economy. That is, local contracts were generally monopolized by the shaykhs, who were routinely paid in cash.[18] In fact, the United States, as a matter of policy, would seek to strengthen cooperative shaykhs through its provision of contracts to them or, as one senior U.S. military officer was to note, "all of it [i.e., money] we funneled through the sheikhs.... We empowered the sheikhs because there really wasn't a government functioning.... And we did all we could to empower the sheikhs."[19]

From the perspective of cooperative tribal shaykhs, they had found the ideal government—or governing authority—with which to work in the form of the United States. As noted, the latter provided the sinews of war and legitimacy and, at the same time, was a governing authority whose interest was primarily in security (as one could argue that even the promotion of development and services were tied to that primal interest) and had little interest in interfering in tribal affairs or in asking too many questions about a shaykh's political activity within his tribe or about his economic dealings. There was even limited oversight into how the shaykhs spent the money that flowed from the United States. As a senior U.S. military officer operating in Al-Anbar noted, "there's a risk, because you're going to give him [i.e., a shaykh] money, and you're not sure where the money's going to go, because it's difficult for you to get into that area, because of security, to ensure the projects are being taken care of."[20] Not surprisingly, the shaykhs could be expected to pocket a good deal of the money forthcoming from the United States for themselves.[21] The shaykhs' expanded personal budgets, in turn, would enable them to extend their power further by such steps as subsidizing their fellow tribesmen who had joined the local police force, as was the case with Shaykh Ahmad Abu Risha, who noted of the source for financing salaries, weapons, and uniforms for the local police, "Those expenditures came out of our own pockets."[22]

Typically, perhaps as ostentatious display is a traditional form of affirming one's power in tribal society, Shaykh Ahmad Abu Risha was not shy about flaunting his new wealth: "stables of Arabian horses, a camel farm, caged fawns, a pink mansion, and a fleet of armored SUVs. Sheik Ahmed owns properties as well as trade and investment companies in the United Arab Emirates."[23] The Iraq Sahwa Council website, indeed, became little more than a celebration of the cult of personality for Shaykh Ahmad Abu Risha.

Yet, at the same time, a scenario for subsequent tribal instability was set. Perhaps not surprisingly, the endemic intertribal competition that characterized Iraqi society could also engender resentment directed not only against rivals or Al-Qaida but also against the governing authority, which could easily be accused of favoring some shaykhs over others and thereby influencing the power hierarchies within and among the tribes for the future. As one disgruntled shaykh put it, "Sheikh Sattar Abu Risha was made too prominent. He was given much more prominence than he deserved . . . he was given too much money under the guise of various projects, meaning arming of the people."[24] The same shaykh, likewise, had criticized an early U.S. commander in Al-Anbar: "He put people who did not deserve to be in leadership ahead of the real leaders. . . . This is what we refused to accept."[25] While the ensuing war against Al-Qaida and the United States' dominant presence could dampen such rivalries, even organizing the Sahwa and building an Iraqi government would likely only postpone the playing out of such tribal rivalries, especially with the retrenchment of U.S. influence.

CHAPTER 7

THE TRIBAL WAR AGAINST AL-QAIDA

In the near term, however, by providing combat support and personal security, U.S. forces made the area safe, providing the shield that enabled the shaykhs to wield their swords against the most pressing shared threat. In many ways, the war against Al-Qaida that ensued after the alliance between the tribes and the United States and the formation of the Sahwa was a bitter one, whose outcome was not a foregone conclusion, at least in the eyes of the local players. Some tribes, in fact, remained neutral, waiting for the situation to sort itself out.[1]

Operations often took the form of struggles within individual tribes, pitting pro- and anti-Al-Qaida tribesmen against each other, as Al-Qaida had recruited from within the tribes. In fact, a local Sahwa commander, Abu Khalid Al-Mujammai, noted that "most of those we arrest or kill are from our own tribe."[2] Pitched battles were rare, though there were some fierce armed engagements between Sahwa forces—often supported by U.S. combat forces—and Al-Qaida. More frequently, however, the dismantling of Al-Qaida's structure took the form of identifying and isolating operatives within a tribe—a task that only the tribe was capable of doing—and informing the authorities, turning them over, or eliminating them directly. As part of the anti-Al-Qaida fight, according to one shaykh, he had personally reported to the authorities 130 members of Al-Qaida from within his tribe, including an Al-Qaida deputy commander and a minister in Al-Qaida's Islamic State of Iraq, which also suggests the depth to which Al-Qaida had penetrated into the tribal fabric.[3] Significantly, as Al-Anbar's chief of police noted, "the tribal shaykhs were targeted by their fellow tribesmen."[4]

The fight against Al-Qaida frequently followed a familiar pattern of tribal tradition. For example, the lifting of tribal protection (which served as a deterrent in the form of fear of tribal revenge) from an individual was a used as an effective means to deal with suspects. Especially in the countryside, removing tribal protection could be tantamount to a death sentence, because without protection a would-be attacker from another tribe or clan need not fear retaliation by the victim's tribe. For example, one of the key recommendations emerging from a 2007 meeting convened by the mayor and the police chief of Falluja with the local tribal leaders designed to counter the insurgents was that the tribes proclaim that they would disown (*bara'a*) any tribesmen who belonged to a terrorist organization, and that their blood could thus be shed with impunity (*hadr dam*), according to tribal tradition.[5] Likewise, in a characteristically traditional manner, the shaykhs of the Anbakiya confederation in Diyala disowned the entire family of a woman who had been accused of having engaged in a suicide operation.[6]

At times, some shaykhs chafed at U.S. limitations, such as in the domain of rules of engagement. As Shaykh Ali Hatim put it, "All we want is a free hand" and argued that it would be better if the Sahwa could just summarily kill anyone they captured from Al-Qaida, rather than turning them over and worrying about courts and human rights issues.[7]

Such internecine confrontations could be painful. As Shaykh Ali Hatim reminded an interviewer, "the jihadi groups are [also] drawn from the tribes."[8] Indeed, in some instances, the majority of a tribe might have been pro-Al-Qaida.[9] One shaykh in Al-Anbar even expressed discomfort when the crackdowns began on Al-Qaida after the tribal shaykhs and U.S. forces had begun to cooperate, noting that "divisions began to appear among the members of the same tribe, as some of the tribesmen refused to attack to fight and eliminate Al-Qaida's presence in the area."[10] In the clashes between the two tribal factions, he regretted, "we lost a lot of men from both camps."[11] For the fight within a tribe, members from one clan (*fakhdh*) in the local police were often used to fight members of Al-Qaida who belonged to another clan in the same tribe, probably as a way to reduce the natural reluctance to fight one's own closest relatives.[12]

Sahwa casualties in the war against Al-Qaida have been substantial. The Sahwa of Diyala, for example, suffered over one thousand casualties fighting against Al-Qaida.[13] Sahwa leaders have also paid a price, as in the 2006-07 period alone, twenty-eight prominent tribal figures were killed.[14] The intensity of the struggle against Al-Qaida is also illustrated by the fact that, because of the need, tribes were willing to override deeply rooted customs against the involvement of tribeswomen in public life by establishing all-women "Daughters of Iraq" units intended to search and prevent female Al-Qaida bombers from mounting attacks.[15] To be sure, as one of the leaders of the Daughters of Iraq, Wujdan Adil, confirmed, "Society in the province was strongly opposed to having women participate in security work." The women's motivation, supporting "security for society and providing an income for their children," was quite similar to that of their male counterparts.[16] Other tribeswomen have also been encouraged to learn how to shoot, and one shaykh in Al-Anbar, underlining the gravity of the situation that would lead to taking such a step, noted that "were it not for the security situation in our country, we would not have agreed to let women bear arms."[17]

The establishment of the Sahwa—as the embodiment of the changed relationship with the tribes—was a key element in the turnaround of the situation with Al-Qaida, as it generated the large standing forces familiar with the local situation that could challenge Al-Qaida, at least with U.S. combat support. The switching of allegiance by a shaykh could have significant influence on security in an area. As Army Colonel Sean MacFarland noted of the situation in Al-Anbar, "Once a tribal leader flips, attacks on American forces in that area stop almost overnight."[18] Al-Qaida's mobility was now hampered significantly. The tribes, being able to limit access and capable of spotting outsiders easily, were key to area control so that it was very difficult for Al-Qaida to operate without at least a tribe's indifference. For example, two tribes in Al-Anbar, after having made a deal with and receiving arms from U.S. forces, were confident that they could now "prevent any outsider from entering their territory," as everyone was now liable to a close inspection.[19] Foreign Arabs were at a disadvantage because they were outside the Iraqi tribal network and thus could not count on any tribal refuge. Even with tribal support, foreign fighters experienced difficulties blending into the rural environment, and now often migrated to the suburbs of Iraqi cities, where they would be less conspicuous, to find refuge.[20] Equally important was the tribes' ability to reveal the location of Al-Qaida arms caches, the loss of which limited its ability to move at an operational level. Earlier, auxiliaries could prepare arsenals which mobile Al-Qaida units could use when arriving in an area, since it was considerably easier than trying to travel with arms and ammunition.

Using any measure of success, the results of the Sahwa operations in cooperation with Coalition forces were impressive. In Al-Anbar, as General David H. Petraeus, Commander, Multinational Force-Iraq, noted, "A year ago the province was assessed as 'lost' politically. Today, it is a model of what happens when local leaders and citizens decide to oppose Al-Qaeda."[21] Monthly attack levels in Al-Anbar had declined from some 1,350 in October 2006 to slightly over 200 in August 2007 and, during the same period, 4,400 arms caches had been discovered, some 1,700 more than had been discovered in all of the preceding year.[22] By summer 2007, Al-Anbar had been largely secured, and Shaykh Ahmad Abu Risha estimated that there were only two to three hundred Al-Qaida operatives left in the province by November of that year.[23] Al-Qaida openly recognized that the Sahwa had become its biggest threat, and even calculated that the creation of the Sahwa had saved U.S. forces from "a disaster."[24]

CHAPTER 8

AL-QAIDA RESPONDS

Al-Qaida was unprepared for the geological shift in the human terrain and the resulting shock and impact of the tribes' new cooperation with the Coalition. If anything, the Al-Qaida leadership in Iraq had been overconfident that the tribal shaykhs, whether willingly or not, supported and would continue to support their organization and that Al-Qaida would remain in permanent control of the areas where they had established themselves. As one of Al-Zarqawi's senior lieutenants, Abu Jafar Al-Ansari, had noted confidently, "As you see, we are completely safe here in Al-Ramadi, and we move around among our beloved brothers the tribal notables and shaykhs, who have opened their hearts and their homes to us."[1] To a significant extent, Al-Qaida's leadership believed that the fact they had recruited from among the tribes would secure Al-Qaida's presence, since a tribe was not expected to turn against its own sons, or as Al-Ansari had asked rhetorically, "How can we imagine that the tribal chiefs would expel their sons or those who support them?"[2]

The intensity and extent of the turnaround in the stance of the tribes to Al-Qaida came as something of a shock. As the Islamic State of Iraq's minister of war later noted bitterly about the tribes, "you kicked us in the face."[3] Also writing later, another Al-Qaida in Iraq figure noted that the appearance of the Sahwa and the ensuing loss of "many men and much territory" had forced his organization to adopt a new strategy: to "play dead" (*al-tazhahur bi'l-mawt*), that is, to go underground.[4] At a tactical level, Al-Qaida units were equally unprepared for such shifts in alliances. For example, in one instance, after a commander of a group in Samarra affiliated with Al-Qaida—and himself a tribal shaykh—had reached a deal with other local tribal shaykhs and U.S. forces to suspend hostilities, an Al-Qaida unit sent to Samarra was surprised and angered by the unexpected turn of events and found it impossible to continue operations and had to leave the area.[5]

When a response came, Al-Qaida, as one could expect, excoriated the Sahwa initiative. Al-Zarqawi, always wary of the tribes, had complained even before the formal beginning of the Sahwa that "some tribal shaykhs have abandoned their religion."[6] In a sermon, Abu Umar Al-Baghdadi, who had become the head of the recently created Islamic State of Iraq, when referring to the most prominent shaykhs in the Sahwa, expressed the depth of anger which Al-Qaida felt: "Oh armies of God and supporters of the sharia, eradicate this noxious bacteria and purify the world . . . [use] any force and pressure and tear apart their limbs, demolish their houses, burn their property, and target their businesses and all their belongings."[7]

A communique that the Islamic State of Iraq issued after Al-Zarqawi's death labeled those who joined the Sahwa "mercenaries." It attributed the tribesmen's "jihadi and tribal" desire for revenge against Al-Qaida for the latter's earlier killing of their relatives (which Al-Qaida now justified by accusing those they had killed of having been "spies and agents") as one motive for their joining the Sahwa.[8] Another explanation for the Sahwa, from Al-Qaida's perspective, was that this was simply a pretext for those who wanted to take power within a tribe.[9] At the same time, as part of its information campaign intended for damage control, Al-Qaida also claimed that three-quarters of all tribal leaders had given the baya to the recently proclaimed Islamic State of Iraq, which was most unlikely.[10]

Al-Qaida's conclusion at the time was that it was obligatory to fight a jihad against such traitorous elements and to impose the Islamic penalties on them for their "apostasy and infidelity."[11] The head of the Islamic State of Iraq, Abu Umar Al-Baghdadi, was even more cutting, characterizing the Sahwa leadership by such epithets as "servants of the Magian Persian parties" and "the Shia's shoes."[12] He also argued for the need to put tribal loyalties aside, as this had been the key to Muhammad's success during the early days of Islam. More directly, he condemned the shaykhs who had turned against Al-Qaida: "May God damn them all."[13] Al-Qaida routinely called the Sahwa "the satanic Sahwa" (*al-sahwa al-shaytaniya*), "the harmful Sahwa" (*sahwat al-darar*), or the "Apostasy Sahwa" (*sahwat al-ridda*).

However, some influential figures in Al-Qaida, based both outside and inside Iraq, seem to have tried to be more flexible and realistic. Bin Ladin, while reminding his audience that religious ties supersede tribal or national ones, nevertheless was still going out of his way in late 2007 to praise Iraq's tribes, speaking of them as "our beloved awesome tribes," promising that they would be rewarded on Judgment Day if they remained loyal and reminding them that the Americans would leave Iraq eventually.[14] Likewise, although Shaykh Ata Najd Al-Rawi, a respected Iraqi figure in Al-Qaida, attributed the transfer of allegiances by the shaykhs to "tribal chauvinism" and to "interests of tribal ambitions," he also admitted the possibility that Al-Qaida had transgressed against the tribes or, as he put it, "We advise our brothers, if it is proven that errors occurred, to correct all their errors against the tribes, and to offer the latter promises and guarantees and pay reparations, and to win them over using whatever means possible." He also highlighted the positive role that cooperative tribal leaders could play for Al-Qaida. For example, he pointed out that with their intimate knowledge of their fellow tribesmen, shaykhs—if favorably inclined to Al-Qaida—could act as an effective security clearance mechanism for prospective members, and he urged referral to tribal leaders before accepting any recruits.[15] At the same time, he advised that if the tribes remained obstinate then "do not show them mercy" and suggested the need to kill some shaykhs "so that they serve as a warning to anyone who thinks to follow along the same path."[16] More analytically, Al-Qaida in Iraq attributed the United States' success in weaning away the tribes to an intensive media campaign against Al-Qaida and to the fact that the United States had "flooded [the area] with money."[17] One Al-Qaida commander blamed the tribes' switching of allegiance on "the most trivial of reasons," such as the desire for jobs as provided by the United States.[18]

Mother Al-Qaida blamed the reverses on a competing nationalist and Bathist outlook in Iraq that it claimed was dominant.[19] Bin Ladin explained the tribes' defection as the result of the Americans' decision, in the wake of the perceived failure of military means, to refocus their efforts to the political arena, as they had sought to "lead the tribes astray by buying their conscience." He claimed that "many tribes," however, had refused to go along, and he regarded such tribes as "the proud free tribes."[20] He praised those tribal shaykhs who gave the baya to Al-Zarqawi's successor as head of the Islamic State of Iraq.[21] Ayman Al-Zawahiri himself exhorted the Iraqi tribes to avoid cooperating with the Sahwa project, appealing to their honor, as he warned that any tribe that betrayed the jihad would be remembered in history as traitors and agents, while those who did not would be remembered with honor.[22]

Al-Qaida at all levels realized that its plans for Iraq had gone badly, and that tribal loyalties had been a significant factor for this deteriorating situation. Although Al-Qaida allegedly had initially expected to field a large local mujahidin force, and claimed it had had 100,000 fighters in the field at one time, a military expert writing in a journal published by Mother Al-Qaida rued, "What happened to them? Don't be surprised if, at most, only one thousand of them remain," and called the result "a military disaster by any measure." Pointing to the Dulaym tribal confederation, the article drew a stark comparison between the first three years when the latter confederation reportedly had prided itself in its defiant resistance whereas "today you have some of the tribal chiefs who are openly and publicly allied to the Americans!" It praised, however, those mujahidin who had remained loyal to Al-Qaida, for although they too were from the same tribes, they had "preferred loyalty to religion over loyalty to tribe."[24]

Al-Qaida, of course, fought back as best it could in what now had become a desperate contest for survival in a hostile environment. In a fight to just stay alive, many foreign fighters left the country. Many Iraqi Al-Qaida fighters, including entire units, joined the Sahwa.[25] Sermons in the mosques had urged Al-Qaida members to do so.[26] Other Al-Qaida fighters apparently joined the Sahwa not out of conviction but as a refuge. From the first, there were indications that at least some of the Sahwa units had been set up with the express purpose of serving as a tribal cover for a continuing relationship with Al-Qaida.[27] Other Al-Qaida fighters took refuge by joining the local police, as in Diyala.[28] Still other fighters sought a more conducive environment in cities, where they had a better chance of blending in. Some members of Al-Qaida who were discontented with its treatment of the population and had urged reform just left the organization, without, however, joining the Sahwa.[29]

A key component of Al-Qaida's response was to again target the offending shaykhs, who were now in charge of the Sahwa forces. Often, the preferred instrument was the use of members from the shaykh's own tribe, as those were most likely to be successful and least likely to trigger tribal revenge. As one Iraqi security source noted of the frequent attempted assassinations of shaykhs, "One finds the executioner and the victim from the same tribe."[30] According to Shaykh Ali Hatim, "Most shaykhs were killed at the hands of their own sons, the sons of their tribes . . . don't think for a minute that someone comes from outside the tribe and can assassinate the shaykh of a tribe. That's impossible."[31] In fact, Shaykh Abd Al-Sattar Abu Risha's assailant in September 2007 had also been his fellow tribesman and bodyguard.[32] Perhaps not surprisingly, Abd Al-Sattar's successor soon thereafter hired foreign workers as cooks, cleaners, and servants for his compound, whom he no doubt viewed as less a risk than even his fellow tribesmen.[33] Multiple attacks continued against the same leading individuals and their families. However, distressing as such attacks might be, they were unlikely by themselves to change the tribes' orientation in Al-Qaida's favor now that there was an alliance with the United States, unless the overall political environment itself changed. Clearly, Al-Qaida's military response to the Sahwa-Coalition onslaught was unlikely to succeed, and the organization would have to reassess its assumptions and strategy if it were to remain an effective player even in the Sunni areas.

CHAPTER 9

AL-QAIDA ADAPTS

Although Al-Qaida was impressed by the scope and impact of the Sahwa movement, at least publicly it believed early on that the Sahwa project was fragile and not deeply rooted in Al-Anbar's tribes.[1] Al-Qaida took emergency measures in an effort at damage control. As noted above, Al-Qaida sought to appeal to the tribes by installing a local individual, Abu Umar Al-Baghdadi, as the new leader of the Islamic State of Iraq, following Al-Zarqawi's death. An Iraqi Al-Qaida figure, perhaps to highlight the organization's respect for Iraqis and its own flexibility, stressed that Al-Baghdadi had originally not even been a member of the organization or a commander and yet had been put in charge.[2] As well, Al-Qaida sought to give the appearance that it would become more discerning in whom it targeted, beginning to emphasize explicitly that it did not target all tribal shaykhs, especially not "honorable" ones, but only those who served as agents and who were involved in the Sahwa.[3] Despite the harsh treatment of many shaykhs by Al-Qaida, the latter remained overly optimistic, and unrealistic, still assuming that over 70 percent of the Sunni tribal shaykhs would adhere to the Islamic State of Iraq.[4]

REASSESSING THE SITUATION

Mother Al-Qaida, in a comprehensive policy review from late 2009 to early 2010, sought to analyze what had gone wrong in Iraq and to provide policy guidance to its followers in that country in order to implement a more successful revised strategy for the future. The document eschews religious exhortations, noting that "it is pointless for us to play the role of a preacher and recite verses from the Qur'an and the hadith," focusing instead on an analysis very much in the realistic mode.[5] Often, such analyses crystallize and systematize verbal discussions and initiatives that have already been occurring within Al-Qaida decision-making circles and among field commanders, and reflect at least an emerging consensus. The intent of such public Al-Qaida documents was also to reinforce guidance already provided to regional leaders in verbal or written form and to inform the rank and file of official policy.

Perhaps the key difference from an earlier strategy Al-Zarqawi had pursued in Iraq was in how to deal with the tribes. The author(s) of the document recognize the success of the U.S. tribal strategy and concede that "no doubt, recruiting the tribes in order to eliminate the mujahidin was a brilliant and bold idea."[6] The document, however, posits that there is still hope for Al-Qaida to regain its lost position. To win over the tribes again, the author(s) admit, is not easy, due to "security and societal obstacles," but, as the document stresses, "this is a plan which is *well worth the effort*." (emphasis in the original)[7] And, moreover, if the "Crusaders" were able to overcome such obstacles, then "the difficulties should not mean that the plan should be rejected outright."[8]

The document concedes that "some areas and villages may hold grudges and be suspicious of the mujahidin," blaming hostile propaganda or even "errors" which some mujahidin may have committed in the past, or because of the dominance of the Sahwa. However, the perceived internal contradictions of what it calls the "infidel Sahwa"—which is said to contain already within it "the elements of collapse and disintegration"—are said to provide critical vulnerabilities that can be exploited. The document expresses the hope that material interests and tribal loyalties would be only temporary elements of cohesion and that they would not be able to serve as a stable basis for the Sahwa.[9]

In addition to an intensified information campaign to explain what the plan for an Islamic State of Iraq entailed, a new approach toward the tribes was suggested in this document. One line of operation that had especially impressed Al-Qaida was the effectiveness of tribally based militias, like the Sahwa, to control an area. In fact, this document urges that this successful initiative be replicated by the creation of similar pro-Al-Qaida tribally based forces. With the introduction of such locally based tribal units to protect Al-Qaida members and to expel the police and the Sahwa, the document emphasizes that the current security situation can be reversed and that all the "erroneous impressions" about the mujahidin will then "evaporate," since the mujahidin will all be among their own fellow tribesmen.[10]

Rather than insisting on specifically Al-Qaida military units, the authors of the document recommend existing local tribal militias or units (*majmuat*) be retained, having a minimal foreign footprint but with Al-Qaida exerting its control by providing the leadership—specifically a military commander and a qadi—as well as providing the ideological orientation for such tribally based militias. According to the document, "as is well known," relying on "mobile military forces" (*al-intishar al-askari*)—which here appears to mean mobile stand-alone Al-Qaida units with outsiders and Iraqis and not tied to a specific tribe or tribal territory—to control areas is "a source of weakness." Rather than railing against tribal loyalties as had earlier been the case, now local tribal forces—composed apparently of fighters not necessarily ideologically committed to Al-Qaida's beliefs—protecting their own homes and their folk are best suited for Al-Qaida's area of control, for "these tribal units draw their power from their local environment, since they represent everyone in the area which they are defending and protecting."[11] These units would be modeled on the Sahwa but, in Al-Qaida's case, would have a jihadist orientation. As the document urged, "*We call on the Islamic State of Iraq to establish jihadi Sahwa Councils.*" (emphasis in the original)[12] However unrealistic such a proposal for creating a jihadist Sahwa might be in the local context, what it does underscore is

Al-Qaida's acceptance of the reality of the continuity and strength of tribal cohesion and of the necessity of accommodating it.

Mother Al-Qaida also advised its followers in Iraq to accept neutrals rather than create enemies by forcing Iraqis to choose sides. In his eulogy for Al-Zarqawi, Bin Ladin himself rebuked the latter implicitly for his rigid extremism, noting that "he [i.e., Al-Zarqawi] had clear instructions to focus his combat against the occupying aggressors, and especially against the Americans, and to treat as neutral all those who wanted to be neutral."[13] A foreign senior observer with close ties to Al-Qaida continued to urge the organization to have a greater flexibility particularly toward the tribes in Iraq, noting that "it is necessary to have an open-door policy toward the neutral groups of the Iraqi people in order to recruit them to the Islamic State of Iraq's project, and especially so the tribes, since they are good people and will provide fresh fighters to the Islamic State of Iraq, as well as expertise and energy which one cannot afford to pass up at all."[14]

In particular, Mother Al-Qaida recognized the need to cooperate to a greater extent with the tribal shaykhs: "This concept presupposes cooperation with the honest tribal shaykhs in establishing security forces from the youth of their tribes for the defense of their territory against the puppet police and the Crusader forces and to cleanse an area of them completely."[15] A key element that sets off this revised strategy is that now, rather than eliminating or bypassing the tribal shaykhs, Al-Qaida in Iraq is instructed to work through the shaykhs. As the document urges, Al-Qaida should now operate in coordination with the tribes and the jihadi Sahwa should be financed by the tribes as well as by Al-Qaida, but that can "only be accomplished by convincing the tribal shaykhs and notables, and then the rest of the people residing in the area can be convinced."[16] Working with the tribal leadership, according to this document, provides a greater likelihood "of obtaining the agreement, loyalty, and support of the people" rather than trying "to control the area by force" and ignoring the notables.[17] In a section entitled "Winning the

Tribal Shaykhs' Loyalty," the document stresses that Al-Qaida must negotiate with the shaykhs, as this will make them believe they are important to Al-Qaida, and make them feel they are doing something useful for their people and their area. This approach is said to induce shaykhs to be more committed and more courageous, provided the idea is presented to them in an effective and convincing manner.[18]

Al-Qaida realized that newly minted shaykhs who were able to wield power—and whom the document derides as "bandits and those with previous baggage"—had entrenched themselves thanks to the armed power and material benefits they had accrued through their alliance with the "Crusaders." These assets allegedly gave such shaykhs a decisive advantage over pro-Al-Qaida elements—labeled "the honorable shaykhs and the youth." But, by the same token, and whether correctly or not, Al-Qaida believed that the new power elite and their new "law of the jungle" and "moral libertarianism" had alienated it from the majority of the tribesmen and that would undermine popular acceptance of the Sahwa.[19]

Some Sahwa leaders had indeed been sensitive initially to the appearance of receiving significant U.S. support, in part because of apparent condemnation from Iraqi critics living abroad and from shaykhs opposed to the Sahwa.[20] In response, Shaykh Fawaz Al-Jarba, a senior shaykh of the one-million-member-strong Shammar tribal confederation and a prominent figure, had in fact gone out of his way to publicly deny that there had been any combined operations with U.S. forces. For his part, another shaykh sneered (albeit unconvincingly) at those who claimed that "'the Americans finance them, that the Americans give them billions;' come on, uncle, just tell me what it is they give us? Ask the Americans themselves, uncle, and I challenge the Americans, I challenge them from where I sit whether they have given us a single cent.... By God the Almighty, we have not taken from them either weapons nor money, nor anything at all."[21]

There are indications that rethinking along Mother Al-Qaida's lines had also been occurring at least among some members of Al-Qaida in Iraq, particularly those in the local leadership who recognized that there were problems. For example, a commander who had recently broken with Al-Qaida, had believed that targeting the Sahwa, instead of wooing back its members and focusing attacks against the Americans, had been a major error and had alienated the Sunni population.[22]

At the same time, some of the original limitations of Al-Qaida's appeal to the tribes appear to persist in the strategy outlined in Mother Al-Qaida's policy review document. For example, the emphasis on wooing the tribal youth remained in force. Al-Qaida in Iraq was advised to select military commanders who have experience, patience, and the sophistication needed specifically to work effectively with tribal youths.[23] Indeed, tribal youths are seen as key in "convincing" merchants and others who are employed to donate money for the projected Al-Qaida-run tribal self-defense forces.[24]

Similarly, the policy review document's calls for an application of the sharia continued an earlier line of operation. The document acknowledges that the motivations for the establishment and spread of the Sahwa had been not only material incentives but also a "hate for the Islamic sharia and for the obligations which its principles entail and for its mores, and a desire to be free of all of that in pursuit of passions and pleasures."[25] Yet, at the same time, the application of the sharia remains a central tenet of Al-Qaida's worldview, and something that cannot be abandoned with impunity. The declared objective as stated in this document was still to continue "raising the banner of the sharia so that the people can be judged by it, which is an obligation at the very heart of religion, and not something marginal which one can postpone until it becomes possible."[26] In its advice to Al-Qaida in Iraq, Mother Al-Qaida continued to oppose customary law for the tribes of Iraq, noting that it was a throwback to the jahiliya period and contrary to Islamic law.[27] However, the focus now was to use the Sharia against "thieves and bandits"—implicitly rather than, as before, against anyone who might not adhere to the letter of the law—which presumably would make its application more palatable.[28] As the document acknowledges, living under the sharia "appears to some to be a frightening and terrifying prospect," but the document also exudes confidence that once people actually experience sharia, they would come to feel otherwise.[29]

Ultimately, the question was not whether Al-Qaida had abandoned its basic principles and objectives but whether it had adapted sufficiently to overcome earlier barriers to effectiveness and whether the situation on the ground had also changed enough to make Al-Qaida's modified approach meaningful.

CHAPTER 10

THE TRIBES AND THE IRAQI GOVERNMENT: A ROCKY RELATIONSHIP

With the progressive reduction in U.S. military and political involvement, the human terrain once again was shifting. In particular, as part of the phased handover of responsibility for the Sahwa from the U.S. forces to the Iraqi government in the December 2008 to April 2009 period, the identity of the government changed for the Sahwa to that of a local player. The relationship between the tribes and the Iraqi government would have been a difficult one even without the presence of Al-Qaida, and the result has been an operational environment that is more favorable for Al-Qaida, by engendering potential critical vulnerabilities that the latter can seek to exploit. In fact, Al-Qaida viewed the relationship between the Sahwa and the Iraqi government as a critical vulnerability to exploit, with Ayman Al-Zawahiri noting that the "the Sahwa has been undermined and has become threatened by the Shia [i.e., Iraqi] government."[1] The relationship between the Sunni tribes and the central government even during the common war against Al-Qaida was often marked by mistrust and mutually exclusive expectations and objectives. The tribes' quest for power and autonomy, supported by its ready-made Sahwa armed muscle, was bound to make any partnership with the Iraqi state an uneasy one at best.

A CLASH OF POLITICAL CULTURES: CENTRALIZATION VS. DECENTRALIZATION

Realistically, given the country's political culture, any Iraqi state would be predisposed to centralize power and would look at a phenomenon such as the Sahwa—or at the factor of assertive tribes that lay behind the Sahwa militia—with concern as a potential or active threat. The relationship between the Sunni tribes and the government has been exacerbated by the perception in the eyes of most Sunnis of a government, army, and security force that are predominantly Shia, with significant influence from—or even domination by—Iran.[2] The government, for its part, has eyed Sunni regions with suspicion as being potentially disloyal, as being willing to cooperate with neighboring Sunni regimes, and as being tied to the past Saddam regime. To be sure, sympathy for the Bath party does continue to be active within some tribes , which is not surprising, given the links of some tribal leaders with Saddam before 2003. For example, Shaykh Ahmad Abu Risha defended the Bathists, stressing that "the Bathists are Iraqis and we want them to continue living safely in this country. . . . Why should we force the Bathists to leave Iraq? . . . There are six million Bathists we should win over." And, he praised the army under Saddam, in which he himself had been an officer.[3] In 2011, a number of major Sunni tribal shaykhs asked the government to rescind the 2008 "Accountability and Justice" law that Sunnis have viewed as a tool for revenge against former Bathists.[4] With the additional element of Al-Qaida in play, it was to be expected that the government's suspicions of the Sunni tribes and of the Sahwa would increase even more. Characteristically, Prime Minister Al-Maliki fretted in public that the Sahwa had become penetrated by both the Bath and Al-Qaida and claimed that it was "working to create another Saddam."[5]

The Iraqi government that eventually came into being, with its Shia coloring, was never quite comfortable with how the Sunni Sahwa was established, thereby sowing the seeds of mistrust from the start. Shaykh Fawaz Al-Jarba of the Shammar confederation was later to claim that as early as 2004 he had proposed to the Iraqi government to set up a Sahwa-like tribal force, but "we could not do it at the time."[6] What is more, according to Shaykh Wisam Al-Hardan, "The political entities started pressuring the American commanders in Anbar not to help us. We met with Al-Maliki, and a verbal confrontation ensued, and we threatened him. If we were not given any assistance from them, we were going to push the terrorists into their territory, close the borders, and let them worry about the terrorists."[7] Shaykh Abd Al-Sattar Abu Risha again sought support from the Iraqi government in 2007, but he complained that this was slow in coming and fellow shaykhs from Al-Anbar threatened that if Baghdad did not provide such support, Al-Anbar would set up its own autonomous canton, hardly a gesture that would have reassured the central government.[8] A Shia journalist, perhaps reflecting government views, expressed his misgivings early about the Sahwa, drawing attention to the fact that the Sahwa's creation had bypassed the Iraqi government in an extralegal move and that arming Sunni tribes would weaken the government in the long run.[9]

Tribal shaykhs, in the absence of a strong central government, had already sought to flex their muscles immediately after the collapse of the Saddam regime, even on the international scene. For example, the Shaykhs' Council, established by local tribal initiative after the fall of Saddam, had soon thereafter even begun dealing directly with the United Nations, the Arab League, and various Arab governments.[10] A press report, citing unnamed "sources close to the Iraqi government," had called President George W. Bush's visit to the Sahwa leader Shaykh Abd Al-Sattar Abu Risha in September 2007 "a not very friendly signal, which contradicted protocol and embarrassed the politicians who were brought in after midnight to meet with the U.S. president in the strongholds of the tribal militias."[11]

Shortly thereafter, a tribal delegation from Al-Anbar was invited to Washington in 2007 to meet President Bush and other senior government officials, and Shaykh Ali Hatim noted that Shaykh Abd Al-Sattar Abu Risha would be "the interlocutor between the General Council of Arab and Iraqi Tribes and the American side," that is, that the tribes would bypass the Iraqi government in dealing directly with the United States.[12] The Iraqi government was reportedly angry that the U.S. government had not even informed it when the invitation had been extended to the Anbar Sahwa leaders for that visit, as the Iraqi prime minister's adviser for tribal affairs, Karim Bakhati, noted in a thinly veiled rebuke that "one would have thought that [the invitation] would have been sent through the Iraqi government," and concluded that "sending the invitations in this manner bypasses the authority of the central government."[13] He also reiterated that "it is indispensable that the central government be aware of all initiatives whether from the American side or from any political formation."[14] Nevertheless, the following year, the head of the Council of Tribal Shaykhs, Shaykh Majid Abd Al-Razzaq Al-Ali Sulayman, would visit the Egyptian foreign minister in Cairo, in a clear show of defiance to the Baghdad government.[15] The fact that, reportedly, encouragement and money for the Sahwa also came from Saudi Arabia and Jordan, where many of the Iraqi shaykhs resided, must also not have pleased the Baghdad government, which often has had tense relations with its Sunni neighbors.[16]

When the U.S.-Iraq strategic framework agreement was being debated in 2008, Shaykh Ahmad Abu Risha expressed his strong support—which in and of itself the Iraqi government would have welcomed—but at the same time reminded listeners of his visit to Washington and of the assurances that President Bush and other government officials had given him personally on the subject of a future U.S. withdrawal, which probably again irritated Baghdad officials.[17] The government's long-standing, deep-seated hostility of the Sahwa did not bode well for the latter in the future, as an Iraqi Army general told the press, "These people [i.e., the Sahwa] are like cancer, and we must remove them."[18]

The U.S. handover of responsibility for the Sahwa to the Iraqi government crystallized the need to accommodate competing demands and visions between the government and the Sunni tribes and highlighted the need to develop a new relationship. Friction between the Sahwa and the central government was indicative of a deeper mutual suspicion, as Sunni tribal leaders have sought more power by at times crossing the boundary of their local authority, and thus representing a threat from the perspective of the central state. In the largely Shia south, it seems that the central government has in general been able to work out a somewhat more stable balance with tribal leaders, perhaps aided by the shared Shia linkages, as well as by a mutual interest to counter the Sadr and other Shia militias that challenge the power both of Prime Minister Nuri Al-Maliki and the tribal shaykhs. In fact, in the largely Shia areas of central and south Iraq, Prime Minister Al-Maliki established in early 2008 the Tribal Support Councils (*Majalis Al-Isnad Al-Asha'iri*), structures resembling the Sahwa and intended to organize tribal support for security. However, unlike the Sahwa, the initiative came from the central government, and the support councils were widely viewed as an instrument for Prime Minister Al-Maliki to influence and control tribal shaykhs, rather than as a threat.[19]

The government has been particularly wary of the Sahwa becoming a parallel Sunni armed force. As part of the handover, Al-Maliki expressed his concern at a press conference that the government needed to ensure it had a monopoly over armed force and announced that it would limit Sahwa powers of arrest, while expressing the need "to close out the Sahwa file."[20]

The issue of the Sahwa is also of concern to the broader Shia community, and this was echoed in 2007 by the then-leader of the Supreme Islamic Iraqi Council (one of the larger Shia parties), the late Abd Al-Aziz Al-Hakim. In a holiday sermon, he stressed that the Sahwa must be a reinforcement to the government, "not a replacement for it," especially in mixed areas, and that "weapons must only be in the hands of the government."[21]

Major General Mahdi Sabih, commander of the Ministry of the Interior's security forces, reflected the government's mistrust of the Sahwa when he expressed his unease that the Sahwa had become "a third security force" in addition to the army and the national police, and he rejected Sahwa requests to establish a separate ministry to handle their affairs. He also claimed that U.S. support had encouraged the shaykhs to demand more privileges, which would result in "security chaos," while noting that some tribes had even set up their local Sahwa without any real need to do so and that the latter had become little more than employment offices for the shaykhs' relatives.[22]

Perhaps fueling government concerns has also been the fact that the Al-Anbar Sahwa had tried to expand beyond a local area of operations by their activities in neighboring Salah Al-Din Province and by seeking to open an intelligence office in Baghdad.[23] Iraqi tribes can extend over wide areas, and tribes in Al-Anbar had members who had settled in cities, for example, so it was not surprising that those tribes would also seek to operate in Baghdad and elsewhere outside their home province.[24] However, the government, not unexpectedly, refused permission for the Al-Anbar Sahwa's desired intelligence office in Baghdad, probably apprehensive about seeing such armed groups controlled by individuals with a power base beyond the government's reach.[25]

In fact, Shaykh Abd Al-Sattar Abu Risha had aspired to be recognized as the leader of the Sahwa in all of Iraq, according to his brother and successor, Ahmad, who likewise told President Bush when the two met that he represented all the shaykhs of Iraq.[26] Arguing that Al-Anbar was most deserving of such leadership because of the success achieved there, Abd Al-Sattar Abu Risha had hoped to convert the Sahwa into a national political force—no doubt with himself as leader.[27] His brother Ahmad, for his part, had been rumored in the run-up to the 2010 elections to be seeking the presidency for himself. He was also thought to have lobbied Gulf sources for money and support, thereby no doubt further alienating Prime Minister Al-Maliki, who would have viewed such aspirations as a threat to his own precarious position.[28] Significantly, during a conference in 2010 of tribal shaykhs and notables, which Prime Minister Al-Maliki attended, the tribes' spokesman, Shaykh Abbud Wahid Al-Isawi, requested that the government establish a separate tribal "National Council" in order to enable the tribes to "play a role in national affairs," asserting that "we are Iraq, both its history and future."[29]

In many ways, the Sunni tribal shaykhs have been able to entrench themselves at the local level, and any centralization would involve a loss of their privileges and, by extension, those of their fellow tribesmen. With the buildup of the Sahwa, tribal leaders in the Sunni areas had seen their chance to develop political control over their home areas, and had used the Sahwa period to establish their authority over the local administrative machinery. For example, before the handover of control from the U.S. forces to the Iraqi government, some Sahwa leaders sought to assume local government functions, such as Shaykh Mustafa Kamil Al-Jiburi, head of the Sahwa in South Baghdad, who announced that his organization intended to "rebuild the infrastructure of the schools, clinics, streets, and electricity."[30] In Al-Anbar, tribal shaykhs, through their clients, even established control over the local university.[31]

Sunni shaykhs also tend to dominate provincial councils, with most council members themselves being shaykhs, thereby ensuring a built-in situation of conflict with officials appointed by and responsible to the central government.[32] As Shaykh Umar Al-Jiburi, head of the Independent Iraqi Tribal Assembly, asserted, "Tribesmen ... must have the greatest say in selecting the members of the local municipal councils and of the local government" and affirmed that the "tribes are the locus of the distribution of power, with their votes, in selecting the provincial councils and the Parliament."[33] As a leading shaykh in Al-Anbar had noted with pride, the Sahwa expected to be treated as an equal player, alongside the government and the U.S. forces for, as he stressed, "we are not government employees."[34]

Not surprisingly, the government spokesman, Ali Dabbagh, had complained that "the Sahwa councils in some provinces have become substitutes for the government and the state and its machinery, and therefore the government is concerned that the Sahwa may expand at the expense of the state's authority."[35] As a case in point, in Salah Al-Din Province, tribal shaykhs held a meeting at which they decided to remove a local police chief and to retain the local Sahwa commander, even though the province's deputy governor had wanted the latter removed.[36] Significantly, during a meeting in Al-Anbar with tribal leaders in October 2010, Prime Minister Al-Maliki chided the shaykhs to stop interfering in the security establishment's affairs and to stop obstructing operations.[37] On the other hand, as Shaykh Naji Al-Mahallawi of Ramadi warned, "We will not allow anyone to neglect the tribal role." Accusing the mayor of Falluja of doing just that, the shaykhs on Al-Anbar's Provincial Council removed him from office, with one shaykh noting menacingly that "we will not permit anyone who tries to reduce our role as tribes to remain in office."[38]

In particular, Al-Anbar has displayed resistance to central government control. For example, the province's Sahwa leader, Shaykh Ahmad Abu Risha, asserted that the national Ministry of Oil did not have a right to drill on Al-Anbar's territory and warned that the Sahwa would use force to prevent that. Abu Risha also stressed that the local tribal chiefs were opposed to an Iranian pipeline crossing Al-Anbar to Syria for gas exports destined for Europe.[39] Likewise, the head of Al-Anbar's Provincial Council demanded that the central government permit the exploration for oil in Al-Anbar rather than elsewhere, but local authorities at the same time warned that unless the central government agreed to their terms, they could not guarantee the security of foreign companies.[40] In Diyala, too, there has been clear evidence of this continuing residue of distrust toward the central government. As an interview in the Iraqi press with Diyala's governor indicated, the feeling in the province is that the Baghdad government has been using excuses to avoid providing even the aid it had pledged. For example, promised investment funds had not been disbursed, while of the four hundred schools needed, only two had been built. According to the governor, "the [government] ministries are waging a war against Diyala," and he claimed that the latter's inhabitants "are treated like second-class citizens."[41] Predictably, the central government's clumsy directive that Diyala send four of its electric generating plants to Basra—a sensitive issue in light of the chronic power shortages—led to a vociferous refusal on the part of the Diyala Provincial Council.[42]

Tribal shaykhs understandably relish their new-found status and would be reluctant to relinquish power to any central government. While some Sahwa commanders might be willing to accept an official government post to enable them to govern while maintaining appearances, even Izzat Al-Shabandar, a top player in Ayad Allawi's political coalition and therefore likely to try to curry favor with the Sunni community, saw the shaykhs' assertiveness as "a threat" and admitted that "ending the Sahwa is more difficult than setting it up was."[43]

However, Iraq's tribal leaders have expected to continue playing a significant political role, believing they represent a dominant sector of society. As the head of Iraq's Council of Tribal Shaykhs representing the country's largest tribes, asserted confidently, "The tribes are the decision makers and the effective power on the ground, and we will take our rights whether today or tomorrow."[44] Shaykh Ali Hatim expressed the tribes' perspective of self-importance when he remarked, "We, the tribes, are above the occupier, above the government, and above the entire world. We do not fear nor are we awed by anybody."[45] Even the chief of police in Al-Anbar, Major General Tariq Yusuf Al-Thiyabi, himself a member of the powerful Albu Thiyab tribe in Al-Anbar, insisted on the legitimacy of the tribes' role in society on religious principles: "God the Almighty (may He be Praised) recognizes us, the tribes, in the Qur'an."[46]

(Mis) Managing the Sahwa and the Tribes

To make matters worse, the Iraqi government has often mismanaged its dealings with the Sahwa and with the Sunni tribes in general. Prime Minster Al-Maliki, for example, sought to weaken the autonomy of the Sahwa by setting up rival organizations, such as a new tribal council under the direct authority of the central government.[47] While Al-Maliki was interested in developing ties with the Sunni tribes in view of the impending March 2010 elections, the process proved difficult, as shaykhs in one meeting with his representative expressed skepticism about his intentions. The fact that the meeting was also attended by U.S. military officers ensured some civility, but the government representative's assertion that "the Sahwa was imposed on us because of the security situation" and his rhetorical question, "does the Sahwa have any legal standing?" highlighted the lack of mutual trust.[48] Moreover, the paramount chief (*shaykh al-mashayikh*) of the large Shammar confederation, who was residing in Damascus, noted that the shaykhs living in Syria had refused outright to meet and reconcile with Prime Minister Al-Maliki, claiming he was too pro-American and pro-Iranian.[49]

In the case of the Sahwa, Prime Minister Al-Maliki in 2009 reportedly had wanted to close out the file in just three months.[50] That timetable in itself clashed with the Sahwa's own horizon, for the latter's representative, Shaykh Thamir Al-Tamimi, had posited that the Sahwa should be maintained as long as there was a security threat in the country, including from Shia and Kurdish militias—in effect, putting off the Sahwa's disbandment into the distant future.[51] However, handling the Sahwa has apparently proved more difficult than expected, and the government's treatment of the Sahwa and, by extension, of the tribes, has contributed to alienating many shaykhs and tribesmen, and risks creating a more favorable operational environment for Al-Qaida.

One of the most troublesome issues for the Sahwa has been that of pay and benefits. Interruptions and irritations connected with the payment of salaries by the government to the Sahwa fighters have alienated Sahwa fighters throughout the system and have made them more receptive to blandishments by Al-Qaida. In some extreme cases, as in Diyala, pay to 4500 Sahwa fighters had been interrupted for more than a year.[52] In Diyala, the frequent delays in pay have led Sahwa members to conclude that the government simply did not care.[53] What is more, on payday, some Sahwa members grumble about being harassed and humiliated gratuitously.[54] Work stoppages have been common when salaries have been late, which had also been the case at times even when the United States was still in charge.[55] Some Sahwa fighters have walked off the job to protest late pay, such as those who abandoned their checkpoints in Diyala.[56]

Pay issues have at times been so exasperating that Sahwa personnel in Baghdad threatened to rejoin Al-Qaida if the situation did not improve.[57] In the Baghdad region, one frustrated Sahwa commander contrasted Al-Qaida and other insurgent groups' readiness to "shower" money on the local Sahwa with "up to now we have not received anything except promises" from the government.[58] Another commander in Baghdad fretted that if his sixty men were to leave because of the issue of late pay, "I will not be able to carry out patrols on my own." He had already lost 20 percent of his force over decreased pay after the transfer of the Sahwa to the Iraqi government, and he feared that more would rejoin Al-Qaida.[59]

While the administrative inefficiencies of the Iraqi government may explain some of the deterioration in support, Sahwa leaders and fighters attribute such problems to deliberate policies by a hostile government.[60] The government, for its part, has argued that the membership lists that the Sahwa put forward often contain duplication and fictitious names as a way to increase revenue from salaries for nonexistent personnel. Such padding of the rolls would not be surprising. For example, of the 3000 names on one Sahwa roster presented to the government, only some 1800 had turned out to be genuine.[61]

Al-Qaida, the Tribes, and the Government

Sahwa commanders, for their part, have understandably been angry when pay for their fighters was chronically late, and have threatened to withdraw their services if the government did not show respect for them as tribal shaykhs by ensuring that pay would arrive on time.[62] A former Sahwa commander from Ramadi, Shaykh Rad Al-Sabah, admitted that he had left the Sahwa because the Iraqi government had neglected the organization. He complained that "what has been offered to the fighters in Al-Anbar up to the present has been paltry in comparison to the sacrifices they have made. Those who were wounded or even permanently disabled fighting Al-Qaida do not have medical care." He taxed government promises made in public as "electoral propaganda" and pointed to the "very low" pay of 120,000 dinars ($102) per month for Sahwa personnel, categorizing that as "sad."[63] The government had reportedly promised to treat the families of Sahwa fighters killed in the line of duty in the same manner as those from the army, but one Sahwa commander in Diyala, Adnan Al-Jiburi, disagreed that the promise was being upheld, saying, "That has not been the case up to now."[64]

As the commander of the Sahwa in Samarra, Majid Abbas, complained in 2010, overall funding by the government was seen as insufficient, and this also affected operational readiness. "Ever since the transfer of responsibility to the Iraqi government, we have been suffering from a lack of support and routinely do not receive our salaries.... We are now obliged to buy our own weapons and ammunition."[65] The Sahwa has also complained of not receiving the necessary explosives detectors to do their job; one Sahwa unit staged a walkout from checkpoints in Babil in protest because of that issue, as well as due to delays in pay.[66]

Unemployment and the need to find the wherewithal to keep a family alive have become increasingly acute as financial support for the Sahwa has diminished, exacerbated by a perception of government indifference. Being released from the Sahwa, or even delays in pay, could mean genuine hardship for tribesmen and their families. Alternative sources of income now or in the foreseeable future are limited, especially as unemployment remains a problem in Iraq in general. According to figures released by the country's Ministry of Planning and Cooperation, unemployment surpassed 25 percent in 2010 and was reported to be especially severe among the youth, while a 2007 report by the same ministry had indicated that the rate of poverty in rural areas stood at 39 percent.[67]

Significantly, in Diyala, violence is seen as the major cause for the fact that 80 percent of the private sector has been destroyed or paralyzed, leading to the loss of 60,000 local jobs.[68] Even in the Baghdad region, once the country's industrial heartland, some 80 percent of the factories lie idle while the remaining 20 percent are operating at less than one-half of their capacity.[69] Prospects for employment in the agricultural sector, which some Iraqi experts assess as having collapsed due to a lack of government support, and related issues of desertification and irrigation, are no better.[70] What is more, despite Iraq's considerable oil-generated wealth, corruption and partisan differences are likely to limit the funds necessary for adequate development in those regions of the country not seen as supportive of the ruling government, thus continuing to offer openings for the effect of Al-Qaida's information campaign and material incentives to the tribesmen to sympathize with the latter.[71] Not coincidentally, Hikmat Jasim Zaydan, the deputy governor of Al-Anbar, warned that the unemployed—including many university graduates, whose unemployment was at "very frightening" levels—would provide a recruitment pool for the insurgents, a situation he blamed squarely on the government.[72]

The reduction in economic and social aid from the central government has also proved to be an area of considerable friction with the tribes. At a macrolevel, money for projects and aid directed through the shaykhs has diminished from earlier levels which, in turn, reduces both the trickle-down effect to members of the tribes as well as money to the shaykhs, weakening the latter's ability to provide employment and to cement the allegiance of their subordinates. What made the disenchantment even more bitter was that tribal leaders, naturally, believed it was their forces that had been key in the war against Al-Qaida. As the head of the Dulaym confederation, Shaykh Ali Hatim, saw it, during the early days of the fight in Al -Anbar, "It is the tribes who are doing the fighting, while the police are in support, and the [Iraqi] army is just sitting."[73] In a way, perhaps the tribal leadership had always expected more than was realistic in the way of support for their position, while ordinary tribesmen, too, had rising economic and security expectations which were difficult to meet, even during the period of U.S. control. One inhabitant in Tikrit summed up his view of the U.S. record: "We expected more—better infrastructure and better services—yet electricity supply is still only a few hours a day. Petrol is a disaster, with long, long queues."[74] Some had already felt let down by the Americans once the immediate danger had passed. As one Sahwa commander in Abu Ghraib observed, "The Americans got what they wanted. We purged Al-Qaida for them, and now people are saying why should we have any more deaths for the Americans. They have given us nothing."[75]

DEMOBILIZING AND INTEGRATING THE SAHWA

The envisioned integration of fighters into the government sector, as part of a demobilization of the Sahwa, has been beset by problems and has only further fueled discontent within the tribes. There was disagreement from the first about how many Sahwa personnel would be integrated into the security forces and army, and the country's Sunni vice president at the time, Tariq Al-Hashimi, warned that a failure to carry out an effective integration would lead to major problems. A Sahwa representative, for his part, insisted that the government had agreed to absorb all Sahwa fighters, and that as part of the handover from U.S. forces, the Sahwa had asked the United States to guarantee that it would pressure the Iraqi government to absorb all Sahwa members but that the United States had refused.[76]

The government's subsequent policy of limiting integration to 20 percent of the Sahwa and its refusal to stand up any new Sahwa units led tribal shaykhs to complain. The head of the Council of Iraq's Sahwa, Shaykh Fadil Al-Janabi, for example, characterized the envisioned number to be integrated as "very small." Shaykh Ali Hatim, for his part, asserted that the government's proposal was "a great injustice to the rights of the tribes" and asked indignantly, "Why are the members of the tribes not allowed to join the security sector except in specified proportions?"[77] Soon disagreements surfaced as to what had been agreed, with government spokesman Ali Al-Dabbagh reiterating that it had approved the integration of only 20 percent of the Sahwa fighters into the security services, while Thamir Al-Tamimi, the Sahwa's advisor, was adamant that the government had agreed to absorb into the security forces all Sahwa fighters who met the requirements, while those who did not would be given government jobs elsewhere.[78]

Salih Al-Matlak, a Sunni opposition member in Parliament, confirmed the Sahwa's fears when he noted about the promises to absorb Sahwa fighters that "the government made promises such as this just to be polite to the American administration and used the tactic of procrastinating and gaining time in order to postpone the issue."[79] Government spokesmen, in veiled warnings, have continued to emphasize that the Sahwa was set up without the government's approval and that it could, if it desired, "suppress the Sahwa account without fear," even if it had not done so up to now.[80]

Sahwa commanders in general have continued to complain that the intended 20 percent target for fighters to be absorbed is simply not enough.[81] One Sahwa leader, Asad Al-Fawaz, typically warned that if the government ignored earlier commitments to integrate the Sahwa, that "will push the Sahwa members to drift back into Al-Qaida's embrace, which will obliterate all the successes in security achieved during the preceding phase."[82] Of course, many former insurgents now in the Sahwa had originally belonged to groups with a Bathist or other orientation, and could be expected to revert to their former allegiance rather than join Al-Qaida. However, even if Sahwa fighters and those in the security services did not join Al-Qaida, their removal from progovernment ranks could still favor Al-Qaida by weakening the overall government effort.

In some provinces, the integration of Sahwa fighters has been more thorough. In the mixed-sectarian Wasit Province, for example, in addition to the projected 20 percent recruited into the security forces, the other 80 percent were at least promised jobs elsewhere in the government sector, although the small number involved (909) may explain the apparent anomaly in this instance.[83]

The Ministry of the Interior, for its part, also claimed that it simply lacked the funds to absorb additional Sahwa fighters.[84] Most government officials have justified the slow integration of Sahwa personnel largely on security grounds. As one Shia lawmaker from Al-Maliki's political party put it, "There are good Awakening members. But there are others who have simply changed their T-shirt ... who do not believe in a new Iraq. We don't want these elements to infiltrate our security forces.[85] The government cited the need for careful screening for recruits in the security forces and the army, since there was a concern that some elements of the Sahwa were really still linked to Al-Qaida and were serving as sleeper cells. As Vice President Adil Abd Al-Mahdi remarked, "Sometimes, we are unable to distinguish between the genuine [Sahwa] forces and spurious ones. Some of them claim to be Sahwa forces, but are waiting for the right time to strike."[86] Indeed, as part of the integration, some tribes nominated former Al-Qaida members in Diyala to be census takers in the government's planned population census, although that could lead to problems, as the often-postponed census is a politically charged issue.[87] However, the fact that unnamed Iraqi government officials reportedly openly expressed a reluctance to absorb all Sahwa fighters into the army and security forces specifically out of a concern "to maintain the sectarian balance" may reinforce Sunni skepticism.[88]

Sahwa forces have been progressively depleted, not only by the gradual integration into the government sector but also by the apparent disillusionment among many fighters with the inadequate government support. Thus, in Diyala, where at its peak the Sahwa had had 14,000 fighters, by late 2010 there were just over 6,000, but only 2,000 of the reduction was accounted for by integration into the security forces.[89] Likewise, in Samarra, of the original 4,800 fighters, by 2010 there were only 2,300. While 750 had been absorbed into the local police, another 1,750 had simply left the Sahwa "in order to earn a living," as was also the case in Kirkuk, where—according to their commander—400 of the original 900 personnel had left "because of low salaries."[90] In one part of Baghdad, the number of Sahwa fighters decreased from 2,500 to 250, only in part due to integration into government ranks.[91] In Al-Anbar, the number of Sahwa fighters absorbed into the security services has been especially low, with Shaykh Ahmad Abu Risha claiming they totaled only eighty.[92] One Sahwa member in Ramadi, Al-Anbar, complained that the national and local government "have not given anything to the Sahwa members who were the ones who made the great sacrifices.... The [Sahwa fighters] have not been given appropriate job opportunities in the government sector, contrary of what the officials announced in the media."[93]

Even those Sunni tribesmen who have been able to enter the country's security apparatus, moreover, have felt insecure. The government abolished the ranks of about 450 police personnel who had been promoted when they were integrated from the Sahwa during the period of U.S. control, arguing that most were illiterate and citing the need for professionalism. At the same time, however, Shaykh Ahmad Abu Risha warned that "the government must think hard in applying appropriate solutions to the holders of honorary ranks."[94]

At the same time, Sahwa members who have been integrated into the government sector were often dissatisfied with their experiences. When offered government employment, members of the Sahwa have preferred security jobs rather than those in the civil side of the government, which usually pay less, and they have also demanded that their time in the Sahwa be factored into their seniority.[95] As one former Sahwa fighter complained, despite having faced great dangers in the fight against Al-Qaida, "we are surprised by . . . the jobs [we received], which are not appropriate to our dignity and our capabilities . . . such as in the sanitation or agricultural components of the state sector."[96] Other jobs were also temporary at best. For example, in Diyala, although more than 5,000 Sahwa fighters were given jobs in the local government, this was only on the basis of temporary projects.[97] Reportedly, the civilian government sector has even discharged many Sahwa fighters it had hired originally, citing their lack of qualifications.[98] The government suggested recently that it would be creating an additional 115,000 government jobs and promised that the Sahwa fighters would get some of them.[99] However, there may be economic limits to the number of Sahwa veterans who can be integrated into the Iraqi government bureaucracy, which is already bloated and underemployed.[100] Finding security or government jobs for relatives and clients is a litmus test for a shaykh's influence, as he competes with other shaykhs or would-be shaykhs, and the decreasing employment opportunities could weaken a shaykh's authority.[101]

As of October 2010, only some 52,000 Sahwa fighters remained on the official rolls, according to government statistics.[102] However, as one shaykh pointed out, not all those tribesmen who had fought against Al-Qaida had joined the Sahwa formally, and he insisted that these informal Sahwa fighters, too, deserved to be rewarded just like those who had joined officially.[103] While the remaining personnel in the Sahwa may appear to be a relatively small number to worry about, even those ex-Sahwa members who have been integrated into the local police retain their tribal loyalties and can be considered tribesmen in uniform. As the senior police official in Ramadi had conceded in 2007, while the senior officers took their orders from the U.S. Army, rank-and-file policemen took their orders from their own tribal shaykhs.[104] Indeed, the head of the Directorate General of Intelligence and Security in Al-Anbar was himself a shaykh and his brother was the paramount shaykh of the Dulaym confederation.[105] Significantly, when the Sahwa fighters in Diyala protested the arrest of some of their members by walking off duty, they were joined in solidarity by 3,500 of their former fellow Sahwa fighters who had earlier been absorbed into the police.[106] Local leaders, for their part, have been in a position to pressure the provincial police—often their fellow tribesmen—to release suspected members of Al-Qaida, as was the case with the 1,800 arrests in 2010 in the Mosul area, of whom 1,600 had to be released after the intervention of local political figures.[107]

When tribesmen had been recruited into the police, the shaykhs had strenuously opposed using their fellow tribesmen who joined the police force outside their tribal area, presumably as this would have diluted their influence over such personnel and tribal cohesion. As it was, one shaykh could even use the nine local police stations that he controlled—no doubt manned by fellow tribesmen—as a venue where he could beat information out of detained Al-Qaida suspects.[108] Conversely, the national police administration sought such out-of-area assignments for locally recruited police specifically to limit tribal influence.[109]

Some in the government, however, apparently did not consider the Sahwa issue as a significant problem. One official from Muqtada Sadr's party, for example, in 2009 held that "any fears are unjustified," insisted that integration was proceeding on schedule, and was confident that dissatisfied fighters would be unlikely to revert to the insurgency.[110] However, at the same time, a Sahwa commander from South Baghdad (where there were still about 20,000 personnel), had countered that none of his men had been absorbed yet, despite many meetings with the government and with some fighters having submitted the required paperwork five times. Moreover, the same commander complained that Sahwa fighters had received their monthly salaries only twice in the nine months since the handover from U.S. forces.[111]

By late 2010, the government seemed anxious to close out the account within the coming few months, according to the central government committee in charge of Sahwa affairs. Zuhayr Al-Chalabi, the committee's chairman, announced that a demobilization center would be created for the Sahwa, that the shaykhs, the older fighters, and farmers—that is, those considered unfit for security careers—would be given a cash bonus, and that in the meantime, salaries for the remaining Sahwa members would be made comparable to those in the security forces, while the army committed itself to providing protection for the Sahwa personnel.[112] How difficult it may be to resolve such issues is reinforced by the fact that even as late as mid-2011, the Sahwa's representative in Diyala was still complaining about the same issues and accusing the government of not having fulfilled most of its promises.[113]

The government, as of May 2011, was intent on crafting a law to restrict the possession of arms to the state, citing in particular the tribes and Sahwa as being a problem in this respect.[114] While perhaps a reasonable move intended to increase security and stability, to disarm the tribally based Sahwa—much less the tribes themselves—could prove difficult, not only because of the tribes' resistance to a diminution of their power in an uncertain security situation and enduring concerns about the Baghdad government, but also because weapons are not only a tool but also a potent symbol of manliness and tradition in tribal society. As Shaykh Ali Hatim noted, "We will not hand over our weapons . . . why should we hand them over? Is that not part of my worldview—just like I have my religion, so also I have my weapons. That is, I believe that weapons are a part of who I am."[115] In fact, as the announced time for a complete American withdrawal approached, the purchase of weapons in certain tribal areas began to rise.[116] And, it is not just the Sunni tribes who are reluctant to turn over their weapons, as the mostly Shia tribes in the south have also gone on record as refusing to disarm, no doubt making Sunni tribes even more wary.[117]

As of May 2011, Shaykh Ali Hatim Al-Sulayman, shaykh of the Dulaym confederation, was openly pronouncing the end of the Sahwa and calling on the remaining fighters to leave the field and let the government forces and the terrorists fight it out by themselves, predicting with some glee, "Let us see how powerful the security forces are against this [Al-Qaida] challenge without the support of the Sahwa."[118]

THE ISSUE OF GOVERNMENT HARASSMENT

What is seen as government harassment and discrimination has also played a significant role in fomenting anxiety and dissatisfaction among Sahwa personnel and within the Sunni tribes in general. One of the most controversial phenomena has been the government crackdowns that have accompanied Al-Qaida's increased activity and the government's doubts about the Sahwa's reliability. The number of Sahwa personnel arrested took on sizeable proportions, such as the sixty fighters and commanders detained during the first six months of 2010 in Diyala, with the latter claiming that those arrests were based on fraudulent charges stemming from spite and generated by pro-Al-Qaida elements.[119] Rumors of more than a thousand such outstanding warrants for past activities, when many Sahwa personnel had been part of the insurgency, prompted hundreds of Sahwa fighters in Diyala Province to abandon their posts, with one local Sahwa commander concluding that such unfounded arrests were just being used as "a weapon to eliminate the Sahwa."[120] In fact, in Diyala some five hundred warrants for local government employees—presumably ex-Sahwa members now in government service—who were accused of supporting the insurgents in the past also led to many fleeing to avoid arrest in 2010.[121] One Sahwa commander in South Baghdad characterized such arrests as "laughably sad," and blamed the relatives of dead Al-Qaida fighters for now bringing suits in court accusing Sahwa fighters of crimes, and the Iraqi government for being only too ready to accept such claims for its own purposes.[122] In Salah Al-Din Province, Sahwa members accused the central security forces of stopping them routinely and accusing them of having belonged to Al-Qaida in the past.[123]

Government arrests have even involved significant personages in the tribes, such as Shaykh Husam Al-Mujammai, head of the Sahwa Council in Diyala, in July 2010, at the hands of security forces sent from Baghdad. Sahwa leaders in the province interpreted this arrest as "the security apparatus' carrying out a plan to eliminate [the Sahwa]."[124] Later, government forces arrested the Sahwa Council commander's uncle on charges of terrorism, not only highlighting the deteriorating relations between the Sahwa and the government but also, if the charges are accurate, the continuing ties between Al-Qaida and the tribes.[125] In September 2010, special forces brought in from Baghdad arrested two shaykhs from the Jiburi tribes, with no reason given, and their families claimed that the police also beat them during the arrest.[126] Likewise, the head of Saddam's tribe and his son were arrested in October 2010 on suspicion of financing terrorist groups.[127] Al-Mulla Nazhim Al-Jiburi, the controversial cleric who had been a former Al-Qaida figure but had later become a Sahwa commander and was detained in 2009 on charges of kidnapping for ransom and for sectarian killings, was released and arrested again in 2010, this time on charges that he was sheltering five would-be women suicide bombers in his house, but was released subsequently.[128] Such arrests have continued, including that of the commander of the Sahwa in Rawat, Al-Anbar, in 2011.[129] Suspicion of the government on the part of the tribes reached a point where some shaykhs in Al-Anbar accused the security forces of having been behind the 2011 kidnapping of a leading shaykh and his son.[130]

One of the highest profile cases was the arrest of the Central Baghdad Sahwa commander, Ali Al-Mashadani, in 2009, on charges of murder and extortion of protection money from merchants, which led to armed clashes between the Sahwa and the Iraqi army and police, as well as resentment against U.S. forces, who had supported the latter during the operation. The resulting displacement of the local

Sahwa facilitated a renewed Al-Qaida presence in the area.[131] On that occasion, Prime Minster Al-Maliki stressed that this was "a message to all those who follow the same path as that gang," adding that "some believe they can continue to be far from the eye of the state and the security apparatus ... but they are all under our watchful eye and observation and the day is coming when all of them will get their just reward."[132] Sunni politicians, on the other hand, called such arrests "collective punishment," and the police acknowledged "some individual excesses" on its part.[133]

No doubt some of the Sahwa groups did have among their members those with criminal records and those who had taken advantage of their subsequent membership in the Sahwa to continue such activities. However, the Sahwa generally viewed government crackdowns as unjustified in light of the Sahwa's contribution to the fight against Al-Qaida. Sahwa fighters have protested such arrests, at times by withdrawing their services, as in Diyala, when all 13,000 personnel walked off the checkpoints and other duties following the arrests of 425 of their fellow members on criminal charges. This work stoppage was accompanied by a protest rally by tribal leaders, as well as by commanders of former insurgent groups.[134] Even if there were legitimate charges pending, Husam Al-Mujammai, head of the Sahwa Councils in Diyala, pointed out that such arrests "will lead to clearing the field for Al-Qaida and creating the maneuver space for the latter's renewed activity."[135] Leaders of the Diyala Sahwa Council have cautioned that the arrest of dozens of Sahwa commanders would have a negative impact on the reversion of Sahwa personnel to Al-Qaida, while the Sahwa spokesman, Thamir Al-Tamimi, warned "against the marginalization of the Sahwa's role" in Baquba and stressed that "the security successes achieved would not have happened had it not been for the support and sacrifices of the Sahwa."[136]

Tribal leaders feel threatened and unsure of the future because of such government treatment. In one case, some 150 indignant tribal notables in Baquba demonstrated in protest in front of the local governor's office, arguing that "any one of us can be targeted in the future." The shaykhs threatened to call large-scale demonstrations and to end cooperation with the government if their concerns were not addressed. One shaykh, Hamid Al-Lahibi, in a thinly veiled threat, even warned that "the tribes will escalate their peaceful complaints if those arrested are not released."[137] In Salah Al-Din Province, the Sahwa in 2010 distributed leaflets threatening to hold demonstrations against the local government to demand their rights, claiming that now they "are being marginalized and treated as enemies ... and are being thrown into prison and are not compensated at all, unlike the case with the army and police," and demanded "fair play in getting jobs."[138] In early 2011, the Council of Shaykhs in Salah Al-Din Province warned that continuing arrests by the Ministry of the Interior "threaten society's unity" and would lead to a "loss of trust in the government."[139] The arrest of the head of the Council of Shaykhs in Ninawa Province, likewise, sparked protests by the tribes, who called for an end to such practices.[140] The government has also arrested local contractors on charges of dealing with Al-Qaida—more than two hundred in the Mosul area alone—and the tribes have also criticized such arrests, rationalizing such cooperation by alleging that "contractors in Mosul cannot do business if they do not turn over part of their profits to Al-Qaida."[141]

There has been an increased sense of threat within the Sunni community in general, sometimes fed further by such reports as that of the return in August 2010 of a notorious Shia militant from Iran who had killed many Sunnis, and the assumption that a majority Shia-government would not help.[142] Some tribal chiefs have accused the national security police of corruption, alleging that Al-Qaida members who were arrested would be released in return for bribes, further undercutting the Sahwa's trust in the effectiveness of the government.[143] Local officials in Salah Al-Din Province, in fact, accused the security forces of arresting businessmen and notables with the sole intent of extorting money in exchange for their release.[144]

Credible reports of secret prisons, where Sunni detainees are held under atrocious conditions, no doubt contribute to a further erosion of confidence in the government within the Sunni community.[145] Most of the Sahwa leaders who are arrested are usually released within a short time—reportedly thanks to U.S. pressure—but this must still be a demeaning and unsettling experience, as ordinary Sunnis often linger in prison even when they are eventually proved innocent. In fact, as an unnamed Iraqi security source admitted, such arrests and the experience and indoctrination in prison are creating "new extremists," and in Diyala Province, such individuals, once released, now account for about a third of all armed attacks.[146]

The Problem of Personal Security and Government Neglect

Another facet of considerable resentment within the Sahwa and the Sunni tribes has been a perception that the government has not been doing enough—or even cares—about the security of Sahwa personnel and their families. This factor has become a major concern with the U.S. retrenchment and Al-Qaida's resurgence, as the Sahwa found itself in a precarious position after the loss of its foreign patron, with tribal leaders often perceiving themselves to be vulnerable simultaneously both from a reinvigorated insurgency and from the Iraqi government.[147] For now, despite the retrenchment, U.S. forces are still available to supply combat support to local forces against Al-Qaida attacks, as in the case of a combined operation to repel a raid that Al-Qaida mounted in Falluja in September 2010, an action that elicited a response with fire support by U.S. helicopters.[148] U.S. ground forces also continue to operate jointly with Iraqi government forces against Al-Qaida.

Understandably, Sahwa leaders are especially concerned about their own safety after the anticipated U.S. withdrawal.[149] At times, expressions of disillusionment within the Sahwa have rebounded against the United States itself, creating potential reservations among the local population about committing themselves to similar militias in other theaters. As one Sahwa commander put it, "The Americans are duplicitous and treacherous, and dispose of papers they are finished with by burning them.... Unfortunately, earlier, we were obliged to work with them in order to secure our area, not to protect their soldiers who were being killed on a daily basis by Al-Qaida.... I advise everyone not to cooperate with them in the future, since their fate will be the same as that of the tribal Sahwa in Iraq."[150] Not surprisingly, Al-Qaida's number-two leader, Ayman Al-Zawahiri, was to use the Sahwa experience in Iraq as a warning to those collaborating with the United States in Afghanistan, asking rhetorically, "Have they [i.e., the Americans] reserved seats for their [i.e., the collaborators'] families on the last American aircraft that will leave Afghanistan, or will they abandon them to face a fate similar to the Sahwa in Iraq?"[151] The Iraqi government has tended to downplay such fears and, according to Zuhayr Al-Chalabi, the government official in charge of Sahwa affairs, it has been "the politicians who are sowing these fears" for their personal benefit.[152]

The government has taken a number of measures that, as part of a process of demobilization, might be understandable. However, Sahwa fighters and their tribal communities have seen such measures as unwarranted in light of the continuing precarious security situation, and some Sahwa commanders blame this lack of government support for rendering Sahwa personnel vulnerable to Al-Qaida.[153] For example, the authorities collected many small arms from the Sahwa in the Baghdad area, and Sahwa leaders believed that policy made it more difficult for them to protect themselves from revenge attacks by Al-Qaida.[154] By 2010, the government in some areas, such as in Diyala Province, had also restricted the Sahwa's authority to arrest suspected Al-Qaida elements and limited the Sahwa's right to bear arms outside designated security zones. The argument, probably with some justification, was that the Sahwa had misused its powers for personal ends, including to extort money, and that with the Sahwa personnel armed and in civilian clothes it was impossible to distinguish them from Al-Qaida.[155]

The case surrounding the withdrawal of government gun permits illustrates the underlying friction and mistrust between the government and the Sahwa and the latter's fears for the personal safety of their personnel. In 2010, the government apparently decided to withdraw at least some gun permits, accusing the Sahwa of abuses, with some Sahwa commanders giving fraudulent gun permits to other tribal chiefs, which Al-Qaida had then used to smuggle weapons, as did the tribal chiefs to shift weapons from one area to another.[156] Sahwa representatives countered that even if some had misused such permits, that was no reason to withdraw them from everyone.[157] The Diyala Sahwa threatened to quit en masse if the permits were withdrawn, with the Sahwa commander in Baquba noting that "the weapons we carry guarantee our defense and that of the areas within our area of responsibility" and adding that without such gun permits "we will be forced to pull back so that we do not become an easy morsel for Al-Qaida."[158] The head of the government's Reconciliation Committee, Zuhayr Al-Chalabi, hurried to try to assure the Sahwa, declaring "that is not correct," and claiming what was involved was only a case of identity badges having expired, although he also reasserted that no one could bear arms without a valid government permit.[159] The local Sahwa organization, however, reiterated that what was indeed in play were the gun permits themselves. The police then placed the blame for the initiative on the army, which had wanted to reissue new permits in the wake of the arrests of some Sahwa members for aiding Al-Qaida, and assured the Sahwa that the withdrawal of permanent permits would apply only to those Sahwa personnel who had been detained.[160] This case, whatever the details, highlighted the Sahwa's mistrust of the government and the latter's clumsy, uncoordinated, and arrogant handling of relations with the Sahwa.

Understandably, progovernment shaykhs and notables have been especially concerned about their personal security, given their high profile. In the wake of the assassination of one of his subordinate shaykhs, the panicked paramount shaykh of the Albu Alwan tribe called on the government to launch an immediate and genuine investigation, wildly blaming Iran, the United States, and Zionism for the shaykh's death and warning that without effective protection shaykhs would not be able to carry out "the central government's decisions."[161] Some Sahwa commanders in Diyala reacted to the increased personal threat by demanding the immediate execution of Al-Qaida commanders, rather than letting them languish in jail, and called for an application of Saddam's harsh methods and public executions to serve as a deterrent.[162] The government's decision to end the salaries of the Sahwa leaders' bodyguards in 2010 was a very risky move, as it would increase the shaykhs' already high vulnerability to assassination attempts as the threats from Al-Qaida increased, thereby putting the entire Sahwa structure in jeopardy. The government relented only with reluctance, in an effort to retain the loyalty of tribal leaders, but agreed to a palliative of increasing the shaykhs' salaries and paying for only three bodyguards for each Sahwa commander.[163]

Chapter 11

The Evolving Tribal Environment

As a result of the political and economic dynamics noted above, the tribal environment—in its tribal-government, intertribal, and intratribal dimensions—has been changing, and doing so in many ways that are favorable to renewed Al-Qaida activity. For the Sunni tribal shaykhs, whether to cooperate with Al-Qaida is likely to depend on a complex calculus in an evolving situation, involving such elements as rivalries with other tribes; whether personal benefits outweigh a reduction in a shaykh's influence; the significance of irritants in the social arena; the extent of support for Al-Qaida within their own tribe; rivalry with other leadership elements within their tribe; and their ability to use Al-Qaida as a counterweight to other threats such as the government or other sectarian communities.

Tribal resentment over the handling of the Sahwa is emblematic of a broader discontent in the Sunni tribal community with the government in Baghdad. Tribal leaders, both Sunni and Shia, have traditionally been among the staunchest supporters of a unified Iraq, seeing the concept as the best guarantee for their continued influence.[1] However, in the wake of the results of the 2010 elections and of government harassment, there appears to be a spike in backing across Sunni society for a separate Sunni canton, which the central government cannot but resent. As Ahmad Dhiyab Al-Jiburi, an *imam*—or mosque official—in Baghdad, noted, "We participated in the parliamentary elections and won, but we were unable to achieve our constitutional due, and we are now calling for the establishment of a special zone, since we got nothing from the government except arrests and attacks.... Wherever we go, they say, 'You are terrorists.'"[2]

The continuing arrests of Sahwa personnel have been a particular flashpoint fueling talk of an Al-Anbar canton, which Shaykh Arif al-Alwani threatened would happen "if we do not find in the government a sympathetic ear and if we do not get cooperation."[3] Renewed talk of a separate Sunni canton, this time in the context of Iraqi expatriate businessmen in Jordan who were providing money to entice tribal shaykhs to support the idea, may exacerbate relations between the Sunni tribes and the government even further.[4] One local politician noted that demands had also appeared for autonomy for Diyala Province specifically in order to provide protection from the central government's security forces.[5] In fact, some Sunni tribes asked for the intervention by the Organization of the Islamic Conference, the Arab League, and the United Nations, claiming that the alleged attacks to which they were being subjected by government forces amounted to nothing short of phased ethnic cleansing.[6]

Shaykh Abu Risha's recent hard-line stance in the dispute over the district of Al-Nakhib between Karbala and Al-Anbar Provinces illustrates the potential troublemaking ability of local tribal figures backed by their own military clout. Karbala Province has demanded that Al-Nakhib District, transferred to Al-Anbar in 1968 by the ruling Bath regime, be returned to its control. Abu Risha, citing the district's shared tribal and communal links with Al-Anbar, has refused to discuss the issue, truculently challenging the demands and interjecting a sectarian element: "Those individuals who are demanding that Al-Nakhib be joined to Karbala on historical grounds must first demand back the Iraqi lands which Iran seized."[7] His subsequent ambitious 2011 proposal to establish a "nonsectarian" canton comprising Al-Anbar and the largely Shia province of Karbala—which no doubt would add to his power—while so unrealistic that even largely Sunni political parties and shaykhs rejected it, nevertheless was sure to irritate the government.[8] Although positions on a single or several Sunni cantons, in fact, often reflect tribal rivalries, even one of the shaykhs in Al-Anbar who opposed a canton nevertheless pointed out that the "injustice and marginalization" felt by the local population fueled such initiatives.[9]

Perhaps as a result of a growing alienation from the government, Sunni tribal loyalties now seem to trump earlier political splits, and one journalist suggested that the government should no longer mention the tribal affiliation of terrorists now, since tribes feel insulted and tend to rally spontaneously in support of a fellow tribesman, whoever he might be.[10] The adversarial relationship between the government and the tribes can surface even with fortuitous incidents such as the one in which seven tribesmen arrested on charges of terrorism in 2010 were killed while in custody of the national police, accompanied by allegations of torture. Shaykh Hamid Hayis, a prominent Sahwa leader, remonstrated angrily that "for the Iraqi government, the cheapest lives are those of the sons of Al-Anbar, as if they are second-class citizens." He also criticized the government for not sending condolences to the victims killed by Al-Qaida, either. He hinted at the government being motivated by sectarianism for such policies, which he concluded, "does not bode well for the future." A public funeral for the tribal victims of the police was attended by local tribal shaykhs, suggesting that the victims' tribal status outweighed even possible membership in Al-Qaida when the government was to blame for their deaths.[11]

INTERTRIBAL RIVALRIES AS A POTENTIAL CRITICAL VULNERABILITY

Rivalries among and within tribes have always complicated unity and ensured built-in competition that could lead some tribes or subtribes to consider renewed ties with Al-Qaida. Almost unavoidably, one could have expected that an influx of significant support for the Sahwa from a patron—in this case, the United States—

would stimulate existing local rivalries and contribute in the long run to perpetuating an unstable and potentially volatile tribal situation. Whether relating to a temporary U.S. governing authority or to a perceived hostile Iraqi government, the tribes would have viewed an unsettled and unpredictable security environment not only as a threat but also as an opportunity to seize whatever fleeting advantages might be available, encouraged to adventurism and the use of force if for no other reason than to make provision for an even more uncertain future.

Indicative of the intertribal competition that is always under the surface, when the shaykhs from all the tribes were together in one area, they would show solidarity and normally would cover up for one another in front of the U.S. military authorities. However, once on their own, the same shaykhs were more than willing to provide damaging information about other shaykhs' tribes.[12] Characteristically, the lack of tribal unity in Al-Anbar preceding the 2010 elections meant that the tribes' potential political impact was diluted, with different tribal shaykhs often backing different parties or individuals.[13] In West Baghdad, according to U.S. military officers, even an assassination attempt of the local Sahwa commander was traced back to "a rival tribe's wish to replace him as the head of his organization."[14] Not surprisingly, the success of the Abu Risha tribe was contested subsequently by shaykhs in rival tribes.[15] Often, tribal rivalries have gravitated around control of material benefits, such as the lucrative contracts to man security checkpoints, and were a factor even during the U.S. administration of the Sahwa.[16] In one such case in Haditha, Al-Anbar, in 2010, the apparent cause of an armed clash between tribes—reportedly resulting in dozens of casualties—was competition over control of the local administration.[17] Also in Al-Anbar, tribal notables complained that the police (read, those with links to rival tribes) compete with them for contracts, as some senior officers owned their own companies.[18]

As one could expect in the intensively competitive intertribal environment that characterizes the Iraqi scene, when the Sahwa was established, some tribes had not welcomed it or joined up, the decision often being based on a rival tribe's position. In Kirkuk, for example, not all tribes had attended a meeting with U.S. forces, the national police, and the army to establish the Sahwa, reportedly specifically because of "rivalries among the Sunni Arab tribes" in that region.[19] In Al-Anbar, the tribes had been split even when they all opposed Al-Qaida, with some tribes adhering not to the Sahwa but to a rival tribal organization—the Council of All Arab and Iraqi Tribes—with the head of the latter, Shaykh Abd Al-Rahman Muhammad, dismissing the Sahwa as "a bunch of thieves and armed gangs who are using the Salvation Council of Al-Anbar as a pretext to gain government support and to continue their terrorist plans."[20] Some tribes did not feel comfortable cooperating with foreign forces. As one shaykh in Diyala noted, "The tribes are split between supporters and opponents of cooperation with the American forces in the latter's fight against Al-Qaida. Some of these tribes face accusations of treason for standing with the Americans." Even some tribes who disliked Al-Qaida apparently had an equal distaste for the Americans and would have preferred to deal with Al-Qaida on their own.[21]

Also, as noted earlier, tribal shaykhs are well represented in, and in some cases control, the provincial administration. Discontent with the provincial government can be used by rival tribal leaders as a political hammer, putting the provincial officials in a difficult situation and potentially making them resentful for having to bear the burden of the central government's unsuccessful policies, as when some tribal shaykhs in Al-Anbar met with provincial officials in 2010 to complain about the poor public services being provided.[22] In this vein, there were reports of criticism of Shaykh Ahmad Abu Risha, since his clients in the provincial council were seen as having failed to deliver services and effective protection to the population, even though it was probably beyond his power to do so.[23]

Such intertribal fissures have been an ongoing factor, although they had become potentially more disruptive after the handover of the Sahwa to the Iraqi government and the removal of U.S. forces as a perceived impartial arbiter.[24] As such, these internal rifts within the Sunni community can provide a ready-made critical vulnerability for Al-Qaida to exploit, not unlike the opportunity that U.S. forces used in 2005 in cooperating with two tribes against another rival tribe in Al-Anbar when it was claimed that the latter had been siding with Al-Qaida.[25]

INTERNAL TRIBAL DYNAMICS: THE SHAYKHS' PREDICAMENT

The government's attitude toward the Sahwa and the Sunni tribes in general has also put tribal shaykhs in a precarious position vis-à-vis their own tribesmen, as the tribal leaders once again face genuine threats to their material interests and prestige and, ultimately, to their power. The pay issue, for example, was not only salient because of its effect on individual fighters in the Sahwa, but also because it had a negative impact on their commanders—the tribal shaykhs—since problems with pay reduced the latter's role as a source of benefits to their fellow tribesmen and, therefore, undermined their authority. As one shaykh in Diwaniya warned on the issue of pay problems for Sahwa personnel, "The authorities in the province must take care to respect the shaykhs by paying salaries on a regular basis. I will abandon my post if the pay is late because I cannot control the fighters without money."[26] Less government money also means a smaller force under the shaykhs' command to support their authority.

Tribal shaykhs, as self-appointed representatives, often have taken the lead in seeking economic help from the government. The chief of the Mujamma tribe, Shaykh Husam Al-Mujammai, underscored the need for the government to address, at a macrolevel, issues such as unemployment, poverty, lack of public services, and education as "the causes for the growth of the armed groups."[27] In Ninawa Province, the tribal shaykhs also asked Iraq's central government for aid for major development projects and other services "as a priority," and also felt neglected.[28] Even Shaykh Ahmad Abu Risha, a Sahwa stalwart, has been nostalgic about Saddam in this regard, contrasting the aid Saddam had provided and the factories he had opened in Al-Anbar with the current dismal economic situation.[29]

Such advocacy by the shaykhs could potentially reinforce their leadership positions within their tribes if they are successful, but, at the same time, makes them vulnerable to losing prestige and authority if they fail to obtain any tangible returns for their tribesmen. The government has sought to mollify the tribes by issuing public praise for the shaykhs and promising development aid and services, such as at a meeting in October 2010 with some three hundred tribal shaykhs and notables in Diyala.[30] However, reflecting an apparent widespread skepticism with government promises and growing alienation, one shaykh noted, "Diyala Province over the years has seen numerous such national reconciliation meetings, and most of them produce similar recommendations and decisions. . . . What is necessary is for those recommendations to be implemented."[31]

To a significant extent, many shaykhs, despite their undeniable success, still continue to feel insecure in their positions. With the rise of the Sahwa movement, a slate of existing and newly promoted shaykhs was able to establish or fortify positions within their tribes. At the time, one of the main concerns for some shaykhs and aspiring shaykhs who were on the ground no doubt has been, as a senior U.S. military officer operating in Al-Anbar noted, the fear that the senior shaykhs from their tribe would return from abroad to "reestablish . . . a traditional tribal relationship," that is, to displace those who had either been appointed by Saddam or had taken advantage of the current turmoil to secure their positions.

Working with U.S. forces was evidently an opportunity to cement their own positions and to forestall any power play by the traditional shaykhs who were still abroad.[32] Newly promoted shaykhs, like Rad Sabah Alwani, however, were not apologetic, noting that "we became sheiks because we use force. Iraq needs men who use force."[33] U.S. forces had recognized the power struggle between junior shaykhs such as Abu Risha and the senior shaykhs abroad, and that the United States could be decisive in supporting cooperative individuals.[34] As the governor of Al-Anbar was to note after the U.S.-tribal alliance was established, nowadays, "each sheikh wants to have his say. Previously only the paramount sheik ruled."[35] In fact, according to one senior U.S. military officer, the senior shaykhs would become jealous if he paid too much attention to lesser shaykhs.[36] As such, many shaykhs very likely remain very sensitive to potential discontent within their own tribes that rivals could exploit.

Shaykhs have tended to monopolize U.S.-funded contracts for projects for themselves and their relatives or clients, providing the shaykhs with a potent tool to affirm their authority and the loyalty of their tribesmen as the source of the latter's benefits. However, this advantage of the shaykhs has irritated others not connected to the source of power as clients. As one potential businessman complained about the concentration of contracts in the hands of the shaykhs: "The only people who are benefiting now are the sheiks. Now the sheiks can do anything."[37] The trickle-down effect of benefits for ordinary tribesmen, whether in the form of public services or direct payments, has been hampered by what some local critics were calling "siphoning off"—by Sahwa leaders, that is tribal shaykhs—of "much of the billions of dollars of American and Iraqi financing intended for reconstruction."[38] Shaykhs are sensitive to such existing allegations, and Shaykh Ali Sulayman of the Dulaym was predictably anxious to deny them by stressing that "the tribal shaykhs have never ever coveted contracts . . . nor do they seek political power for material gain."[39]

What has changed most perhaps from the early days of the revolt against Al-Qaida is that ordinary tribesmen may now be disillusioned about a lack of overall government support and the resulting limited trickle-down to them through their shaykhs. Moreover, these tribesmen are more anxious about the future now that the United States is no longer a realistic option as an ally and benefactor, and less confident that their shaykhs can deliver what they promise. The danger is that a reduction in benefits stemming from a tribesman's relationship with his shaykh could lead to a weakening of the cohesion of the tribal fabric and a fraying of loyalties to a tribe's leadership and increased instability within a tribe. Such a development may not only mean a reduced willingness to fight against Al-Qaida, but could also make tribesmen more susceptible to recruitment efforts by Al-Qaida.

Challenges to the shaykhs within the tribes have included those from rivals who are Al-Qaida members. Once again, there are suggestions that these rivals come from the lower strata, with a shaykh calling one such rival "a man of no value . . . an illiterate" and "a lesser member of the tribe."[40] For all his bluster in disparaging the reenergized Al-Qaida cadres in his tribe, that shaykh was clearly also anxious because "he has little to show for his tribesmen. Electricity is sparse; there are no hospitals and no jobs."[41]

Internal tensions between the leadership and the rank and file within the Sahwa have also surfaced, creating potential problems in cohesion that could have direct implications to Al-Qaida's advantage. For example, shaykhs have routinely insisted on receiving the complete salary for their Sahwa fighters directly. In some Sahwa units at least, the commander would then keep $50 for each individual and pass on only $250 as their salaries. There was always grumbling by Sahwa personnel because of this widespread practice, and some fighters would even come to a U.S. base and demand that the Americans distribute the salaries directly to the fighters. However, U.S. practice had continued to be paying the shaykh directly, as that was easier, and no doubt reinforced the latter's authority.[42] In one instance, Shaykh Ahmad Abu Risha himself came in for criticism when he had not provided money for salaries for a Sahwa office he had opened in the Karbala area. His local representatives excused themselves feebly by claiming that "the lack of money is the result of the travels outside Iraq by Shaykh Ahmad Abu Risha, the president of the Sahwa Conference of Iraq."[43] In Diyala, Sahwa fighters were indignant that their commanders were collecting salaries for fraudulent paper members—in itself indicative of eroding respect for their shaykhs—and they were disappointed that even after informing the army about their commanders' corruption, nothing had been done about it.[44] Perhaps typical of the disenchantment of Sahwa personnel was the attitude of a former fighter from the Habbaniya Sahwa, in Al-Anbar, who maintained that "I did not get any consideration from those in charge of the Sahwa in my area. Despite my repeated requests to the officials of Al-Anbar Province and my continuous search for a job, it was no use; I received many promises but up to now none has been fulfilled."[45]

Some Sahwa commanders are willing to lend their men money to tide them over, but that means the shaykhs' own income sources must remain secure.[46] Tribal shaykhs have tried to rebuild economic leverage through the control of alternate job sources, such as nominating candidates for guards to safeguard oil company facilities.[47] Some shaykhs have even reportedly been demanding royalties for any oil extracted from traditional tribal lands.[48] Such initiatives, however, bypass the government and may also be seen as unwelcome by the latter. In some cases, the shaykhs themselves have been shortsighted in this regard, as they have worsened the employment situation in Al-Anbar by importing foreign workers who are willing to work for less money, whose lives are more expendable, who are more pliant than local tribesmen, and who are willing to take jobs that carry a stigma in Iraqi society.[49]

Shaykhs might be especially sensitive to economic discontent among their fellow tribesmen in light of the upsurge of protest in the Middle East, as the general malaise in a tribe could turn against the shaykhs as well as against the government. In the wake of the continuing deterioration of the economic situation in Al-Anbar, by 2010, for example, even an individual who had suffered earlier at the hands of Al-Qaida in Al-Ramadi now complained, reflecting a general disgruntlement with the status quo, "Everything has turned sour for us now. There are no services; we don't have jobs; poverty is killing us. What are they waiting for? Do they want us to beg in the streets so that we can live? Is that what they're waiting for?" And, he warned, "By God, if there is no change, blood will flow ankle deep and violence and killing will return once again to this province."[50] It appears that shaykhs have taken precautions to forestall threats that popular anger will turn against them, as media reports indicate that tribal shaykhs have often been at the forefront of demonstrations in Sunni areas but, unless they achieve tangible results, this ploy may be futile. Frustrated tribesmen, deciding that loyalty to their shaykhs was not providing the expected benefits, could turn to Al-Qaida who, although not able to provide the material bounty available to the tribes during the American period, could at least provide some relief and serve as a vehicle of protest. Or, even if a tribesman did not join Al-Qaida, a sense of alienation might predispose him to not take risks and exert himself opposing Al-Qaida for no expected return.

Chapter 12

Al-Qaida's Own Carrot-and-Stick Approach

Al-Qaida has found itself challenged on how to implement in concrete terms a revised strategy in light of its reassessment of tribal policy and how to take advantage of the dynamic domestic environment, especially as the Sunni tribes try to deal with what they perceive to be an indifferent or hostile government and other threatening domestic forces. As part of its operational strategy, Al-Qaida has been engaged in a process that in some of its elements mirrors that which the United States had used successfully. Central to Al-Qaida's strategy has been to seek to exploit the tribes' grievances while retaining the ability to punish any hostility.

The implementation of tribal policy in light of Al-Qaida's reassessment has most often taken the form of a carrot-and-stick method. This approach reflects a greater balance and flexibility than was the case with the arbitrary and rigid imposition of its doctrine and methods in an earlier period, which had contributed to so much resentment among the tribes and had led to such a resounding failure for Al-Qaida. By 2010, Al-Qaida's leader, Abu Umar Al-Baghdadi, had encapsulated Al-Qaida's policy in the motto that the Islamic State of Iraq would be a force that would "gladden the dear friend and sadden the hypocritical enemy," echoing eerily the motto coined earlier by the Marine Corps leadership for its own policy in Iraq: "No better friend, no worse enemy."[1]

AL-QAIDA GOES NATIVE

As part of its adaptation, there has been a general intentional "Iraqization" of Al-Qaida, which could facilitate implementing a revised policy toward the tribes, and specifically its integration into the local tribal society, which would enhance Al-Qaida's force protection capability and increase operational effectiveness in local society. Although foreigners never comprised more than a small portion of Al-Qaida's total personnel in Iraq, they often had held visible positions. With the death, arrest, or withdrawal of most foreigners, the result has been a smaller foreign footprint.[2]

To a significant extent, this refurbished Al-Qaida has often relied on detainees released from U.S. prison camps as part of the U.S. drawdown, both as returning members as well as new recruits. According to a senior Iraqi army source, as many as 80 percent of those released had joined or rejoined Al-Qaida and other insurgent groups.[3] Paradoxically, it appears that the recruitment and the development of new leadership cadres often occurred inside the U.S.-run detention centers, as is the case with the Islamic State of Iraq's most recent two top leaders, who are the products of jihadi training they received while interned in Camp Bucca.[4]

Not surprisingly, Iraqi Al-Qaida operatives can blend in more easily with the local population and are more familiar with the local terrain and society than was the case with the foreign Arabs. Al-Qaida believes that U.S. forces or the Iraqi government find it hard to track what it calls its "new generation."[5] An unnamed senior Iraqi police official confirmed this problem, especially since "the problem is that the enemy's intelligence is better than ours."[6] The government has argued that tracking down Al-Qaida members in a rural environment should be easy, as opposed to those elements operating in Baghdad, and that their continued presence indicated that at least some tribes in the countryside were providing shelter and support to Al-Qaida members.[7]

In Diyala, according to the head of the provincial Sahwa, Husam Al-Mujammai, Al-Qaida has been encouraging its fighters, recently released from American-run prison camps, to marry widows of dead Al-Qaida members, especially those who had earlier joined the Sahwa, in order to blend into the local tribal population and set up sleeper cells.[8] Family ties are usually still strong, and apparently Al-Qaida has sought to take advantage of that by convincing at least one son to join in order to ensure a family's loyalty.[9] However, indicative of the intensity of passions still being unleashed by Al-Qaida, even families can be torn apart—although relatively rarely—with pro- or anti-Al-Qaida individuals willing to betray or even kill their own family members over the issue of Al-Qaida.[10]

SPLITTING THE ENEMY

An important element that Al-Qaida has employed to rebuild its position in Iraq has been to split the anti-Al-Qaida bloc and, in particular, to draw away elements from the Sahwa. In some ways, Al-Qaida has sought to implement the reverse of what the successful U.S. policy had been in this regard.

Al-Qaida believes that the Sahwa would not have been successful if other groups in the resistance had not also broken with Al-Qaida when their interests had clashed with the latter's upon the proclamation of an Islamic state and the imposition of the sharia because, according to Mother Al-Qaida, "These factions (*fasa'il*) thereby had lost their raison d'être."[11] In that vein, Al-Qaida has appealed to religious and nationalist resistance groups that had gone over to the Sahwa in significant numbers and who were heavily dependent on tribal elements for their manpower. Even when unable to attract such groups in their entirety, Al-Qaida has sought to peel away and recruit, or in some cases rerecruit, dissident elements within those groups, especially after Al-Qaida's two hard-line leaders, Abu Hamza Al-Muhajir and Abu Umar al-Baghdadi, were killed in April 2010.[12] In the case of the Islamic Army (*Al-Jaysh Al-Islami*), for example, Al-Qaida reportedly was able to split the latter in 2010 and recruit some of its members by appealing to the younger cadres, as well as attracting segments of fighters from the Jaysh Abu Bakr, Jaysh Al-Fatihin, Ansar Al-Sunna, Jaysh Al-Mujahidin, and Asa'ib Al-Iraq Al-Jihadiya.[13]

Al-Qaida's intent seems to be to at least neutralize current enemies, even if they cannot be drawn outright into Al-Qaida's camp. In that light, unlike Al-Qaida's earlier policy, it is now acceptable for tribes to remain neutral. Abu Hamza Al-Muhajir (the Islamic State of Iraq's minster of war and head of Al-Qaida in Iraq) described some tribes who "are focused on their farming and neither attack us nor cooperate with the occupier" as acceptable and, although noting that they were not carrying out their religious duty, nevertheless "we give them the benefit of the doubt, and God willing they will come around in the near future."[14]

AL-QAIDA'S CONTINUING EXPLOITATION OF SECTARIANISM

The enduring reality of Iraq's sectarian divisions continues to present a critical vulnerability that Al-Qaida has also tried to exploit, with respect to its relations with the Sunni tribes. While its extreme attempts to exploit sectarianism in the past had often backfired, Al-Qaida seems to be reprising this effort, albeit in a more selective manner. A key difference from the earlier period is that the Shia community, as a target, has become a supporting effort for Al-Qaida rather than the focus of effort, which is now the Iraqi government. At least in mixed areas, where the Sunni population may see itself as threatened by other sectarian groups—specifically by the Shia or the Kurds—Al-Qaida may actually be viewed as a balancing force and a shield against local enemies and, thus, have a more welcoming environment than might otherwise be the case.

Sectarian tensions have continued to mar relations between the Sunni tribes and the government, as well as with other communities. For example, relations between the national police and the Sahwa were tense from the very first, with the latter accusing the police of being controlled by "the political parties," that is, by the Shia element, a situation that had required U.S. mediation.[15] One shaykh had even accused the government of inciting Shia militias to fight against the Sahwa.[16] Fear of other communities is especially prevalent in the mixed Diyala Province, where Sunni Arab tribes often feel threatened by Kurdish and Shia militias in the absence of government protection or even with the perceived connivance by the authorities. For example, Sunnis in Diyala have accused the Shia police of persecuting Sunnis.[17] Typically, in Diyala, it was the Kurdish community leaders who have pushed the hardest for military action against Al-Qaida.[18] Use of the 34th Army Brigade in Diyala—a Kurdish Brigade—that fought in most engagements against the Sunni insurgents, led to complaints by one local deputy that it was being used because of its ethnicity, like a militia, and he called its use "illegal."[19] Likewise, in Diyala, the Sahwa protested the government's use of the Kurdish Peshmerga militia in joint operations with the army.[20] In Ninawa Province, Sunni tribal leaders in 2010 were complaining of "repeated violations of the law" by the Kurdish Peshmerga who "kill, terrorize, and arrest" the inhabitants of the province and accused the government of not doing anything to prevent that.[21]

Predictably, one of Al-Qaida's constant propaganda themes to the Sunnis has been that it would protect the them from attacks by other communities.[22] Not surprisingly, Abu Hamza Al-Muhajir stressed that Al-Qaida had established the Islamic State of Iraq specifically in order to protect the Sunni community from the aggression by the Shia.[23] The extent to which Al-Qaida succeeds in mobilizing support within the Sunni tribes will depend, to a certain extent, on the organization's perception of the Iraqi government's policies and the government's effectiveness in addressing the Sunni tribes' need for security. Al-Qaida has been able to gain at least some advantage by exploiting such sectarian tensions. In fact, the Islamic State of Iraq's leader, Abu Umar Al-Baghdadi, attributed the continuing loyalty of tribes in the Kirkuk area to Al-Qaida to its cooperation in the fight against the Peshmerga. As a former Al-Qaida figure who switched to the Sahwa also admitted, the Sunni population in areas such as Mosul preferred Al-Qaida to the Kurdish Peshmerga.[25]

Al-Qaida has also sought to heighten sectarian tensions with attacks against selected Shia militias and individuals from tribes of different sects, as in the mixed Hilla area, hoping thereby to draw the tribes into feuds along a sectarian basis, although in one case, at least, the affected tribes reconciled and traced the real culprits.[26] Al-Qaida has also mounted large-scale attacks against the Shia community, as during the Shia Forty Days Pilgrimage in Karbala in early 2011. A particular concern for the Iraqi government has been a Sunni Sahwa leader, apparently implicated in one of Al-Qaida's attacks in Karbala, which prompted Prime Minister Al-Maliki to establish a committee tasked with a full-scale review of Sahwa commanders throughout the country.[27] Nevertheless, in a nod to greater realism, Al-Qaida reportedly has even begun to form tactical alliances with selected Shia armed groups and with Shia organized crime gangs.[28]

AL-QAIDA RE-TACKLES THE TRIBES

Al-Qaida's effort to win back ordinary tribesmen has been a key objective and the organization has enjoyed some success, thanks to the deteriorating conditions under which the tribesmen in the Sahwa have had to work and the friction between the tribes and the government. There has been a gradual softening on the part of Al-Qaida in Iraq, although the message it sends is still mixed. On the one hand, there was a conciliatory tone in an interview in April 2009 with Abu Hamza Al-Muhajir, who stressed that, even though members of the Sahwa had committed crimes, "our arms and hearts are open to all of them who repent to God," and he expressed the hope that even those tribes that had cooperated with the United States would repent.[29] Abu Hamza Al-Muhajir also urged the nationalist-oriented resistance to fight in the name of religion. He acknowledged that Al-Qaida had also been at fault, noting in general terms that "we have never claimed to be perfect, and today and tomorrow we admit that there have been mistakes."[30] When he addressed the "sons of the tribes," Abu Umar Al-Baghdadi cast his argument in terms of there being worse options than Al-Qaida. For example, he maintained that Iraq's Shia government and the United States had held many more prisoners—including women—than had Al-Qaida, and that it opposed the government and the "Crusaders" who were responsible for many more rapes than was Al-Qaida.[31]

In an effort to improve its image in Iraq, Al-Qaida specifically refuted accusations that it targeted tribesmen, pointing out that most Al-Qaida members also came from the tribes: "Isn't it stupid to say that we target our own fathers, maternal and paternal uncles and brothers, and our own tribe?" Moreover, Al-Qaida also stressed that it did not target tribal shaykhs and that it had no intention of challenging the shaykhs' legitimacy, while at the same time still threatening those shaykhs who cooperated with the Sahwa. As Abu Hamza Al-Muhajir asked rhetorically in 2008, "Why should we target those tribal shaykhs who their own people have selected?" However, he was quick to add, "But I don't think you or anyone else would hold against us the killing of any of the Sahwa's puppet shaykhs.... We are proud to cut off their heads.... Which one of you, honestly, was not happy when Abu Risha was killed?"[32]

As part of the campaign designed to attract the tribes again, in 2010 Al-Qaida made a concerted effort to deny past crimes attributed to them, including passionate denials by the new head of the Islamic State of Iraq, Abu Umar Al-Baghdadi.[33] While admitting that innocent people had been killed, Al-Qaida blamed uncontrolled elements for earlier excesses, citing poor control over unrestrained youth and an intake of unscreened inappropriate elements, and assured its audience that evildoers were being expelled from the organization.[34]

There are some indications that Al-Qaida's appeals, in particular, have had some resonance among the tribal youth. For example, the official Al-Jiburi tribal website showcases Al-Qaida material and that phenomenon is probably related to the younger, computer-savvy tribesmen who manage and access such sites. Indeed, the police authorities in Diyala became so concerned about the use of very popular internet cafes to spread "extremist ideas" and to recruit members for Al-Qaida that a special police branch was set up in 2011 to monitor such venues.[35] Likewise, in the Mosul region, in a telling incident, the police went on alert after pro-Al-Qaida slogans were found on the walls of schools and inside classrooms, suggesting some rural youths at least are still attracted to Al-Qaida.[36]

In order to neutralize Sahwa fighters, Al-Qaida has used traditional values of honor and shame. Abu Hamza al-Muhajir, for example, asked Sahwa members to think about who would marry their daughters, or what their sons and grandsons would say when others called them "sons of traitors and agents" and warned, "Beware that your sons do not spit on your grave."[37] Drawing away Sahwa fighters has included offering material incentives, and one Sahwa commander in Bayji warned that "Al-Qaida is spending large sums of money in order to attract back Sahwa members."[38] According to a Sahwa commander in Baghdad, Al-Qaida targets, in particular, unpaid Sahwa fighters.[39] In Diyala, likewise, Al-Qaida was making special efforts to recruit unemployed youth and Sahwa veterans, offering them money.[40] In the northern part of the Baghdad region, some 15 percent of the Sahwa fighters were said to have reverted to Al-Qaida by late 2010.[41] Likewise, in Diyala, estimates were also that 15 percent of the former Sahwa fighters had reverted to Al-Qaida by 2010.[42] Indicative of the ongoing competition between Al-Qaida and the shaykhs, the Sahwa in Diyala, headed by Shaykh Yusuf Haylan of the Mujamma tribal confederation, had originally recruited from among its own tribesmen, who had been part of Al-Qaida. Now, a commander in that Sahwa was urging the government to rehire Sahwa veterans who had been dismissed, with the specific purpose of preventing Al-Qaida from again recruiting its former members.[43]

In order to secure more resources to support its policy financially, Al-Qaida has been rebuilding its economic network by relying on local sources. New initiatives include extracting a tax or protection money (*al-khawa*) from merchants and levying a tax on truck traffic in Mosul, apparently with only limited police interference.[44] In Diyala, Al-Qaida was reportedly also stealing oil along the pipeline from the Khanaqin oil fields and from the refinery at Bayji.[45] Also in Diyala, according to local security sources, Al-Qaida relies for a significant portion of its finances on money collected from gas station owners.[46] In this respect, Al-Qaida appears to have integrated itself into local society in the Sunni areas, establishing front contracting companies or simply "taxing" other businesses to generate revenue, although its role reportedly has become accepted because of the accompanying greater order and diminished amount of random violence, at least in Ninawa Province.[47]

Moreover, at least in financing, Al-Qaida's focus appears aimed more at urban sources and less at those in direct competition with the tribes than was the case before. For example, rather than earlier attempts to compete with the tribes for control over the main trade routes, today Al-Qaida seems to prefer to generate income by charging truckers of imported goods at the point of arrival in a city, such as is the case in Mosul.[48] In fact, suggesting renewed commercial cooperation with the tribes in Al-Anbar, in 2010 Sahwa leader Ahmad Abu Risha had to negotiate a settlement with Shia tribes in a case involving the theft of autos by Al-Qaida operatives and their subsequent apparent fencing through the Dulaym tribes.[49]

Iraqi intelligence confirmed that in 2010 Al-Qaida was also making approaches to tribal shaykhs to recruit them, prompting a senior security officer to issue a reminder that "it is impossible for them [i.e., the tribal shaykhs] to be with the government in the morning and with Al-Qaida at night" and warning the shaykhs not to succumb to Al-Qaida's plans since the latter was doomed to defeat.[50] An unnamed senior Iraqi security source noted that Al-Qaida has been using intermediaries to deliver messages and sermons aimed at tribal leaders in charge of Sahwa forces.[51] Some prudent tribal shaykhs appear to have kept a foot in both camps, as certain shaykhs in the Sahwa might also have a brother or son with Al-Qaida and, in one case, a shaykh's brother was even an amir, or commander, in the local Al-Qaida.[52]

A parallel line of operation for Al-Qaida has been to target those Sahwa leaders and other tribal shaykhs whom it considers to be uncooperative in order to pressure tribal leaders to change sides or at least to neutralize them. The Iraqi media is full of accounts of continuing successful and failed attacks against shaykhs in the Sahwa and against their families and retainers. Some tribal/Sahwa leaders have been the object of multiple assassination attempts, with the Diyala Sahwa leader, Shaykh Husam Al-Mujammai, alone having been the target of seven such attacks.[53] Sahwa intelligence sources feared that Al-Qaida had made plans to assassinate more than thirty shaykhs.[54] At the same time, by mid-2010, Al-Qaida was handing out leaflets in Diyala seeking to drive a wedge between Sahwa commanders and ordinary fighters, calling on the latter to pass false information against the commanders to the police so the shaykhs would be arrested.[55]

A good example of the carrot-and-stick method is provided by Al-Qaida's foray into the territory of the Karaghul tribe in Al-Anbar. On that occasion, Al-Qaida engaged Iraqi army forces and urged the local tribal shaykhs to join it, but at the same time also threatened to expel some people from their homes, presumably if they did not cooperate.[56] Al-Qaida believed that reaching agreement with a tribe would mean that it would not join the Sahwa, as Abu Bakr Al-Baghdadi indicated had been a measure of success in Ninawa Province.[57] On the other hand, Abu Hamza Al-Muhajir still fulminated that if the Sahwa elements continued as they had, "then with God's help their heads will not escape us and we will quench ourselves with their blood."[58]

Al-Qaida's binary tribal policy, set against a background of friction between the government and the Sunni tribes, seems to have been successful in putting considerable pressure on the tribal leadership, whether within the Sahwa framework or outside it. Even when Sahwa personnel were integrated into the government sector, Sahwa leaders for the most part were not, leaving the leaders particularly vulnerable to Al-Qaida attacks. In the wake of increasing pressure from Al-Qaida and faltering support from the government, Sahwa commanders found themselves in a dilemma. In the case of the Abu Ghraib Sahwa, of the seventeen commanders still on duty (nine had already been killed and four arrested), in November 2010, twelve departed the area with their families and household goods. According to one of those who remained, Shaykh Muhammad Al-Dulaymi (nom de guerre: Captain Muhammad), the reason for such departures was not only the threat from Al-Qaida but also the fact that the army had withdrawn the gun permits from the commanders' bodyguards and that salaries were frequently late.[59]

As a result of Al-Qaida activity, some tribal shaykhs appear to have become more cautious, even if not supportive of Al-Qaida. Thus, after the September 2010 Battle of the Palms in Al-Hadid, Diyala, in which the Iraqi army performed in a lackluster fashion after surprising an Al-Qaida grouping (reportedly including the Islamic State of Iraq's leader), local tribal shaykhs—no doubt under pressure—had to commit themselves to clearing out the palm groves and agricultural areas that had served as an operating base for Al-Qaida and not providing shelter for terrorists, whether they came from their own tribe or were outsiders.[60] In itself, this situation suggested that up until then, the tribal leadership had not been proactive in securing their areas, and the fact that such a formal ceremony was felt to be necessary may be an indication of a growing problem with commitment. As a local official in Diyala noted, in the rural—that is tribal—areas of the province "some of the people . . . still sympathize with the Al-Qaida leaders and provide them with logistic support."[61]

In Salah Al-Din Province, tribal leaders likewise met with government representatives in December 2010 to pledge themselves publicly to fight against the terrorists and to support the government against them. The event enabled tribal shaykhs to feel pride about the continuing importance of tribes, as Shaykh Aziz Al-Janabi waxed proudly that "tribes in Iraq play an active role in everything . . . everywhere in Iraq."[62] At the same time, however, the need for such renewed public reassurances of loyalty might suggest lingering government doubts on the tribes' position vis-à-vis Al-Qaida.

AL-QAIDA'S COMBAT OPERATIONS

A combination of factors, of which an increasingly disillusioned Sunni tribal base may be key, has enabled Al-Qaida to rebuild at least part of its military capability and allowed it to intensify its kinetic operations. To some extent, the Sahwa's reduced force structure—as a result of either disillusionment with the government or of the absorption of some of its fighters into civilian government jobs outside their home areas—has facilitated Al-Qaida's task of reconstitution and increasing its operational tempo, since a full-time armed force within the tribes that had been an obstacle has now diminished in numbers and commitment. The reduction in Sahwa ranks has also given Al-Qaida greater freedom of movement, with neither the depleted Sahwa nor the security forces able to control all the territory and, in particular, has led to the loss of intelligence about Al-Qaida, including that provided by the local eyes in the street able to recognize strangers.

Perhaps responding to the earlier Iraqi Sunni dismay with civilian casualties resulting from indiscriminate attacks, Al-Qaida has revised its target selection. Al-Qaida's refocused strategy appears to dovetail with the guidance provided in the section entitled "Targeting Strategy" from the most recent Al-Qaida policy review. This document determined that the "greatest priority" is to target the most effective cadres in the best units of the Iraqi army and police, as well as engineers and trainers, since this approach, which it termed "focused targeting," is expected to have the greatest impact.[63]

Recently, Al-Qaida's emphasis has been on more precise strikes against government officials, police and army officers, and security facilities, as well as against Sahwa commanders, while indiscriminate bombings resulting in large-scale civilian casualties—though not absent—have become relatively less common than before, at least against fellow Sunnis.[64] In addition, the highly publicized grisly executions, a hallmark of the Al-Zarqawi period, which had engendered so much negative publicity, have ceased.

To be sure, the overall number of Iraqis killed has decreased dramatically over time, and in 2010, officially totaled 4,561 (as well as 12,749 wounded). However, 98 percent of those casualties were concentrated in Baghdad and the four largely Sunni provinces.[65] While there are daily media reports of arrests of operatives, including commanders, and of the discovery of arms caches, this also indicates a continuing Al-Qaida force structure of some significance. An unidentified Iraqi security source estimated Al-Qaida fighter strength in 2010 at 12,000 plus over 10,000 auxiliaries, confirming that Al-Qaida remains a factor to be reckoned with.[66]

The Iraqi media is still filled almost daily with reports of small-scale failed or successful attacks by Al-Qaida against individuals, patrols, and vehicles (mostly with explosives or with firearms equipped with silencers) in Baghdad and the provinces. The problem became so serious that in July 2011 the Iraqi government decreed that the manufacture or possession of silencers would be an offense punishable by death. Such attacks are punctuated by less frequent but more spectacular strikes against secure government facilities such as the Ministry of Justice and the Baghdad City Council (October 2009); the Center for Criminal Investigations (January

2010); the Trade Bank (June 2010); the government complex in Ramadi (December 2010); military facilities (April 2009, August 2010, and January 2011); the police recruitment center in Tikrit (January 2011); police headquarters in Diyala (January 2011); as well as against non-Sunni civilian targets such as Baghdad's Our Lady of Salvation Church (November 2010) or the Shia Mausoleum of Imam Al-Hasan Al-Askari near Tikrit (February 2011). Even the attacks in Baghdad—where the most lucrative targets are—are said to be closely linked with support from the rural areas, according to Lieutenant General Diya' Husayn, the director of Counterterrorism and Organized Crime in the Ministry of the Interior.[67] For example, the Al-Qaida suicide bomber who attacked an army recruiting station in Baghdad in October 2010, Wisam Al-Naimi, although a resident of Baghdad, had (as his name indicates) connections with the large tribal confederation of that name.

In addition, Al-Qaida appears to have begun using traditional guerrilla tactics in the tribal areas, specifically that of attacking the army and security forces in the expectation that those forces, unable to retaliate against its operatives, would retaliate against the population. The intended effect of eliciting collective punishment would be to drive a wedge between the tribal population and the government, thus providing new recruits for Al-Qaida. For example, when a roadside bomb blew up an Iraqi army vehicle in the Abu Ghraib tribal area in April 2010, the army retaliated by closing off the area, bursting into homes, and allegedly arresting, beating, and killing locals, including women. A reporter commented that this had become the standard operating procedure for the army and police after every security incident. When the locals complained to the government about their treatment at the hands of the army, the grievance was compounded by the attitude they met from the authorities. The head of security for Baghdad Province laid the blame on the shoulders of the local population, stating that not providing information meant that they, at the very least, had been careless and uncooperative with the security forces, and attributed whatever excesses occurred to the fact that the local population had allowed the attack to develop.[68] Such collective punishments at the hands of the national police, likewise, only seemed to increase popular discontent.[69] The Sahwa's representative, Shaykh Thamir Al-Tamimi, has posited that the army's arbitrary arrests after all such security incidents is a result of a lack of available local intelligence, which has disappeared with the demobilization of the Sahwa, whose fighters were familiar with the local environment.[70]

Moreover, the recent attacks highlight what appears to be worrying penetration by Al-Qaida of the security institutions and, more broadly, its insinuation again into the tribal system. The government continues to harbor lingering doubts about the reliability of those Sahwa fighters already absorbed into the security forces out of concern about penetration by Al-Qaida. In Diyala, according to its police chief, even three members of the provincial council were in jail for allegedly aiding terrorists, while there was an outstanding arrest warrant for a tribal shaykh on the same charge. Al-Qaida had also penetrated the local police force and was now in a position to change names and issue forged documents.[71] The two October 2009 attacks in Baghdad, which alone had caused some 1,000 casualties, led a member of Iraq's Parliamentary Security and Defense Committee to argue that such repeated attacks indicated that the security services were penetrated.[72] Similarly, when the government center in Ramadi was bombed in December 2010, a member of the Al-Anbar Provincial Council concluded that "the incident today is clear evidence of the dominance of armed groups affiliated with Al-Qaida, since they have individuals inside the police who are providing them updates and who are enabling their activity."[73] Significantly, when security forces from Baghdad mounted a raid against suspected Al-Qaida interests in Falluja in 2010, the local police force was not allowed to participate.[74] Again, when the Iraqi army and military police took control of Falluja in response to the antigovernment protests in the Spring of 2011, according to press reports, the government forces made sure they neutralized the local police first.[75]

Locals in Al-Anbar, in fact, are critical of the local police for having become timid and avoiding danger: "The police today are the ones hiding from Al-Qaida."[76] Even Al-Qaida's integration into the local economy in Ninawa Province, for example, was also said to be possible because of its penetration of the local government, which provides Al-Qaida with timely and detailed information on new contracts into which it can muscle its way.[77]

The latest attacks by Al-Qaida against specific individuals have often had the hallmark of inside jobs and are likely to reduce the government's trust of former Sahwa fighters now in the security services even further. According to the Baghdad Security Operations spokesman, the mounting number of assassinations of government officials is either based on information leaked from inside the security services or is actually carried out by personnel serving in the security services.[78] By late 2009, some 70,000 members of the security forces (total strength 650,000) had already been purged, and although there may have been multiple reasons, one can presume that at least quite a few had Al-Qaida connections and that the issue remains a problem.[79]

Al-Qaida has clearly also penetrated many Sahwa units. As a Sahwa commander in Diyala admitted, "Al-Qaida has spies within our ranks and it is very difficult to uncover them."[80] Perhaps this interpenetration is not surprising given one Sahwa leader's estimate that 60 percent of the Sahwa was composed of former insurgents.[81] In effect, Al-Qaida members had initially joined the new Sahwa as a way to avoid the crackdown. The original influx of members had resulted in many Sahwa fighters who still sympathized with Al-Qaida, and some tribesmen reportedly continue to cooperate with the organization even while in the Sahwa.[82]

This persistence of old loyalties for Sahwa fighters for Al-Qaida is confirmed by media reports from the field. As one Sahwa commander in Baquba noted, "We have been surprised many times to learn when we have arrested terrorists that they were still operating in our ranks."[83] For example, when the special police from Baghdad arrested fourteen individuals in a village in Diyala following a bomb attack against the local police, eight of those detained were found to be members of the Sahwa.[84] According to Iraqi police sources, even a number of Sahwa commanders had already been arrested in Diyala on suspicion of cooperating with Al-Qaida.[85] One Al-Qaida operative in Diyala revealed under interrogation after his arrest that he was, in fact, also a commander in the Sahwa.[86] In May 2009, forces from the Ministry of the Interior, deployed from Baghdad, arrested another two Sahwa commanders in Diyala for allegedly belonging to Al-Qaida.[87] In March 2010, the commander of the West Baghdad Sahwa was arrested on charges of terrorism.[88] In January 2011, security forces arrested Sabah Al-Janabi, the commander of the Jurf Al-Sakhr Sahwa, in Babil Province, on charges of being the local commander of Al-Jaysh Al-Islami, one of whose factions is now again affiliated with Al-Qaida.[89]

In the Abu Ghraib area, so great was the mistrust of the Sahwa that the security forces refused to share intelligence with the local Sahwa.[90] In Diyala, by 2010, the government felt compelled to establish joint Sahwa/police cells with the express purpose of monitoring the 8,000 current and the undetermined number of former Sahwa fighters, an indication of the recognition of the challenge that Al-Qaida posed within the Sahwa organization.[91] In some cases, Sahwa members who had failed to get official recognition by the government reportedly had allowed Al-Qaida to mount operations.[92] In Diyala, some fighters serving in the Sahwa simply stopped cooperating with the authorities; according to the province's security forces commander, "They are not telling us if Al-Qaeda is in the area. They are not warning us.... A lot of them are definitely helping the insurgents."[93] In at least some instances, it appears that the local Sahwa might cooperate with U.S. forces during the daytime, but then gunfire and rockets would still be directed at U.S. bases at night, indicating that the Sahwa, at the very least, was not always reacting forcefully to the Al-Qaida presence, if not actually cooperating with the latter.[94]

Significantly, a tribal shaykh from Diyala urged the government to close down the "security centers" (that the Iraqi army had set up in September 2008 and that were manned by Sahwa personnel and run by a tribal shaykh) and even the parent Sahwa organization itself, since in his view the Sahwa had by now become just "armed militias which include large numbers of Al-Qaida leaders and fighters" who had joined originally out of self-protection to survive the earlier military crackdowns.[95] The recruitment of former Al-Qaida personnel into the Sahwa, which had earlier been seen as an achievement, has more recently been viewed as a threat. Husam Al-Mujammai, in fact, was calling for the need to purge such elements from the "security centers" in 2010.[96] Significantly, in late 2010, there were murky reports of an attempted coup against the local government in Diyala, involving Al-Qaida operatives and others on the inside, and necessitating the intervention of special security forces from Baghdad.[97] That Al-Qaida was involved is suggested by the fact that car bombs and suicide vests to be used in the attack had been assembled in the palm groves, a traditional stronghold for Al-Qaida in the province.[98]

There is a plausible correlation between, on the one hand, Al-Qaida's penetration of the Sahwa and of the security apparatus following the integration of Sahwa personnel and other tribal elements and, on the other, the growing sense of alienation within the Sunni community in general. Even if not openly cooperating with Al-Qaida, Sahwa personnel or local police—mostly local tribesmen, whether themselves veterans of the Sahwa or of other insurgent groups or not—might begin to show a growing reluctance to operate aggressively against Al-Qaida, either out of sympathy or out of disenchantment with their own lot and with government policy, and as a way to hedge their bets in an uncertain future.

A CONTINUING UNSTABLE TRIBAL ENVIRONMENT

Current indications are that relations between the Sunni tribes and the government will remain tense and may even deteriorate in the future, perhaps offering Al-Qaida greater scope for activity. To be sure, in the wake of the hung elections of March 2010, embattled Prime Minister Al-Maliki did seek to curry the Sunni tribes' favor, as he scrambled for any support he could find, and promised to address their grievances and raise the Sahwa's salaries and benefits.[99] However, most Sunni tribes seem to have supported Ayad Allawi and his coalition in the elections. The fact that Allawi was outmaneuvered in the formation of the new government was likely to mean even less influence and fewer benefits for the Sunni tribal shaykhs, weakening their own standing within their tribes and likely to contribute to a continuing fractious relationship between the Sunni tribes and Baghdad.

To be sure, the Al-Maliki government did establish a new Ministry for Tribal Affairs, ostensibly in recognition of the tribes' importance, and appointed a tribal shaykh, Jamal Al-Btikh, as its first minister in February 2011. Previously, a tribal affairs department lodged within the Ministry of the Interior had managed the tribal sector. In part, the creation of the new ministry and the appointment of Shaykh Al-Btikh, a member of Parliament from Ayad Allawi's Al-Iraqiya coalition, may have been done in order to entice Al-Btikh to break with the latter. In effect, within a few weeks of his appointment, Al-Btikh was to lead a walkout of a bloc of eight parliamentarians from Allawi's coalition and the establishment of a new party, thereby weakening Allawi, who was Prime Minister Al-Maliki's main political rival.[100]

Tribal shaykhs were hopeful the new ministry would be a vehicle to transmit their demands to the government, with the shaykhs from Al-Anbar and Salah Al-Din, for example, asking Al-Btikh to relay the "people's demands" being voiced in the demonstrations to Prime Minster Al-Maliki.[101] Al-Btikh did seek to promote tribal interests, calling for a greater role for the tribes in national security and for the government to subsidize the shaykhs financially.[102]

At the same time, the ministry was apparently under pressure from the government to function as a means to control the tribes. The ministry, for example, warned tribal shaykhs that "infiltrators" would use the protests to spark chaos.[103] Al-Btikh himself offered his services in analyzing the pressure points in the tribal system for the government to leverage, to help the government eliminate "negative phenomena" such as blood money, and in general to help the government rebuild the tribal system—all measures apparently intended to appeal to the government as a way to control the tribal sector. However, Al-Btikh appeared to have become increasingly disillusioned, noting that "some seek to minimize the ministry's importance and to marginalize its role," seeing it as a ministry "with no real mission," and had to quash rumors early that he was quitting.[104] As of June 2011, the ministry still had no building, website, or budget, suggesting that the government did not view the issue of tribal relations as a high priority.[105]

Perhaps more significantly, how the Iraqi government handles the mounting popular protests that have echoed similar ones elsewhere in the Middle East could prove to be a key factor in affecting the attitudes of the Sunni tribes and of the Sunni community in general, and could be a factor in Al-Qaida's prospects in Iraq. Unconfirmed Iraqi government security reports have alleged that Al-Qaida planned to exploit the protests for its own ends, but such protests reflect a more broadly based level of discontent with issues such as unemployment, corruption, and a lack of services and security. Such grievances are often interpreted as an indication of the government's indifference and hostility to the Sunni community.

In general, the government's handling of the situation up to now may augur badly for how it will deal with the environment in which Al-Qaida operates. The Iraqi army has so far responded to protests in Al-Anbar with such typical measures as a security crackdown involving the arrest, death, and wounding of demonstrators; the imposition of a general shutdown of Falluja and Ramadi; and the attempted arrest of Shaykh Hammud Al-Jumayli, who was the head of a committee set up to respond specifically to the demonstrations. Relations between the Iraqi army and the public deteriorated, and the shaykhs in Al-Anbar accused the army of using excessive force against the protesters, "such as had not been the case in earlier times" (that is, in Saddam's day) and claimed the army was as bad as Al-Qaida.[106] Shaykh Ali Hatim of the Dulaym, in turn, demanded that Prime Minister Al-Maliki withdraw the army immediately from Al-Anbar.[107]

More recently, an increasingly frequent demand voiced in demonstrations in Sunni tribal areas has become that for a total withdrawal of U.S. forces from Iraq (as well as the end of Iranian influence), with tribal shaykhs in Al-Anbar, Salah Al-Din, and Ninawa Provinces, in particular, being the most vociferous on this issue.[108] The government's heavy-handed response to such demonstrations, punctuated by the firing on demonstrators in Mosul at the hands of the Iraqi army's 2nd Division in April 2011, has generated an escalation of tensions between the Sunni tribes and the government.

To be sure, the Iraqi government recognizes the continuing importance of the tribes for security and of the shaykhs in guiding and controlling the tribes. Significantly, a document leaked to the Iraqi press that provided government guidance to army units on dealing with the ongoing protests, directed army commanders to inform the shaykhs officially that they would not receive any government money if any of their fellow tribesmen participated in demonstrations.[109] However, as the shaykhs have themselves often organized and led such protests, the government has also cracked down on the shaykhs, arresting six local shaykhs in Ninawa Province and dozens more in Salah Al-Din Province in the wake of demonstrations, risking alienation of that important element of leadership.[110] Not surprisingly, the shaykhs of Ninawa Province—who styled themselves the "representatives and leaders of Iraq"—reacted by warning Prime Minister Al-Maliki that insulting the shaykhs was "a red line which we will not permit to be crossed by anyone whoever he may be or he will see a violent response [if he does]."[111]

Government spokesmen, such as an operations commander in Mosul, have accused "terrorist actors" and especially "cursed Al-Qaida" of fomenting such protests.[112] Whatever the actual extent of Al-Qaida's involvement and influence in such protests, the tensions between the government and the tribes and the resulting congruency of interests between the tribes and Al-Qaida are likely to provide the latter with a more conducive operational environment and favor continued instability.

Conclusions and Prospects

Based on this study, one can draw several conclusions with a general or specific application to Iraq.

Iraq's Tribes Continue to Be an Important Element for Al-Qaida's Prospects

Iraq's Sunni tribes remain an important element in the country's political life and in the security equation; they are and will continue to be the major arena for Al-Qaida's recruitment efforts and operations. Al-Qaida views the Sunni community as its natural constituency and the tribes, in particular, as a critical requirement for its ability to conduct combat operations. Al-Qaida relies on the tribes for its manpower, logistics, force protection, mobility, and intelligence, and without at least some support from this sector, its operational effectiveness would be crippled. As a corollary, depending on the level of support it can generate from the Sunni tribes, Al-Qaida can pose a major threat to the Iraqi government or at least it can deny to the latter the ability to establish a stable and secure situation for the foreseeable future.

Without a strong working relationship between Baghdad and the Sunni tribes—to include strong security and economic support from the central government—the Sunni tribes by themselves would find it difficult to deal effectively with the continuing threat posed by Al-Qaida. Conversely, distancing the tribes from Al-Qaida is necessary in order for the Iraqi government to attain success against Al-Qaida. As seen in this study, the successful U.S. strategy of an indirect approach for degrading Al-Qaida's capabilities relied significantly on an effective handling of the country's Sunni tribes. As such, it will be necessary for the Iraqi government to craft realistic and effective policies that will address the Sunni tribes in order to undercut tribal support for Al-Qaida if the latter is to be defeated decisively.

AL-QAIDA'S "FOREIGN" CHARACTER CAN BE A CRITICAL VULNERABILITY

As indicated by the Iraqi case, local resentment of Al-Qaida's cadres as foreigners can have a negative impact for the organization's effectiveness. Outsiders not only may be insensitive to the local culture but are also prone to arouse resentment just by being outsiders, especially in tribal societies where mistrust of outsiders is ingrained. Mother Al-Qaida realizes that local populations can be sensitive to the perception that outsiders are in positions of control. Al-Qaida is aware that native cadres understand the local society and operational situation best, but in some cases cadres educated in Al-Qaida's system and selected by the latter's leadership—much less ordinary fighters filling those criteria—are simply not available when needed in certain theaters. For example, according to Sayf Al-Adl, a member of Al-Qaida's inner circle at the time and the handler for Al-Zarqawi, the objective of Al-Qaida's effort to co-opt Al-Zarqawi was to use him in connection with Palestine, since "Al-Qaida and its ideas did not have many followers in Palestine and Jordan." Al-Zarqawi was even seen as able to "recruit brothers from Jordan, Palestine, Syria, Lebanon, Iraq, and Turkey, "since these regions were very important to us, and because we knew that we were weak there," which would thus enable Al-Qaida "to reach an important region of the Arab-Islamic world."[1]

Al-Qaida's frequent reliance on nonlocal cadres suggests a latent critical vulnerability for the organization, which can be targeted at its expense in other theaters, especially in those areas where tribal societies are predominant. Psychological operations and the crafting of inducements intended to highlight the gap between the local societal leaderships and populations and Al-Qaida's "foreign" character can be effective, as was the case in Iraq.

AL-QAIDA CAN ADAPT

Despite Al-Qaida's past failures with Iraq's tribes, it is an adaptive organization and has shown itself capable in Iraq of reassessing its assumptions and of adjusting policy to changing conditions on the ground, often through an interaction of guidance from Mother Al-Qaida and lessons learned by local Al-Qaida leaders, especially once Al-Zarqawi was removed from the scene.

Al-Qaida's interaction with Iraq's complex tribal society has been a difficult process for which it was ill prepared initially and that has proven to be an often painful learning experience. As a basically alien organization, insofar as its leadership was concerned during the Al-Zarqawi period, Al-Qaida initially lacked a sound appreciation of Iraq's tribal society and a willingness to approach the tribes on their own terms. What is more, Al-Qaida's often erroneous original assumptions and ideological inflexibility hampered a more rapid learning curve and even dampened an interest in understanding local society, especially during the early period of operations. This rigidity often not only prevented the exploitation of potential advantages but also contributed to the embracing of unrealistic expectations and the crafting of unworkable and unsuccessful plans.

Al-Qaida has been able to recognize that it has made mistakes and that it needed to revise its assumptions and strategy if it were to improve its performance or even survive. To be sure, the movement's fundamental ideological underpinnings will still limit the extent of its flexibility when ideology and realpolitik requirements compete, and adaptation is not likely to be in the realm of policy objectives as much as it is likely to be in that of strategies and tactics. Nevertheless, in the case of its interaction with Iraq's tribes, Al-Qaida has exhibited the ability to learn from experience and has modified its approach at least sufficiently to place it in a position to try to take advantage of an evolving political situation and of the emerging critical vulnerabilities that the latter presents.

Every society has its own characteristics and presents unique challenges for Al-Qaida. However, Al-Qaida's willingness to learn, at least to some extent, in Iraq may suggest a potential general lesson learned for Al-Qaida that may be transferable to other theaters and could perhaps help it as it deals with other tribal societies: namely that understanding a tribal society, appreciating its interests, and approaching tribes with some flexibility rather than seeking to impose a standardized ready-made template without regard to local culture are necessary for operational and strategic success.

Supporting Proxy Local Forces in a Counterinsurgency Has Consequences

Within the context of fighting an insurgency, encouraging and supporting any armed local constituency such as Iraq's tribes may be a reasonable or even an unavoidable option at a particular juncture in time for an outside power in dealing with that insurgency. In particular, in tribal areas, local forces may be the most effective tool in a counterinsurgency, thanks to their knowledge of the human and physical terrain. Nevertheless, dealing with subnational forces can be a volatile factor, which can shift with changing interests and a dynamic situation in interaction with other players in the country.

Moreover, even if successful in terms of increasing security, fielding local forces may lay the groundwork for longer-term consequences with which a local government will have to deal eventually. In particular, the arming of any subnational group will challenge the development of an emerging government's authority and may heighten the likelihood of future violence. As part of the process of supporting such subnational armed forces, an outside power must ensure that a realistic and effective demobilization plan is in place when and if the need for such forces ends, whether the outside power is still in charge or whether authority has been transferred to the local government.

More generally, over the long term, supporting a tribal system can impede or derail the development of a more stable civil society. In Iraq, certain urban circles have continued to exhibit considerable hostility to tribal values and influence, seeing in them a premodern mode of thinking and way of life, and urban intellectuals sometimes criticize tribalism openly.[2] One opinion piece in the Iraqi media rued the encouragement of the tribes, and especially of their armed role, calling the situation "a new feudalism" and "tribal sectarianism" with tribal shaykhs having extended their influence into the cities and consolidated relations based on fear and dominance, with life and death power over individuals.[3]

IT IS POSSIBLE—AND VITAL—TO SHAPE AL-QAIDA'S OPERATIONAL ENVIRONMENT

Perhaps what is key is an appreciation that deliberate actions by other players can make the environment in which Al-Qaida operates more benign or more difficult for the organization and that shaping the environment can make the difference between success or failure in the fight against Al-Qaida.

Shaping of the operational environment affecting Al-Qaida in Iraq involves to a significant extent influencing the competition between Al-Qaida and the government for the support of the Sunni tribes. The tribes themselves are active players rather than just passive recruitment pools and, at the same time, the tribes' actions and relations with Al-Qaida cannot be seen in a vacuum. Rather, the tribes' activity is best understood within a framework of their interaction with both Al-Qaida and the government. As such, how the Iraqi government manages the tribes is a key variable that can have an impact on Al-Qaida's prospects. Iraq's Sunni tribes, in a sense, are still an asset to be won over, wholly or in part, by either Al-Qaida or the government. In the absence of an effective national political and economic integration of the Sunni community, which Al-Qaida's policy will unavoidably seek to obstruct, Al-Qaida can be expected to continue to have an entree in the Sunni community and, in particular, among the Sunni tribes.

Of course, Al-Qaida will not be passive and it, too, will continue to try to shape the environment. Unless the Sunni tribes are distanced from Al-Qaida, the latter can be expected to remain as a disruptive factor, provided it too is not seen by the tribes as inimical to their core interests. What the Iraqi government must strive to do is to avoid putting the Sunni tribes in a position where they perceive their own interests to be closer to those of Al-Qaida rather than to those of the government.

An Outside Power's Ability to Shape the Domestic Social and Political Environment May Be Limited

An external player such as the United States can advise and encourage both the Iraqi government and the Sunni tribal leadership. However, the effectiveness of such outside influence on shaping the domestic environment in which Al-Qaida operates may be limited—and increasingly so given the expected withdrawal of most of the U.S. military with a near-term horizon. To be sure, the United States' political involvement and a robust contractor presence to deal with civilian and military tasks are expected to continue and will still translate into some influence. However, Iraq's domestic players will be most responsive to the short-term requirements of their primary constituencies upon which their power depends. Other outside players—such as Saudi Arabia, Jordan, or Syria—can also influence the Sunni tribes through aid, trade, training, or the provision of safe haven. However, the promotion of regional governments' own national interests as the basis for such policies may well undercut such broader objectives as Iraqi integration and a strong and stable Iraqi government, and may embolden the Sunni tribes while alienating the government in Baghdad.

At the same time, one cannot judge a local government by the same standards as one would a temporary authority, with the latter's short-term focus and external power base. In particular, a local government's reliance on its domestic constituencies may well constrain policy choices and limit its ability and willingness to implement the systemic changes and compromises to address the demands of subnational groups, which are at times necessary for success and stability in such a situation as is found in Iraq. The current Iraqi government, with its continuing core dependence on the Shia majority community may be hampered in its ability to shape the security environment in the preferred direction in order to minimize or preclude exploitation of the latter by Al-Qaida.

In fact, in the wake of the inconclusive showing by Prime Minister Al-Maliki's political party in the 2010 elections, the Iraqi government can be expected to be under pressure from new coalition elements, such as the resurgent Shia leader Muqtada Al-Sadr, who has insisted that members of his *Jaysh Al-Mahdi* militia be integrated into the army and police as existing units, as well as has demanded specific ministries in the new government and control of the administration in several provinces. This pressure thus limits the government's flexibility even further with respect to the Sahwa's—and the Sunni tribes'—demands and reinforces Al-Qaida claims of the Shia-coloring of the state and the security apparatus.[4]

* * *

Al-Qaida's resurgence, despite its limitations, presents a continuing security challenge in Iraq, and the tribal factor remains a significant element in the security equation. To be sure, barring a disintegration of the current Iraqi government, it is highly unlikely that Al-Qaida would be able to seize control of any significant area, much less of the country, as the Iraqi state structure and the security apparatus have become sufficiently rooted and powerful enough to deal with such a threat. Rather, the greatest danger that Al-Qaida presents—as long as it can rely on sufficient support in the Sunni community and in particular among the Sunni tribes—resides in its ability to create chronic security problems, affecting stability and an already difficult economic situation negatively and hindering national integration by heightening tensions between the Sunni community on the one hand, and the central government and the non-Sunni communities on the other.

The present upsurge of popular discontent in Iraq, similar to the current upheavals elsewhere in the Middle East, could constrain further the Iraqi government's options for managing domestic politics and security. Prime Minister Al-Maliki could become increasingly focused on dealing with domestic protests, such as began—albeit still on a manageable scale—in early 2011. If threatened with instability, one can expect that Al-Maliki would redirect resources with a priority to the Shia community, which he must satisfy first, even at the expense of Sunni areas, with grievances leading to a greater Sunni-government split.

While it is difficult to forecast the dynamics of such protests, as recent events elsewhere in the region have demonstrated, any significant distractions in this direction, much less a collapse of the present Iraqi government and the long-term political disarray that would likely follow—possibly with a greater or even dominant role for the largely Shia military and security apparatus—would reduce government support for the Sunni tribes even further, relieve security pressure on Al-Qaida, and allow the latter greater room for maneuver, especially in the Sunni areas, thus putting many of the past hard-won security and political gains at risk.

Similarly, the effect of the death of Usama Bin Ladin in May 2011 is difficult to gauge at the time of the completion of this study. One can expect a period of disarray within Mother Al-Qaida as new leadership and strategies are sorted out, which may well confuse and demoralize Al-Qaida in Iraq, especially if Al-Qaida as an organization were to fragment into completely uncoordinated local affiliates. Al-Qaida in Iraq, always a hodgepodge of factions and organizations, could split apart with the removal of Bin Ladin as a symbol of unity. Nevertheless, local factors in Iraq—at least in the short run—may prove to have a greater effect on determining the demise or continuation of the role that Al-Qaida plays in the equation between the Sunni tribes and the government.

Notes

Introduction

1. Carl von Clausewitz, *On War*, ed. and trans. by Michael Howard and Peter Paret, (Princeton: Princeton University Press, 1984), 75, 77, 81.

Chapter 1: The Human Terrain: The Tribal Factor in Iraqi Society

1. See Amatzia Baram, "Neo-Tribalism in Iraq: Saddam Hussein's Tribal Policies, 1991-96," *International Journal of Middle East Studies* 29 (February 1997): 1-31; Faleh A. Jabar, "Sheikhs and Ideologues: Deconstruction and Reconstruction of Tribes under Patrimonial Totalitarianism in Iraq, 1968-1998," in Faleh A. Jabar and Hosham Dawood, ed., *Tribes and Power: Nationalism and Ethnicity in the Middle East* (London: Saqi, 2003), 69-109, hereafter Jabar and Dawood, *Tribes and Power*; and Hosham Dawood, "The Stateization of the Tribe and the Tribalization of the State: the Case of Iraq." Ibid., 110-35.

2. "Al-Wala' li'l-ashira, hal yahkum qarar al-nakhib?" [Will Tribal Loyalty Determine the Voter's Decision?], *Aswat Al-Iraq* (Baghdad), 28 January 2009, hereafter "Al-Wala' li'l-ashira, "http://ar.aswataliraq.info.

3. "Asha'ir Al-Anbar farraqatha al-masalih al-siyasiya fi rihlat al-bahth an al-nufudh wa'l-sulta" [Political Interests on the Path to Seeking Influence and Power Have Divided the Tribes of Al-Anbar], Ur News Agency (Baghdad), 23 July 2010, hereafter "Asha'ir Al-Anbar," www.uragency.net/index.php?aa=news&id22=9657; and Firas Al-Ghadban Al-Hamdani, "Mahzalat istiratijiyat al-ruqiy bi'l-jamiat al-iraqiya" [The Promotion Strategy Charade in Iraqi Universities], *Babil* (Baghdad), 31 August 2010, www.babil.info/printVersion.php?mid=27114.

4. Muhammad Al-Nahr, "Al-Asha'ir al-iraqiya wa-shuyukhha wa'l-amaliya al-dimuqratiya" [The Iraqi Tribes, Their Notables, and the Democratic Process], *Al-Rafidayn* (Baghdad), 9 August 2010, hereafter Al-Nahr, "Al-Asha'ir al-iraqiya," www.alrafidayn.com.

5. "Al-Wala' li'l-ashira," *Aswat Al-Iraq*, 28 January 2009. Iraqi doctors nowadays complain that relatives of patients who die demand "tribal judgement" (*al-fasl al-asha'iri*) to collect blood money. "Mutatallabat al-atibba' bi'l-fasl al-asha'iri wa-tahdidhum min qibal ahali al-marda tadfa atibba' Baghdad ila al-itisam" [The Demand on Doctors to Submit to Tribal Judgment and Threats from the Patients' Relatives Impel Doctors to Go on Strike], Wikalat Khabar li'l-Anba' (Baghdad), 14 January 2011, www.khabaar.com/popup.php?action=printnews&id=13048. It took a formal agreement between the government and the tribes to finally end this practice. "Al-Sihha wa-amaliyat Baghdad wa-'l-asha'ir yuwaqqiun wathiqat sharaf tamna mutalabat al-atibba' bi-diya" [The Ministry of Health, the Baghdad Operations Office, and the Tribes Sign a Gentlemen's Agreement Forbidding the Demand of Blood Money from Doctors], *Al-Muwatin* (Baghdad), 28 June 2011, www.almowatennews.com/popup.php?action=printnews&id=23002.

6. Muhammad Al-Wandi, "Al-Mujtama al-iraqi ... al-izdiwajiya wa'l-asha'ir" [Iraqi Society ... Duality and the Tribes], *Al-Sabah* (Baghdad), 14 September 2009, www.alsabah.com/paper.php?source=akbar&mlf=interpage&sid=90009; and "Qawanin al-ashira tatgha ala qawanin al-dawla wa-tatadakhkhal fi mashakil al-wizarat" [Tribal Law Prevails over State Law and Intrudes in Problems between Ministries], *Al-Badil al-Iraqi* (Baghdad), 14 May 2011, www.albadeeliraq.com/spip.php?page=imprimir_articulo&id_article=14377.

7. Al-Nahr, *Al-Rafidayn*, 9 August 2010. Such new titles include Amir of the Tribe (*amir al-ashira*), Head Amir of the Tribe (*amir umara' al-ashira*), or Head Notable (*ayn al-ayan*).

8. Rad Al-Hamdani, interview by Ilhami Al-Maliji, "Suqut Baghdad al-sari mufaja'a mudhhila!" [The Rapid Fall of Baghdad Was a Stunning Surprise], *Al-Ahram* (Cairo), 3 July 2004, hereafter Al-Hamdani, "Suqut Baghdad," http://arabi.ahram.org.eg/arabi/Ahram/2004/7/3/WRLD9.HTM. For an insightful overview of the role of tribes in Iraq's current situation, see Montgomery McFate, "*The "Memory of War: Tribes and the Legitimate Use of Force in Iraq,*" in Jeffrey H. Norwitz, ed.,

Armed Groups: Studies in National Security, Counterterrorism, and Counterinsurgency, (Newport, RI: U.S. Naval War College, 2008), 291-310.

9. There were early calls in the Iraqi media for the tribes to play such a stabilizing role, especially in the wake of the spree of looting and crime that followed Saddam's fall. Ibrahim Al-Mashhadani, "La-tashum al-asha'ir fi mukafahat al-jarima" [Let the Tribes Participate in Fighting Crime], *Al-Jarida* (Baghdad), 15 September 2003, 4.

10. "*Al-Majd* fi arwiqat majlis al-shuyukh al-iraqi" [*Al-Majd* in the Tents of the Iraqi Shaykhs' Council], *Al-Majd* (Baghdad), 31 May 2003, 2.

11. Muhammad Ali Muhy Al-Din, "Al-Urf al-asha'iri faq al-qanun" [Tribal Custom Is above the Law], *Al-Hiwar Al-Mutamaddin* (Copenhagen), 27 October 2009, www.ahewar.org/debat/show.art?aid=189624; and Haydar Al-Jarrah, "Zhawahir shadhdha lakin-naha umur adiya jiddan fi Al-Iraq" [Perverted Phenomena, But Completely Normal Affairs for Iraq], Shabakat Al-Naba' Al-Malumatiya (Washington, DC), 24 January 2011, www.annabaa.org/nbanews/2011/01/260.htm.

12. Ibid.

13. Ferry Biederman, "Arrest Raises Fears in Saddam's Tribe," *Asia Times* (Hong Kong), 18 December 2003, www.atimes.com. The preceding shaykh, in fact, had been gunned down by unknown assailants. "Head of Saddam's Tribe Gunned Down in Tikrit," *USA Today*, 1 July 2003, www.usatoday.com.

14. Ala' Al-Samarmad, "Awa'il al-madumin wa'l-mutaqalin tutalib bi'l-diyya" [The Families of Those Executed or Arrested Demand Indemnification], *Al-Ayyam* (Baghdad), 26 June 2003, 3. Some of the cases had lain dormant for twenty years.

15. "Sunnat Al-Iraq wa-tumuh al-awda ila al-sulta; Al-Qawa'im al-alamaniya taktasih Al-Mawsil wa-Salah Al-Din wa'l-Anbar" [Iraq's Sunnis and Their Desire to Return to Power; The Secular Parties Sweep Mosul, Salah Al-Din, and Al-Anbar], Shabakat Al-Naba' Al-Malumatiya, 10 March 2010, www.annabaa.org/nbanews/2010/03/134.htm.

Chapter 2: Al-Qaida Tackles the Tribes

1. In fact, this issue had been key to the split between Usama Bin Ladin and the senior jihadist figure Abd Allah Azzam, as the latter had promoted the integration of the Arab mujahidin into the local tribal structure and had intended them to instruct the Afghans on religion and to help the latter institute the sharia, whereas Bin Ladin had wanted the Arab mujahidin to focus on training and logistics for operations in other theaters. According to Azzam's widow, Umm Muhammad, interview by Muhammad Al-Shafii, "Zawjat al-zaim al-ruhi li'l-afghan al-arab: Qatl Masud wasma kabira fi tarikh Bin Ladin" [The Widow of the Spiritual Leader of the Afghan Arabs: The Killing of Masud Is a Big Blemish on Bin Ladin's Legacy], *Al-Sharq Al-Awsat* (London), 28 April 2006, www.aawsat.com/print.asp?did=360386&issueno=10013.

2. Abu Musab Al-Zarqawi, interview by the Media Section of Al-Qaida in Mesopotamia, "Hiwar ma Al-Shaykh Abi Musab Al-Zarqawi" [Interview with Shaykh Abu Musab Al-Zarqawi], 1427/January 2006-June 2006 (Al-Zarqawi's death), hereafter "Hiwar ma Al-Shaykh Abi Musab Al-Zarqawi," http://tawhed.ws.pr?i=6679.

3. Abu Hafsa Al-Ansari, interview by Abd Allah Al-Tamimi, "Abu Hafsa Al-Ansari yakshif li'l-*Watan Al-Arabi* li-awwal marra asrar" [Abu Hafsa Al-Ansari Reveals Secrets to *Al-Watan Al-Arabi* for the First Time], *Al-Watan Al-Arabi* (Beirut), 24 February 2006, hereafter Al-Tamimi, "Abu Hafsa Al-Ansari yakshif," www.muslim.net/vb/showthread.php?t=153691.

4. Talib Aadd, "Qa'id sariyat rasul Allah qad majmuat al-mutatawwiin fi Al-Iraq, lakin-nahu ad yahtif: shukran Bush" [The Commander of the Prophet of God Brigade Led a Group of Volunteers in Iraq, But He Returned Shouting "Thank You Bush"], *Al-Siyasa* (Kuwait), 16 April 2003, 13.

5. "Al-Qaida bi-Diyala tabhath an maladhdhat jadida abr al-rawabit al-asha'iriya wa'l-zawaj al-mutaaddid bi-aramil anasirih" [Al-Qaida in Diyala Seeks New Refuges through Tribal Ties and Plural Marriage to the Widows of Its Members], *Al-Rafidayn*, 25 June 2010, hereafter "Al-Qaida bi-Diyala," www.alrafidayn.com.

6. Abu Bakr Naji, *Idarat al-tawahhush: Akhtar marhala sa-tamurr biha al-umma* [*Governing Anarchy; The Most Dangerous Phase through Which the Umma Will Pass*], (Pakistan: Markaz al-dirasat wa'l-buhuth al-islamiya, 2004), 49-50.

7. "Iraq Chiefs Vow to Fight Al-Qaeda," BBC News, http://newsvote.bbc.uk..

8. Abu Anas Al-Shami, "Al-Jihad kayf nafhamhu wa-kayf numarishu" [How We Understand and Practice Jihad], March 2005, www..al3ah.org/vb/showthread.php?t=122744. Likewise, Abu Hafsa Al-Ansari had expressed the ideal when he said, "I swear by God the Almighty that even if my father, my mother, my brother, my sister, my cousin, my son, or anyone else connected to me by blood cooperates with [the Iraqi government] I will slaughter him without any compunction for him," Al-Tamimi, "Abu Hafsa Al-Ansari yakshif."

CHAPTER 3: AL-QAIDA ALIENATES THE TRIBES

1. Al-Nahr, "Al-Asha'ir al-iraqiya."

2. Shaykh Ali Hatim Ali Sulayman, interview by Majid Hamid, "Sinaat al-mawt" [The Death Industry] program, "Ightiyal shuyukh al-asha'ir . . . al-fail wa'l-asbab" [Assassinations of the Tribal Shaykhs . . . the Perpetrator and the Causes], Al-Arabiya TV (Dubai, UAE), 1 February 2007, hereafter "Ightiyal shuyukh al-asha'ir," www.alarabiya.net/save_print.php?print=1&cont_id=65493.

3. Ibid.

4. Ibid.

5. Interview with Shaykh Ahmad Abu Risha, "Ightiyal shuyukh al-asha'ir." The emphasis on the low socioeconomic status of pro-Al-Qaida elements has been a recurring theme for the shaykhs who backed the Sahwa, various interviews in Colonel Gary W. Montgomery and Chief Warrant Officer-4 Timothy S. McWilliams, eds., *Al-Anbar Awakening, Vol. 2, Iraqi Perspectives; From Insurgency to Counterinsurgency in Iraq, 2004-2009*, (Quantico, VA: Marine Corps University Press, 2009), 103, 104, 108, and 141, hereafter

Montgomery and McWilliams, *Al-Anbar Awakening, Vol. 2*

6. *Li-Llah thumma li'l-tarikh: Liqa' khass ma asir sabiq fi sujun al-rafida bi-Baghdad* [*For the Record and for God: An Exclusive Interview with a Former Prisoner in the Shia Prisons in Baghdad*], (Mu'assasat Al-Ma'sada Al-Ilamiya, November 2010), 5, hereafter *Li-Llah thumma li'l-tarikh*.

7. According to Usama Bin Ladin, "We find that the cohort from fifteen to twenty-five is the cohort with the ability to commit and struggle; that is what we observed during the jihad in Afghanistan, that is that most mujahidin were that age." Usama Bin Ladin, interview by Jamal Ismail, "Bin Ladin wa'l-Jazira wa-ana" [Bin Ladin, Al-Jazira, and Me], 1998, www.arabslink.net. Likewise, Ayman Al-Zawahiri noted that youth were "the jihadi vanguard" and "It is the Muslim youth who must spread the battle against the Jews and the Crusaders over the widest possible area of the world." Ayman Al-Zawahiri, *Taht rayat al-qur'an* [*Under the Banner of the Qur'an*], (Al-Sahab li'l-intaj al-ilami, 19 Dhu al-hijja 1425/30 January 2005), 17.

8. Staff Major General Kadhim Muhammad Al-Fahadawi al-Dulaymi, former Deputy Commander, Al-Anbar Operations Center, interview in Montgomery and McWilliams, *Al-Anbar Awakening, Vol. 2*, 263.

9. Rajiv Chandrasekaran, "In a Hostile Land, Trying Whatever Works; U.S. Officials in Iraq Learn to Adapt to Local Rules," *Washington Post*, 23 December 2003, A1.

10. Shaykh Ahmad Abu Risha, interview by Suhayr Al-Qaysi, "Min Al-Iraq: Ma al-shaykh Ahmad Abu Risha" [From Iraq: With Shaykh Ahmad Abu Risha], Al-Arabiya TV, 25 November 2007, hereafter Abu Risha, "Min Al-Iraq, www.alarabiya.net/save_print.php?print=1&cont_id=42097.

11. Miriam, wife of a senior police officer, interview in Montgomery and McWilliams, *Al-Anbar Awakening, Vol. 2*, 23.

12. Shaykh Ahmad Abu Risha, interview in Montgomery and McWilliams, *Al-Anbar Awakening, Vol. 2*, 46; and Hannah Allam, "Iraqi Insurgents Taking Cut of U.S. Rebuild-

ing Money," McClatchy Newspapers, 26 August 2007, www.mcclatchydc.com/2007/08/27/v-print/19232/iraqi-insurgents-taking-cut-of.html.

13. Or, as one shaykh in Al-Anbar put it, "the al-Qaeda-led extremists had muscled in on the 'trading' across the border," Bing West, *The Strongest Tribe: War, Politics, and the Endgame in Iraq*, (New York: Random House, 2008), 101, hereafter West, *The Strongest Tribe*. Some well-known tribal figures, such as Shaykh Rad Al-Hamdani, soon to be the secretary general of the Shaykhs' Council, had also been suspected by the U.S authorities of smuggling oil, Al-Hamdani, "Suqut Baghdad."

14. Shaykh Sabah Al-Sattam Effan Fahran Al-Shurji Al-Aziz, paramount shaykh of the Albu Mahall tribe, interview in Montgomery and McWilliams, *Al-Anbar Awakening, Vol. 2*, 141.

15. "Muhafizh Ninawa yu'akkid: Al-Asha'ir hiya al-umq al-istratiji li-bina' al-wad al-amni" [The Governor of Ninawa Confirms: The Tribes Are the Strategic Depth on Which to Build the Security Situation], *Al-Rafidayn*, 11 December 2006, www.alrafidayn.com/story/News/11_12_3.html.

16. Mushriq Abbas, "Tajadhubat asha'iriya wa-siyasiya rafaqat siraahu ma Al-Qaida wa'l-Maliki . . . Masira qasira wa-ghamida qadat Abu Risha ila jiwar Bush" [Tribal and Political Mutual Attractions Accompanied His Struggle with Al-Qaida and Al-Maliki . . . A Murky and Short Journey Led Abu Risha to Bush's Side], *Al-Hayat* (London), 16 September 2007, hereafter Abbas, "Tajadhubat asha'iriya," http://international.daralhayat.com/print/155881/archive.

17. Ibid.; and Mark Kukis, "Turning Iraq's Tribes against Al-Qaeda," *Time*, 26 December 2006, www.time.com/time/printout/0,8816,1572796,00.html.

18. *Li-Llah thumma li'l-tarikh*, 3.

19. "Hiwar ma Al-Shaykh Abi Musab Al-Zarqawi."

20. *Li-Llah thumma li'l-tarikh*, 4.

21. As an Iraqi report on tribalism notes, however, the practice within tribes of killing women as punishment for adultery is widespread, even on mere suspicion without proof, although that is normally a family prerogative, and not one for even tribal courts. Tariq Harb, "Al-Ashira fi al-dustur al-jadid wa'l-nizham al-qanuni al-iraqi" [Tribes in the New Constitution and the Iraqi Legal System], *Al-Sabah* (Baghdad), 17 January 2006, hereafter Harb, "Al-Ashira," www.alsabah.com/paper.php?source=akbar&mlf=copy&sid=16682.

22. "Asha'ir Al-Anbar." This was also confirmed by U.S. military observers. Zeke Minaya, "Baghdad Tribes Close to Fighting Al-Qaida," *Stars and Stripes*, 21 May 2007, www.stripes.com/news/baghdad-tribes-close-to-fighting-al-qaida-1.64315.

23. As one shaykh noted, "No no can abandon or get rid of tribal law. The laws and the constitution are not permanent. They change with the governments." Sudarsan Raghavan, "A New Breed Grabs the Reins in Anbar: U.S.-Backed Sheiks Reshaping Own Areas and, Potentially, the Future of Iraq," *Washington Post*, 21 October 2008, A1, hereafter Raghavan, "A New Breed."

24. For example, when Shaykh Salih Ahmad Al-Alwani was assassinated, his tribe's paramount chief highlighted that the victim was especially known for "resolving disputes between members of his tribe and disputes with other tribes." "Ashirat Albu Alwan tutalib bi-fath tahqiq bi-maqtal ahad shuyukhha" [The Albu Alwan Tribe Demands That an Investigation Be Opened into the Death of One of Its Shaykhs], Sharikat Akhbar Al-Iraq (Baghdad), 20 September 2010, www.aliraqnews.com.

25. *Li-Llah thumma li'l-tarikh*, 5. This function of a shaykh whereby the latter guarantees protection to—or redress for—his fellow tribesmen is key to tribal cohesion and to the shaykh's authority. Typically, it was a tribal shaykh in Salah Al-Din Province who announced that his tribe would sue the U.S. forces for having killed a member of the tribe during an anti-Al-Qaida operation. "Quwwa amirikiya taqtul madaniyyan khilal inzal jawwi janub Tikrit" [American Force Kills a Civilian During an Airborne Operation South of Tikrit], *Sumarriya News*, 17 March 2011, www.alsumarianews.com/ar/18858/print-article.html.

26. "Fi sahwa wataniya: Al-Sunna fi gharb Al-Iraq ya'khudhun siraan damiya ma tanzhim Al-Qaida" [In a Patriotic Awakening: The Sunnis in Western Iraq Embark on a Bloody Struggle against Al-Qaida], *Shabakat Al-Naba' Al-Malumatiya*, 28 Ferbruary 2007, hereafter "Fi sahwa wataniya," www.annabaa.org/nbanews/61/509.htm.

27. "Arab al-jinsiya hawalu ifsad al-hayat al-ijtimaiya fi Diyala" [Those with Arab Nationality Tried to Undermine Societal Life in Diyala], *Al-Sabah Al-Jadid* (Baghdad), 24 March 2010, www.newsabah.com; Raghavan, "A New Breed," A1; interview with Shaykh Ali Hatim and Shaykh Muhammad Al-Hayis, "Ightiyal shuyukh al-asha'ir"; and Miriam, interview in Montgomery and McWilliams, *Al-Anbar Awakening, Vol. 2*, 21.

28. "Arab al-jinsiya."

29. Ibid.

30. Asad Allah Al-Hasani, "Waqi al-jihad fi Al-Iraq wa-Afghanistan" [The Status of the Jihad in Iraq and Afghanistan], *Talai Khurasan*, Dhu Al-Qada 1426/November-December 2005, 41-42.

31. Samir Aluww, "Ashira fi Al-Taji tuslim 3 saudiyyin shakkalu mahakim shariya" [A Tribe in Al-Taji Hands Over 3 Saudis Who Had Set Up Sharia Courts], *Al-Zaman* (London), 28 February 2007, www.azzaman.com.

32. Tariq Al-Shammari, "Hadha al-sabab al-haqiqi li-azl Abi Sulayman Al-Utaybi (al-qadi al-shari) li-Dawlat Al-Iraq Al-Islamiya" [This Is the Real Reason for the Ouster of Abu Sulayman Al-Utaybi (the Religious Law Judge) of the Islamic State of Iraq], 26 August 2007, www.muslm.net/vb/showthread.php?t=247718.

33. Al-Mulla Nazhim Al-Jiburi, interview by Majid Hamid, "Al-Mulla Nazhim min Al-Qaida ila majalis al-sahwa" [Al-Mulla Nazhim from Al-Qaida to the Sahwa Councils], "Sinaat al-mawt" [The Death Industry] program, Al-Arabiya TV, 27 April 2008, hereafter Nazhim Al-Jiburi, "Al-Mulla Nazhim min Al-Qaida," www.alarabiya.net/save_print.php?print=1&cont_id=48959.

34. Islamic State of Iraq communique of 25 August 2007 from the Office of the Com-

mander of the Believers, www.hanein.info/vbx/showthread.php?t=77312&page=3.

35. "Al-Anbar min Al-Qaida ila al-sahwa: Inqilab fi al-way am yaqzha abira?" [Al-Anbar from Al-Qaida to the Sahwa: A Revolution in Consciousness Or Just a Temporary Alertness?], *Al-Sabah Al-Jadid*, 14 March 2009, www.newsabah.com.

36. In Abu Anas Al-Shami, "Marakat al-ahzab bi'l-Falluja" [The Battle of the Confederates in Falluja], Shabakat Kalimat Al-Haqq, n.d., www.rightword.net/Anuke/modules.php?name=Sections&op=viewarticle&artid=557.

37. Shaykh Ali Hatim Ali Sulayman, interview by Abd Al-Azhim Muhammad, "Al-Mashhad al-iraqi: Tajrubat taslih al-asha'ir fi al-Anbar" [The Iraqi Scene: The Experiment of Arming the Tribes in Al-Anbar], Al-Jazira TV (Doha, Qatar), 29 July 2007, hereafter Shaykh Ali Hatim, "Al-Mashhad al-iraqi," www.aljazeera.net,

38. *Li-Llah thumm li'l-tarikh*, 3.

39. "Mu'tamar li-asha'ir Karbala' yutalib bi-ilgha' bad al-adat wa'l-taqalid al-asha'iriya" [The Conference of the Karbala Tribes Requests the Suppression of Some Tribal Customs and Traditions], *Aswat Al-Iraq* (Baghdad), 12 December 2010, http://ar.aswataliraq.info.

40. Shaykh Ali Hatim, "Ightiyal shuyukh al-asha'ir."

41. Shaykh Ali Hatim, "Al-Mashhad al-iraqi."

42. Nazhim Al-Jiburi, "Al-Mulla Nazhim min Al-Qaida."

43. "Arab al-jinsiya."

44. Jonathan Steele, "Iraq: Arrests of Sunni Tribal Leaders Risk Giving Al-Qaida a Way Back, Says Iraqi Vice-President," *The Guardian*, 16 September 2008, www.guardian.co.uk/world/2008/sep/16/iraq/print.

45. Shaykh Ali Hatim, interview by Wa'il Isam, "Siraat bayn Al-Qaida wa-jamaat sunniya musallaha fi Al-Iraq" [Struggles between Al-Qaida and Armed Sunni Groups in Iraq],

Al-Arabiya TV, 3 May 2007, hereafter Isam, "Siraat bayn Al-Qaida," www.alarabiya.net/save_print.php?print=1&cont_id=34083.

46. According to Sayf Al-Adl's handwritten memoirs, reproduced in Fu'ad Husayn, *Al-Zarqawi: Al-Jil al-thani li'l-Qaida* [*Al-Zarqawi: Al-Qaida's Second Generation*], (Beirut: Dar al-Khayyal, 2005), 137. Al-Adl was Al-Qaida's handler for Al-Zarqawi in Afghanistan.

47. Abu Umar Al-Baghdadi's sermon "Fa-Amma al-zabadu fa-yadhhabu jufa'an" [For the Scum Disappears; Like Froth Cast Out], 4 December 2007, hereafter Al-Baghdadi, "Fa-Amma al-zabadu," www.iraqipa.net/12_2007/1_5/News/a28_5des07.htm. The title is taken from the Qur'an, xiii/17, *The Holy Qur-an*, (Medina: King Fahd Holy Qur-an Printing Complex, 1410/1990-1991), 679.

48. Al-Baghdadi, "Fa-Amma al-zabadu."

49. Ibid.

50. Harmony document, dated 9 July 2005, (West Point, NY: Combating Terrorism Center, 2006), http://ctc.usma.edu/pdf/CTC-Zawahiri-Letter-Arabic-10-5.pdf.

51. Abu Musab Al-Zarqawi, "Mawqifna al-shari min hukumat 'Karzay al-iraqi'" [Our Legal Position on the Government of the "Iraqi Karzai"], July 2004, hereafter, Al-Zarqawi, "Mawqifna," www.tawhed.ws/r?i=2a0e4j83.

52. See, for example, "Zijat Al-Qaida hikayat mu'lima li-nisa' ughtusibna wa-anjabna atfalan min dun iradatihinna" [The Al-Qaida Marriages Were Painful Experiences for the Women Who Were Compelled and Who Gave Birth Against Their Will], *Al-Sabah Al-Jadid*, 19 December 2010, www.newsabah.com. However, in at least some cases, the families of tribal girls whose relatives were themselves in Al-Qaida appear to have been favorably disposed to marrying foreign Al-Qaida fighters, as was the case of one Saudi, according to his confession in "Irhabi saudi yarwi qissat tajnid Al-Qaida lah hatta itiqalih fi Al-Iraq; Iddaa dhahabhu ila al-hajj fa-taallam ziraat al-qanabil wa-tazawwaj intihariya" [A Saudi Terrorist Tells His Story from Being Recruited into Al-Qaida until His Arrest

in Iraq; He Claimed He Was Going on the Pilgrimage But Instead Learned How to Plant Bombs and Married a Woman Suicidee], *Al-Balad Al-Amin* (Baghdad), 17 October 2009, 23.

53. Nazhim Al-Jiburi, "Al-Mulla Nazhim min Al-Qaida."

54. As confirmed by a report on tribalism, Tariq Harb, 17 January 2006. So great a store do tribes set by this custom that its violation can lead to violence, as in a 2010 incident, when fighting broke out between two tribes at a wedding as a result of violating that custom, causing deaths and injuries. "Maqtal wa-jarh 10 ashkhas baynhum thalath nisa' ala khalfiyat nahwa asha'iriya janub Al-Mawsil" [Ten Dead and Injured, among Them Three Women, in the Wake of a Tribal Nahwa South of Mosul], *Al-Rafidayn*, 15 June 2010, www.alrafidayn.com.

55. In some traditional tribal societies, marrying above one's station and thus violating the principle of *kafa'a* –or equality of partners—is still considered a reason to end marriages. Indeed, a Saudi man was sentenced to three years in prison for forging his genealogy in order to marry above his station. Zayna Ali, "Mufaja'at zawj qadiyyat 'takafu' al-nasab' bi'l-sijn 3 awam" [Surprise for the Husband in the "Equal Lineage" Case with Three Years in Prison], *Shams* (Riyadh), 26 October 2010, www.shms.com.sa/html/story.php?id=113398.

CHAPTER 4: MOBILIZING THE TRIBES AGAINST AL-QAIDA

1. "Qissat al-muwajaha bayn Al-Qaida wa-Hay'at Ulama' Al-Muslimin fi'l-Iraq" [An Account of the Confrontation between Al-Qaida and the Association of Muslim Scholars in Iraq], *Al-Hadath* (Amman, Jordan), 18 December 2006, www.al-hadath.com.

2. As the local Al-Qaida amir in Falluja claiming to speak for Al-Zarqawi insisted, when asked on the stance toward any neutral elements, dismissed them, saying "he who remains silent denies the truth, and is [just] a mute devil." Ibrahim Khayyat and Muhammad Abd al-Razzaq, "Amir muqatili Al-Falluja Abu Usama li'l-*Wasat*" [The Fighters' Amir in Falluja to *Al-Wasat*], interview in *Al-Wasat* (Manama, Bahrain) reproduced in *Al-Hayat*, 3

May 2004, www.darlahayat.net.

3. Layla Al-Shayib, "Ma wara' al-khabar: Sahb tarakhis al-silah al-tabi li-majalis al-sahwa" [Behind the News: Withdrawing Gun Permits from the Sahwa Councils], Al-Jazira, 8 June 2010, www.aljazeera.net; and Khulud Al-Amiri, "Al-Qaida tuhajim al-qura al-shiiya fi Diyala; asha'ir Diyala tutliq mashruan li'l-musalaha" [Al-Qaida Attacks the Shia Villages in Diyala; The Tribes of Diyala Launch a Reconciliation Project], *Al-Hayat*, 8 June 2007, http://international.daralhayat.com/print/141120/archive.

4. Harmony document, undated, (West Point, NY: Combating Terrorism Center, 2006), www.ctc.usma.edu/aq/pdf/IZ-060316-01-orig.pdf.

5. Harmony document, dated 11 December 2005, http://ctc.usma.edu/harmony/pdf/30031006-arabic25639-05.pdf. The author is almost assuredly Atiya Abd Al-Rahman Al-Libi, someone close to Al-Qaida's leaders, as Numan Bin Uthman, the former head of Al-Qaida's Libyan branch, identifies the latter as having written such a letter at the time. Numan Bin Uthman, interview by Kamil Al-Tawil with, "Al-Wajh al-akhar li'l-Qaida" [Al-Qaida's Other Face], part 3, *Al-Hayat*, 27 September 2010, hereafter Bin Uthman, "Al-Wajh al-akhar li'l-Qaida," http://international.daral-hayat.com/internationalarticle/185480.

6. Bin Uthman, "Al-Wajh al-akhar li'l-Qaida."

7. Abd Al-Karim Al-Jizani, "Al-Sira al-ta'ifi wa-taghayyurat al-mawaqif al-matluba" [The Sectarian Struggle and the Required Changes in Position], Shabakat Al-Naba' Al-Malumatiya, January 2007, www.annabaa.org/nbanews/67/314.htm.

8. Majid Hamid, "Ightiyal shuyukh al-asha'ir."

9. "Inqisamat fi sufuf al-muqatilin al-iraqiyyin: al-wala' li'l-ashira yataghallab ala al-wala' li'l-Zarqawi" [Splits among the Iraqi Fighters: Tribal Loyalties Trump Loyalty to Al-Zarqawi], *Al-Rafidayn*, 18 February 2006, http://alrafidayn.com/Story/News/N18_02_1.html.

10. Ibid.

11. "Mas'ul amni yaqul inn intihariyan muaqan fajjar sayyartu fi mawkib Abu Risha . . . wa-shaqiqu yatawaad Al-Qaida bi'l-tha'r" [A Security Official Says That a Disabled Suicide Attacker Exploded His Car against Abu Risha's Convoy . . . His Brother Swears He Will Take Revenge against Al-Qaida], Wikalat Anba' Al-Buratha (Baghdad), 14 September 2007, www.burathanews.com.

12. "Al-Maliki yataahhad bi'l-wuquf ila janib Zawba wa-Albu Faraj tushinn hujuman ala Al-Qaida" [Al-Maliki Vows to Stand By the Zawba, while the Albu Faraj Mount an Attack against Al-Qaida], *Al-Sabah*, 28 March 2009, www.alsabah.com/paper.php?source=akbar&mlf=interpage&sid=39660.

13. Ibid.

14. Interview with Shaykh Ali Hatim by Muntaha Al-Ramhi, Panorama program, Al-Arabiya TV, 16 September 2007, hereafter Al-Ramhi, www.alarabiya.net/programs/2007/09/1839267.html.

15. Interview in Chief Warrant Officer-4 Timothy S. McWilliams and Lieutenant Colonel Kurtis P. Wheeler, eds., *Al-Anbar Awakening, Vol. 1, American Perspectives; From Insurgency to Counterinsurgency in Iraq, 2004-2009*, (Quantico, VA: Marine Corps University Press, 2009), 56, [hereafter McWilliams and Wheeler, *Al-Anbar Awakening, Vol. 1*.

16. Major Niel Smith, USA, and Colonel Sean MacFarland, USA, "Anbar Awakens: The Tipping Point," *Military Review*, March-April 2008, 42-43

17. Montgomery and McWilliams, *Al-Anbar Awakening, Vol. 2*, 108.

18. Ibid., 109.

19. Abu Ahmad Abd al-Rahman Al-Masri, *Dawlat Al-Iraq Al-Islamiya haqiqa la awham, wa-waqi la ahlam* [*The Islamic State of Iraq Is a Fact, Not a Fantasy, and Reality, Not a Dream*], (n.p.: Sariyat al-sumud al-ilamiya, February 2009), 64, hereafter Al-Masri, *Dawlat Al-Iraq*.

20. Staff Major General Kadhim Muhammad Al-Fahadawi al-Dulaymi, former Deputy

Commander, Al-Anbar Operations Center, interview in Montgomery and McWilliams, *Al-Anbar Awakening, Vol. 2*, 263.

21. "Hiwar ma Al-Shaykh Abi Musab Al-Zarqawi."

22. Abu Musab Al-Zarqawi, "Risala min jundi ila amirih" [Letter from a Soldier to His Commander], May 2005, www.qal3ah.org/vb/showthread.php?t=126108.

23. According to Shaykh Abd Allah Jalal, the Head of the Sunni Waqf, in Majid Hamid, "Sinaat al-mawt" [Factory of Death] program, "Ulama' al-din hadaf li'l-Qaida" [The Ulama' Are One of Al-Qaida's Targets], Al-Arabiya TV, 29 June 2009, hereafter Hamid, "Ulama' al-din," www.alarabiya.net/save_print.php?print=1&cont_id=77308.

24. Ibid.

25. Al-Nahr, "Al-Asha'ir." Also reported in Hamid, "Ulama' al-din."

26. Shaykh Sad Al-Shammari, "Al-Jihad fi Al-Iraq haqiqa la tukhfa" [The Jihad in Iraq Is a Reality Which Cannot Be Hidden], Shabakat Akhbar Al-Iraq (Baghdad), 13 August 2010, www.aliraqnews.com. The author of this press account had been a participant in those events.

27. Shaykh Wisam Al-Hardan, interview in Montgomery and McWilliams, *Al-Anbar Awakening, Vol. 2*, 56.

28. Communique from the Islamic State of Iraq, "Jabhat al-takhadhul wa'l-hisad al-murr" [The Betrayal Front and the Bitter Harvest], 7 August 2008, www.hanein.info/vbx/showthread.php?t=77312&page=3.

29. According to Khalid Al-Fahdawi, an official with the Sunni Waqf, Mazin Sahib, "Tanzhim Al-Qaida al-irhabi: bunduqiya li'l-ijar tastahdif ahl al-sunna [Al-Qaida: A Hired Gun Targeting the Sunnis], Wikalat Anba' Al-Mustaqbal (Baghdad), 25 March 2011, hereafter Sahib, "Tanzhim Al-Qaida," www.mustakbal.net/ArticlePrint.aspx?ID=5732.

30. Mother Al-Qaida, in fact, sharply criticized Iraq's Association of Muslim Scholars for

allegedly being willing to accept customary tribal law, Abd Allah Nadhir Al-Qahtani, *Indhar al-anam* [*A Warning to Mankind*], (Markaz Al-Fajr li'l-ilam, 1430/2009), 41, as did Abu Hamza Al-Muhajir in his interview, "Tafrigh al-liqa' al-sawti ma wazir al-harb bi-Dawlat Al-Iraq Al-Islamiya" [Transcript of the Interview with the Minister of War of the Islamic State of Iraq], October 2008, www.soman.net/avb/showthread.php?t=305206.

31. Al-Shammari, "Al-Jihad."

32. "Sahwat Al-Iraq tattahim Al-Islami bi-tashwih sumatha wa-qiyadi fi al-hizb yanfi" [The Iraq Sahwa Accuses the Islamic Party of Slandering It But a Party Leader Denies That], *Al-Sabah Al-Jadid*, 2 September 2009, www.newsabah.com.

33. "Rijalat al-sahwa bi'l-Anbar yuhaddidun bi-haml al-silah bi-sabab tazwir al-intikhabat" [Sahwa Personnel in Al-Anbar Threaten to Use Force Because of the Falsification of the Elections], *Aswat Al-Iraq*, 2 February 2009, http://ar.aswataliraq.info.

34. As in the open letter from the secretary general of the association, Shaykh Harith Al-Dari, to the tribes, 30 November 2007, http://muslm.org/vb/showthread.php?t=266818.

35. Interview with Shaykh Harith Al-Dari, a leader of the association and a supporter of the non-Al-Qaida resistance, by Abd Al-Qadir Iyad, "Harith Al-Dari: Al-Wad fi Al-Iraq siyasiyan wa-amniyan" [Harith Al-Dari: The Political and Security Situation in Iraq], 29 May 2009, Al-Jazira TV, www.aljazeera.net/NR/exeres/483E69DB-DC04-4C92-B777-A9E067B6C1B3.htm.

36. "Amaliya amniya wasia fi Diyala hayth yantaliq al-sayyarat al-mufakhkhakha ila Baghdad" [Extensive Security Operation in Diyala, the Source of Car Bombs to Baghdad], *Al-Sabah Al-Jadid*, 11 April 2009, www.newsabah.com.

37. Shaykh Ali Hatim, interview in Montgomery and McWilliams, *Al-Anbar Awakening, Vol. 2*, 109.

38. Shaykh Wissam Abd Al-Ibrahim Al-Hardan Al-Aethawi, interview. Ibid., 55.

Chapter 5: The U.S. Strategy Matures and the Awakening Develops

1. Joe Klein, "Saddam's Revenge," *Time*, 18 September 2005, http://205.188.109/time/printout/0,8816,1106307,00.html.

2. Interview with Shaykh Abd Al-Rahman Al-Janabi in Montgomery and McWilliams, *Al-Anbar Awakening, Vol. 2*, 71.

3. Al-Hamdani, "Suqut Baghdad." According to the same source, in a meeting with Hume Horan, senior counselor on tribal and religious issues for the Coalition Provisional Authority, in 2003, the latter infuriated the shaykhs by terming the U.S. presence an occupation. Ibid.

4. Perhaps characteristically, early on U.S. forces had arrested—and allegedly mistreated—a senior Dulaymi shaykh, Khalaf Abd Al-Shadid, and four of his sons on suspicion of having harbored some of Saddam's family and senior members of the Bath Party. Ali Al-Sabbak, "Al-Quwwat al-amrikiya tukhalli sabil ahad wujaha' Al-Falluja bad musadarat amwalih" [U.S. Forces Release One of Fallluja's Notables after Seizing His Belongings], *Al-Shira* (Baghdad), 20 March 2003, 2. Likewise, U.S. forces arrested and confiscated the personal weapons of Shaykh Rad Al-Hamdani on charges of cooperating with the Bath insurgency. Al-Hamdani, "Suqut Baghdad."

5. For example, a Marine Corps officer in Al-Anbar said of the shaykh of the Albu Fahd, Nasir Al-Fahdawi, that "you could probably argue that he was the leader of the 1920 Revolution Brigade," one of the resistance groups. Major Alfred B. Connable, interview in McWilliams and Wheeler, *Al-Anbar Awakening, Vol. 1*, 126.

6. Mushriq Abbas, "Al-Alyan yu'akkid annahum khudiu wa-dafau 20 milyun dular li-tashkil lijan amniya wahmiya; al-amirikiyyun takhallaw an al-hiwar ma al-muqawama" [Al-Alyan Confirms That They Were Deceived and Paid 20 Million Dollars to Establish Imaginary Security Committees; The Americans Have Stopped Talking to the Resistance], *Al-Hayat*, 20 November 2006, http://international.daralhayat.com/print/109230/archive. The amount alleged in this case was $20 million.

7. Major Morgan Mann, USMCR, "The Power Equation: Using Tribal Politics in Counterinsurgency," *Military Review*, May-June 2007, 104.

8. See Anthony H. Cordesman, *Iraq's Insurgency and the Road to Civil Conflict*, vol. 2, (Westport, CT: Praeger Security International, 2008), 474-80.

9. Interview with Shaykh Wisam Al-Hardan in *Al-Anbar Awakening, Vol. 2*, 60.

10. Shaykh Wissam Al-Hardan maintains that on the eve of the conference, U.S. officials had provided Shaykh Abu Risha with the text of a manifesto for his use in proclaiming the movement. Interview in *Al-Anbar Awakening, Vol. 2*, 57.

11. Colonel Anthony E. Deane, USA, "Providing Security Force Assistance in an Economy of Force Battle," *Military Review*, January-February 2010, 86; and Todd Pitman, "Sunni Sheiks Join Fight Vs. Insurgency," *Washington Post*, 25 March 2007, www.washingtonpost.com/wpdyn/content/article/2007/03/25/AR2007032500600_pf.html.

12. Video conference with Jim Soriano, Provincial Reconstruction Team leader for Al-Anbar, "Anbar Province Sets the Example for All of Iraq," 2 September 2008, www.state.gov/p/nea/rls/rm/109101.htm.

13. In fact, even the Sahwa in Baghdad, as in the Al-Azhamiya District, had been established "in coordination with . . . tribal chiefs." "Thawrat ahali Al-Azhamiya didd tanzhim Al-Qaida fi Al-Iraq" [Popular Revolt in Al-Azhamiya against Al-Qaida in Iraq], *Nun*, 18 November 2007, www.non14.net/display.php?id=108.

14. "Qa'id sahwat Diyala an zajj al-adid min anasir Al-Qaida fi sufuf al-sahwat" [The Commander of the Diyala Sahwa on Cramming into Its Ranks of Many Members of Al-Qaida], Radio Nawa (Baghdad), 5 June 2010, http://radionawa.com.

15. Interview with Shaykh Thamir Al-Tamimi by Abd al-Azim Muhammad, "Majalis al-sahwa takwinha wa-mahammuha" [The Sahwa Councils: Their Formation and Missions], Al-Jazira TV, 23 January 2008, www.aljazeera.net.

16. Rick Jervis, "General Sees Rift in Iraq Enemy; Local-Foreign Divide Could Aid U.S.

Goals," *USA Today*, 26 January 2006, www.usatoday.com.

17. "Tahawar ra'is majlis sahwat Baghdad Thamir Al-Tamimi Abu Azzam" [Abu Azzam in a Discussion with the Head of the Baghdad Sahwa, Thamir Al-Tamimi], *Al-Sabah Al-Jadid*, 16 March 2008, www.newsabah.com.

Chapter 6: The Shayks' Positions Assured

1. Muhammad Ali Muhy Al-Din, "Al-Urf al-asha'iri faq al-qanun" [Tribal Custom Is above the Law], *Al-Hiwar al-mutamaddin*, 27 October 2009, www.ahewar.org/debat/show.art?aid=189624.

2. "Al-Hayis: Shuyukh Al-Anbar yarqusun li-man yadfa al-mal" [Al-Hayis: The Shaykhs of Al-Anbar Dance for Whoever Pays], *Al-Ra'y Al-Amm* (Baghdad), 17 March 2010, www.alrayy.com/6459.htm.

3. Ibid.

4. "Al-Maliki yataahhad bi'l-wuquf ila janib Zawba wa-Albu Faraj tushinn hujuman ala Al-Qaida" [Al-Maliki Vows to Stand By the Zawba, While the Albu Faraj Mount an Attack against Al-Qaida], *Al-Sabah*, 28 March 2009, www.alsabah.com/paper.php?source=akbar&mlf=interpage&sid=39660. As one Shia shaykh noted of continuing relations with the Sunni tribes of Al-Anbar and Diyala, "We are still as we were, together in good and bad." Ibid. In fact, the paramount shaykh of the Shammar confederation (which itself contains both Sunni and Shia tribes), as part of the Sahwa he established, included also fighters from the Yazidi tribes, which many Iraqis do not consider even to be Muslims. "Asha'ir Ninawa tantafidh didd Al-Qaida" [The Tribes of Ninawa Pounce on Al-Qaida], *Al-Sabah Al-Jadid*, 16 September 2007, www.newsabah.com.

5. Raghavan, "A New Breed," A1.

6. Shaykh Al-Hardan maintained that ninety percent of the Al-Anbar shaykhs had moved to Jordan, interview in Montgomery and McWilliams, *Al-Anbar Awakening, Vol.*

2, 56. Just a bit earlier, Shaykh Abu Risha had been working only as a bodyguard to Al-Anbar's governor. Interview with Shaykh Majid Ali Al-Sulayman. Ibid., 131.

7. Shaykh Jasim Muhammad Salih Al-Suwadawi, interview. Ibid., 70.

8. Dana Hedgepath and Sarah Cohen, "In Ramadi, a Counterinsurgency in Cash," *Washington Post*, 11 August 2008, www.washingtonpost.com.

9. Shaykh Ali Hatim, interview in *Al-Anbar Awakening, Vol. 2*, 118. Actually, at $300 a month, the 54,000 Sahwa fighters in the Baghdad region would have cost about $16 million a month in salaries. According to General David Petraeus, the United States was to spend an estimated $35 million for all the Sahwa during 2007. *Iraqi Benchmarks: Hearings before the Committee on Armed Services, United States Senate, 110th Congress, 7 and 11 September 2007* (Washington, DC: GPO, 2008), 302.

10. Joshua Partlow and John Ward Anderson, "Tribal Coalition in Anbar Said to Be Crumbling," *Washington Post*, 11 June 2007, A11.

11. Iraq Transition Assistance Office Information Management Unit, *Provincial Factbook: Al-Anbar*, May 2009, www.iauiraq.org/documents/239/2Anbar%Factbook.pdf.

12. As Shaykh Abd Al-Sattar had noted, "The coalition is the only thing that makes the central government give anything to Anbar." West, *The Strongest Tribe*, 244.

13. Haytham Halabiya, "Saytaratna bi-haja ila saytarat" [Our Governors Need Governors], *Babil*, 26 August 2010, www.babil.info/printVersion.php?mid=27048. The tribal relationship persisted, as the new army inductees reportedly would continue to pay part of their monthly salaries to their patron shaykhs as a reward for having gotten them into the army. Muhammad Abd Allah Muhammad, "Al-Sahwat wa'l-Qaida" [The Sahwa and Al-Qaida], *Al-Rafidayn*, 4 November 2010, www.alrafidayn.com.

14. As was the case with a delegation of tribal shaykhs from Salah Al-Din Province, "Khilal istiqbalih wafd min shuyukh asha'ir Al-Tarmiya Al-Hashimi yushayyid bi-dawr rijal al-asha'ir fi istitbat al-amn wa-'l-hifazh ala al-huwiya al-iraqiya" [During His Reception of a Delegation of Tribal Shaykhs from Al-Tarmiya, Al-Hashimi Praised the Role of

Tribesmen in Stabilizing Security and in Preserving Iraqi Identity], *Sawt Al-Iraq* (Amsterdam), 13 July 2009, www.sotaliraq.com/iraq-new-printerfriendly.php?id=44740. The shaykhs have continued to use their influence on this issue, as when they pressured the Iraqi government to account for their fellow tribesmen held in Kurdish prisons. "Asha'ir arabiya fi Karkuk tutalib bi-insihab al-bashmarga wa-kashf masir al-mutaqalin [The Arab Tribes of Kirkuk Demand That the Peshemrga Withdraw and an Accounting of the Fate of the Detainees], *Aswat Al-Iraq*, 19 March 2011, http://ar.aswataliraq.info.

15. According to James V. Soriano, Provincial Reconstruction Team leader in Al-Anbar, in McWilliams and Wheeler, *Al-Anbar Awakening, Vol. 1*, 276.

16. Interviews in Montgomery and McWilliams, *Al-Anbar Awakening, Vol. 2*, 93, 130.

17. See the insightful study by Katherine Blue Carroll, "Tribal Law and Reconciliation in the New Iraq," *Middle East Journal* 65 (Winter 2011): 11-29.

18. Greg Jaffe, "Tribal Connections: How Courting Sheiks Slowed Violence in Iraq; Marines Try Payments, Alliances in Anbar Area; Chasing Out al Qaeda," *Wall Street Journal*, 8 August 2007, A1, http://online.wsj.com. As one Marine officer noted, "Every deal goes to the sheik. He then trickles the money down to reward sub-tribes who cooperate and punish those who don't." Ibid. When Saddam had created numerous new shaykhs, he apparently had often selected merchants and contractors, as influential individuals whose loyalty had to be ensured. Ahmad Al-Assafi, "Saddam Husayn ibtakar shuyukh al-tisin wa-Bush shuyukh al-sahwat" [Saddam Husayn Created the Nineties Shaykhs and Bush the Sahwa Shaykhs], Hay'at Asha'ir Al-Iraq, www.ashairiraq.com/index.php?item=read&id=238.

19. Major General John R. Allen in McWilliams and Wheeler, *Al-Anbar Awakening, Vol. 1*, 230.

20. Ibid.

21. That tribal shaykhs could retain significant sums is indicated by such assessments as that by Staff Brigadier Isma'eel Ali Hameed, commander of the 2nd Regional directorate

of Border Enforcement, who opined that contracts were given "to support certain people financially ... a lot of money was stolen." Interview in Montgomery and McWilliams, *Al-Anbar Awakening, Vol. 2*, 225. Shaykh Sabah Al-Sattam, likewise, on the subject of the money given for contracts noted, "Where is it? Nothing. You don't see anything." Interview in ibid., 147. To be sure, intertribal rivalries colored such views, reflecting jealousy over the way contracts were distributed.

22. Shaykh Ahmad Abu Risha, interview in Montgomery and McWilliams, *Al-Anbar Awakening, Vol. 2*, 49. Shaykh Ratta Al-Fahadawi of the Dulaym also provided the local police with equipment and their salaries. Staff Brigadier General Nur al-Din Al-Fahadawi, interview in ibid., 201.

23. Sam Dagher, "Tribal Rivalries Persist As Iraqis Seek Local Posts," *New York Times*, 20 January 2009, A1, hereafter Dagher, "Tribal Rivalries."

24. Shaykh Ali Hatim, interview in Montgomery and McWilliams, *Al-Anbar Awakening, Vol. 2*, 117.

25. Shaykh Ali Hatim, ibid., 117. Shaykh Majed Ali Al-Sulayman echoed these sentiments: "So they [i.e., some shaykhs] have been awarded more than they deserve ... the tribes are very sensitive" and noted that the Americans "made two or three fake sheikhs" and equated the process to that under Saddam, in ibid., 133-34.

CHAPTER 7: THE TRIBAL WAR AGAINST AL-QAIDA

1. Abbas, "Tajadhubat asha'iriya."

2. "Al-Faqr wa'l-jahl awamil ashamat fi tahwil qura min Diyala ila maladhdhat amina li'l-Qaida" [Poverty and Ignorance Are Contributing Factors in Transforming Villages in Diyala into Safe-Areas for Al-Qaida], *Al-Sabah Al-Jadid*, 27 May 2009, hereafter "Al-Faqr wa'l-jahl," www.newsabah.com.

3. Hadi Al-Anbaki, "Shaykh ashira fi Diyala yublig an 130 irhabi min aqriba'ih baynhum qiyadat fi Al-Qaida" [The Shaykh of a Tribe in Diyala Denounces 130 Terrorists

from among His Relatives, Including Al-Qaida Leaders], *Al-Sabah*, 4 August 2008, hereafter Al-Anbaki, "Shaykh ashira," www.alsabah.com/paper.php?source=akbar&mlf=copy&sid=67273.

4. Interview with Major General Tahir Yusuf, "Ightiyal shuyukh al-asha'ir."

5. "Asha'ir Al-Falluja tuhdir dam kull man yartakib amalan kharija an al-qanun" [The Falluja Tribes Allow the Shedding of the Blood of All Those Who Commit Acts Outside the Law], *Al-Adala* (Baghdad), 25 July 2007, www.aladalaanews.net/index_lite.php?show=news&action+print&id=70449.

6. "Al-Anbakiya yulinun bara'athum min anasir tanzhim Al-Qaida" [The Anbakiya Disown the Members of the Al-Qaida Organization], *Aswat Al-Iraq*, 16 October 2008, http://ar.aswataliraq.info/wp-content/themes/aswat/print.php?p=103295.

7. On the Panorama program, hosted by Muntaha Al-Ramhi, "Zhahirat al-sahwa al-asha'iriya fi Al-Iraq" [The Tribal Sahwa Phenomenon in Iraq], Al-Arabiya TV, 18 September 2007, hereafter Al-Ramhi, "Zhahirat al-sahwa," www.alarabiya.net/save_print.php?print=1&cont_id=39267.

8. Interview with Ali Hatim by Rima Saliha in "Asha'ir iraqiya tulin al-harb ala Al-Qaida" [Iraqi Tribes Declare War on Al-Qaida], Al-Arabiya TV, 17 June 2007, hereafter Al-Ramhi, "Zhahirat al-sahwa," www.alarabiya.net/save_print.php?1&cont_id=35579.

9. This was the case with the Isawi tribe, Shaykh Aifan Sadun Al-Isawi, interview in Montgomery and McWilliams, *Al-Anbar Awakening, Vol. 2*, 91.

10. "Fi sahwa wataniya."

11. Ibid.

12. Abu Umar al-Baghdadi, "Al-Bunyan al-marsus" [The Well-Ordered Structure], 15 April 2008, in *Al-Majmu li-qadat Dawlat Al-Iraq Al-Islamiya* [*The Collected Works of the Leaders of the Islamic State of Iraq*], (Nukhbat al-ilam al-jihadi, May 2010), 66.

13. "Khasa'ir sahwat Diyala fi harbiha ma al-tatarruf balaghat akthar min alf shahid wa-

jarih" [The Losses of the Diyala Sahwa in Its War against Extremism Has Reached More Than One Thousand Dead and Wounded], Sumarriya TV, 30 September 2010, www.al-sumarian.tv./ar/print-news-1-55169.html.

14. "Al-Qaida tatawaad bi-istihdaf shuyukh al-asha'ir wa'l-mutarjimin wa-ula amaliyat al-tasfiya bada'at yawm ams al-awwal" [Al-Qaida Threatens to Target Tribal Shaykhs and Interpreters and the First of the Liquidation Operations Began the Day before Yesterday], *Al-Jiwar* (Baghdad), 1 May 2010, www.aljewar.org/news-24059.aspx.

15. Ayman Amin, "Banat Al-Iraq yanjahna fi al-hadd min al-hajamat al-intihariya allati yunaffidhnaha al-niswa" [The Daughters of Iraq Succeed in Limiting Suicide Attacks Carried Out by Women], *Mawtini* (Baghdad), 23 August 2008, www.mawtani.com/cocoon/iii/xhtml/ar/features/iii/features/2008/08/23/feature-01.

16. "Nashitat yu'akkidna ann al-faqr wa'l-jahl wa'l-taqalid al-ashai'riya ahamm asbab muanat al-mar'a bi-Diyala" [Women Activists Confirm That Poverty, Ignorance, and Tribal Traditions Are the Biggest Problems for Women in Diyala], *Sumarriya News*, 8 March 2011, www.alsumarianews.com/ar/18482/print-article.html. In Diyala, there were some four hundred women members, and Al-Qaida has targeted their leadership. "Masdar amni: malumat an niyyat al-musallahin istihdaf banat Al-Iraq fi Diyala" [Security Source: Information about the Intent to Target the Daughters of Iraq in Diyala], *Aswat Al-Iraq*, 30 January 2011, http://ar.aswataliraq.info/printer.aspx?id=271429.

17. "Al-Iraqiyat yattahadna al-rijal wa-yatadarrabna ala istikhdam al-silah li-himayat atfalhinna wa-buyuthinna" [Iraqi Women Challenge the Menfolk and Learn to Use Weapons to Protect Their Children and Homes], Wikalat Al-Nakhil li'l-Anba', n.d., www.nakhelnews.compages/news.php?nid=1209.

18. Jim Michaels, "Behind Success in Ramadi an Army Colonel's Gamble," *USA Today*, 1 May 2007, www.usatoday.com/cleanprint/?1291073743841.

19. "Fi sahwa wataniya."

20. Hisham Al-Rikabi, "Masadir istikhbariya li'l-*Mada*: Al-Qaida talja' ila atraf al-mudun

li-tanzhim sufufha" [Intelligence Sources to *Al-Mada*: Al-Qaida Takes Refuge in City Suburbs to Reconstitute Its Ranks], *Al-Mada* (Baghdad), 8 September 2010, http://al-madapaper.net/popup.php?action=printnews&id=26442. As a Saudi Al-Qaida fighter in Iraq noted, he had had to have crash lessons on the command structure of the tribes and in tribal dialects, much to the amusement of his Iraqi fellow mujahidin, in order to operate safely in the country. According to the memoirs of a Saudi Al-Qaida fighter, Abu Al-Shaqra' Al-Hindukushi, *Mudhakkirati min Kabul ila Baghdad* [My Memoirs from Kabul to Baghdad], part 9, 7, hereafter Al-Hindukushi, *Mudhakkirati*, www.archive.org/details/fromcaboltobagdad.

21. General David H. Petraeus, *Report to Congress on the Situation in Iraq*, 10-11 September 2007, 5, www.defense.gov/pubs/pdfs/Petraeus-Testimony20070910.pdf.

22. Ibid., 4.

23. "Al-Shaykh Ahmad Abu Risha yakshif tafasil jadida an qatil al-shaykh al-shahid Abd Al-Sattar wa yanfa hurub qatilayhi min al-sijn" [Al-Shaykh Ahmad Abu Risha Reveals New Details about the Martyr Shaykh Abd Al-Sattar's Killer and Denies That His Two Killers Have Escaped from Prison], Wikalat Anba' Al-Buratha, 20 November 2007, www.burathanews.com.

24. Al-Masri, *Dawlat Al*-Iraq, 136, 139.

Chapter 8: Al-Qaida Responds

1. Al-Tamimi, "Abu Hafsa Al-Ansari yakshif."

2. Ibid.

3. Interview by the Al-Furqan Agency for Media Productions with the Islamic State of Iraq's Minister of War, Abu Hamza Al-Muhajir, April 2009, hereafter Abu Hamza Al-Muhajir, www.muslim.net/vb/showthread.php?t=342053. 4. Al-Masri, *Dawlat Al-Iraq*, 133-137.

5. Al-Hindukushi, *Mudhakkirati*, part 9, 5-6.

6. Al-Zarqawi, "Mawqifna."

7. Al-Baghdadi, "Fa-Amma al-zabadu."

8. Dawlat Al-Iraq Al-Islamiya, "Bayn al-inhirafat al-manhajiya wa'l-thawabit al-jihadiya" [The Islamic State of Iraq: Between Doctrinal Deviations and Jihadi Steadfastness], 27 August 2007, hereafter Dawlat Al-Iraq Al-Islamiya, "Bayn al-inhirafat," http://m3-f.com/forum/showthread.php?t=548.

9. Ibid.

10. As in Abu Fahd, "Shubuhat hawl Dawlat Al-Iraq Al-Islamiya" [Second-Guessing the Islamic State of Iraq], *Sada Al-Jihad*, Rabi II 1428/April-May 2007, 36, hereafter Abu Fahd, "Shubuhat."

11. Dawlat Al-Iraq Al-Islamiya, "Bayn al-inhirafat al-manhajiya."

12. Abu Umar Al-Baghdadi, "Jarimat al-intikhabat al-shariya wa'l-siyasiya wa-wajibna nahwaha" [The Legal and Political Crime of the Elections and Our Duty with Respect to Them], 12 February 2010, www.atahadi.com/vb/showthread.php?p=q08261.

13. Al-Baghdadi, "Fa-Amma al-zabadu."

14. Usama Bin Ladin, "Ila ahlina bi'l-Iraq" [To Our People in Iraq], October 2010, www.muslim.net/vb/showthread.php?page=6&t=259268.

15. Ata Najd Al-Rawi, "Waqfat ma kalimat al-asad" [Observations on the Lion's Speech], October 2007, hereafter Al-Rawi, "Waqfat," www.aljazeeratalk.net/forum/showthread-php?t=79361.

16. Ata Najd Al-Rawi, "Ya shuyukh Al-Anbar: Al-Maasi la tubarrir al-kufr!" [Oh Shaykhs of Al-Anbar: Wrongdoings Do Not Justify Falling into Unbelief], 13 September 2007, www.muslm.net/vb/showthread.php?t=253640.

17. See the assessment from Mother Al-Qaida on what went wrong in Iraq, *Hakadha in-tahat arad al-afifat wa-biat dima' al-shuhada'* [*This Is How the Honor of the Chaste Ones*

Was Lost and the Blood of the Martyrs Was Betrayed], (International Islamic Media Front, Rabi II 1431/March-April 2010), 12, hereafter *Hakadha intahat*.

18. According to the interview with Abu Turab Al-Jaza'iri, an Al-Qaida commander, "Ma yajri fi Al-Jaza'ir safaha wa-Qaidat Al-Maghrib yusayyirha murahiqun" [What Is Going on in Algeria Is Stupidity and Those Who Run the Maghribi Al-Qaida Are Adolescents], *Al-Arab* (Doha, Qatar), 12 February 2008, hereafter Al-Jaza'iri, "Ma yajri fi Al-Jaza'ir," www.alarab.com.qa/printarticle.php?docId=3229.

19. *Hakadha intahat*, 9.

20. Usama Bin Ladin, "Al-Sabil li-ihbat al-mu'amarat: Hawl Al-Iraq wa-Dawlat Al-Iraq Al-Islamiya" [How to Frustrate Plots: About Iraq and the Islamic State of Iraq], July 2007, hereafter Bin Ladin, "Al-Sabil li-ihbat," www.aljazeeratalk.net/forum/showthread.php?t=95146.

21. Ibid.

22. Al-Sahab Agency's fourth interview with Ayman Al-Zawahiri, *Minbar Al-Muslim*, no. 4, Muharram 1429/January-February 2008, 53.

23. Abd al-Rahman al-Faqir, "Al-Hikma al-rabbaniya fi buzugh majalis al-sahwa al-shaytaniya" [Divine Wisdom in the Emergence of the Satanic Sahwa Councils], *Majallat Al-Mushtaqun ila al-janna*, No. 3, Dhu al-hijja 1430/November-December 2009, 64.

24. Ibid., 65.

25. According to the diary of Abu Tariq, an Al-Qaida local amir, "Daily Diary of an al-Qaeda Sector Leader," in Nicholas J. Schlosser, ed., *U.S. Marines in Iraq, 2004-2008; Anthology and Annotated Bibliography*, (Washington, DC: Marine Corps History Division, 2010), 213, 214.

26. "Al-Qaida fi Diyala min al-masajid ila al-sahwat" [Al-Qaida in Diyala—From the Mosques to the Sahwa], Wikalat Al-Iraq Baytna (Baghdad), 3 July 2010, http://iraq-beituna.net/show.php?sho=19599.

27. According to Iraq's then-Vice-President Tariq Al-Hashimi, "Qa'id fasil musallah yattahim jamaat tamil bi-ghita' asha'iri bi'l-tawatu' ma Al-Qaida" [The Commander of an Armed Group Accuses Organizations of Working under Tribal Cover in Collusion with Al-Qaida], *Al-Hayat*, 1 October 2007,
http://international.daralhayat.com/print/168508/archive.

28. Hadi Al-Anbaki, "Itirafat amir bi'l-Qaida fi Baquba tuthir makhawif muwatini Diyala" [The Confessions of an Al-Qaida Amir in Baquba Arouse the People's Fears in Diyala], *Al-Sabah*, 5 May 2010, hereafter Al-Anbaki, "Itirafat amir," www.alsabah.com/paper.php?source=akbar&mlf=copy&sid=101964. In some cases they are still in the security organizations. "Qal mas'ul majalis al-sahwat fi Diyala, Husayn Al-Mujammai, inn tashkilat al-sahwat fi Diyala la zalat ghayr mutahhara min anasir Al-Qaida wa-mukhtaraqa min qibal anasir amalat ma tanzhim Al-Qaida fi al-sabiq" [Husayn Al-Mujammai, an Official of the Sahwat Councils in Diyala Said That the Diyala Sahwa Units Are Still Not Cleansed of Al-Qaida Elements and That They Are Penetrated by Elements Who Worked with Al-Qaida in the Past], Wikalat Al-Iraq Baytna, 19 June 2010, http://iraq-beituna.net/show.php?sho=18336.

29. Muhammad al-Tamimi, "Qiyadi sabiq fi Al-Qaida li'l-*Hayat*: Iktshaft annana kunna isabat qatl wa-takfir" [A Former Leader in Al-Qaida to *Al-Hayat*: I Saw That We Were a Gang of Killers Who Condemned Others As Unbelievers], *Al-Hayat*, 18 April 2010, http://international.daralhayat.com/print/131597.

30. "Al-Qaida bi-Diyala." The head of the Sunni Waqf, likewise, suggested that the killer of the Sahwa commander in Al-Azhamiya, Baghdad, had been one of the latter's close friends. "Al-Shaykh Mahmud Al-Samidai: Al-Irhabi alladhi qatal qa'id sahwat Al-Azhamiya min maarif al-shahid" [Shaykh Mahmud Al-Samidai: The Terrorist Who Killed the Commander of the Al-Azhamiya Sahwa Was One of the Martyr's Acquaintances], Qanat Al-Furat Al-Fada'iya TV (Baghdad), 9 January 2008, http://alforattv.net/index.php?show=news&action=print&id=16162.

31. "Ightiyal shuyukh al-asha'ir." Wa'il Isam reports on a number of such cases, "Siraat bayn Al-Qaida."

32. Indeed, the woman bomber who had tried to mount the hotel attack in Jordan had also been from Abu Risha's tribe, as had her male relatives whose death fighting with Al-Qaida she was trying to avenge.

33. Fadil Al-Badrani, "Al-Imala al-asiyawiya tunafis fuqara' Al-Iraq" [Asian Labor Competes with Iraq's Poor], *Al-Arab Al-Yawm* (Amman), 1 September 2009, www.alarabalyawm.net/print.php?news_id=181014.

CHAPTER 9: AL-QAIDA ADAPTS

1. As in a communique from the Islamic State of Iraq, "Al-Furqan bayn ibad al-rahman wa-awliya' al-shaytan" [The Distinction between God's Worshippers and the Followers of Satan], 5 September 2007, http://m3-f.com/forum/showthread.php?t=682.

2. Al-Rawi, "Waqfat."

3. According to the interview with Abu Hamza Al-Muhajir, "Tafrigh al-liqa' al-sawti ma wazir al-harb bi-Dawlat Al-Iraq Al-Islamiya" [Transcript of the Audio Interview with the Minister of War of the Islamic State of Iraq], October 2008, hereafter Abu Hamza Al-Muhajir, "Tafrigh al-liqa,'" www.s-oman.net/avb/showthread.php?t=305206.

4. Ibid.

5. *Khutta istiratijiya li-taziz al-mawqif al-siyasi li-Dawlat Al-Iraq Al-Islamiya* [Strategic Plan Intended to Strengthen the Political Position of the Islamic State of Iraq], (Mufakkirat Al-Falluja, Muharram 1431/December2009-January 2010), 16, hereafter *Khutta istiratijiya*. Such analyses are most often anonymous, but carry the imprimatur of an official editing entity controlled by Mother Al-Qaida.

6. Ibid., 38.

7. Ibid., 40.

8. Ibid.

9. Ibid., 39.

10. Ibid., 41.

11. Ibid., 40.

12. Ibid., 39.

13. Usama Bin Ladin, "Ritha' al-shaykh Abi Musab Al-Zarqawi" [Eulogy for Shaykh Abu Musab Al-Zarqawi], Jumada II 1427/June-July 2006, www.tawhed.ws/pr?i=5811.

14. Abu Sad Al-Amili, *Waqfat wa-tawjihat tarbawiya ala tasa'ulat harakiya wa-jihadiya* [*Observations and Educational Guidance about Operational and Jihadi Questions*], 25 Muharram1431/11 January 2010, 144.

15. *Khutta istiratijiya*, 39.

16. Ibid.

17. Ibid., 40.

18. Ibid.

19. Ibid., 38, 39.

20. As claimed by Nizar Al-Samarra'i, a former Bath official now in Syria. Al-Ramhi, "Zhahirat al-sahwa."

21. Ibid. Such shaykhs' insistence on the fiction that monetary and military aid came from the Iraqi government provided some welcome plausible denial against potential criticism of cooperating with a foreign occupier.

22. Amit R. Paley, "Al-Qaeda in Iraq Leader May Be in Afghanistan," *Washington Post*, 31 July 2008, A1.

23. *Khutta istiratijiya*, 39.

24. Ibid.

25. Ibid., 38.

26. Ibid., 39.

27. For example, in Abd Allah Nadhir Al-Qahtani, *Indhar al-anam* [*A Warning to Mankind*], (Markaz Al-Fajr li'l-ilam, 1430/2009), 41. The jahiliya refers to the pre-Islamic period, which in Islamic tradition has become equivalent to paganism, ignorance, and chaos.

28. *Khutta istiratijiya*, 39.

29. Ibid., 41.

CHAPTER 10: THE TRIBES AND THE IRAQI GOVERNMENT: A ROCKY RELATIONSHIP

1. Interview by one of Al-Qaida's news agencies, Al-Sahab, with Ayman Al-Zawahiri. "Haqa'iq al-jihad wa-abatil al-nifaq fi liqa' ma al-shaykh Ayman Al-Zawahiri" [The State of the Jihad and the Prattle of Hypocrisy in an Interview with Shaykh Ayman Al-Zawahiri], June 2009, www.majahden.com/vb/showthread.php?t=27360.

2. Typically, Salih Al-Matlak, a Sunni politician allied to Ayad Allawi, claimed that in Iraq there is "no national will . . . today . . . there only remains an Iranian plan, which is fully active in Iraq, which means, in all honesty, the imposition of Iran's will on the formation of the new government." Salih Al-Matlak, interview by Abd Al-Azim Muhammad, "Tabiat al-ittifaqat bayn al-kutal al-siyasiya al-iraqiya" [The Nature of the Deals among the Iraqi Political Blocs], Al-Jazira TV, 14 November 2010, www.aljazeera.net.

3. Press conference by Ahmad Abu Risha, reported in "Ahmad Abu Risha yatarif annahu kan dabit fi al-jaysh al-saddami almaqbur wa-yadu ila irja 6 malayin bathi mawjudin kharij Al-Iraq" [Ahmad Abu Risha Admits He Was an Officer in Saddam's Defunct Army and Calls for the Return of 6 Million Bathis Now Outside Iraq], Wikalat Anba' Al-Buratha, 5 March 2010, www.burathanews.com/news_article_80076.html.

4. "Shuyukh asha'ir yutalibun bi-ilgha' qanun al-musa'ala wa'l-adala wa-fath makatib li'l-musalaha fi al-muhafazhat" [Tribal Leaders Demand That the Accountability and Justice Law Be Rescinded and That Reconciliation Offices Be Opened in the Provinces],

Al-Qaida, the Tribes, and the Government

Sumarriya News, 6 April 2011, www.alsumarianews.com/ar/19768/print-article.html.

5. "Al-Maliki: Anasir min hizb Al-Bath al-munhall wa-tanzim Al-Qaida ikhtaraqa quwwat al-sahwa" [Al-Maliki: Elements of the Dissolved Bath Party and of Al-Qaida's Organization Have Penetrated the Sahwa Forces], *Al-Ra'y Al-Amm*, 4 April 2009, www.alrayy.com.

6. Interview with Shaykh Fawaz Al-Jarba, Al-Ramhi.

7. Shaykh Wisam Al-Hardan, interview in Montgomery and McWilliams, *Al-Anbar Awakening, Vol. 2,* 59. Al-Hardan added that "there was pressure from these political entities on the ambassador, and the ambassador on Bush, and back." Ibid., 60.

8. According to a government representative, Brigadier General Mukhallaf Dairi, "Maqtal saba junud amirikiyin . . . wa-Talibani ila Al-Wilayat Al-Muttahida li'l-ilaj" [Seven American Soldiers Killed . . . Talibani to the United States for Treatment], *Al-Hayat*, 21 May 2007, hereafter "Maqtal saba,"
http://international.daralhayat.com/print/143983/archive.

9. Salah Bassis, "Taslih al-asha'ir" [Arming the Tribes], *Al-Sabah*, 24 July 2007, www.alsabah.com/paper.php?source=akbar&mlf=copy&sid=46550. To be sure, when the Sahwa was established later also in Salah Al-Din Province in 2007, this was done with greater coordination with the Iraqi government, which granted permission for the raising of such forces. Interview with Shaykh Fawaz Al-Jarba, Al-Ramhi.

10. Al-Hamdani, "Suqut Baghdad."

11. Abbas, "Tajadhubat asha'iriya." Sahwa leaders resented the use of the pejorative term "militia," implying a lack of legitimacy, which appeared even on the forms the government sent to those Sahwa fighters who wished to apply to join the security forces. Udayy Hatim, "Min haraka iraqiya musallaha ila tayyarat siyasiya" [From an Iraqi Armed Movement to Political Factions], *Al-Hayat*, 16 November 2008, hereafter Hatim, "Min haraka iraqiya," http://international.daralhayat.com/print/229160/archive.

12. Jawdat Kazhim, "Al-Hukuma al-iraqiya tatarid ala adam iblaghha bi'l-dawa allati waj-

jahha Bush . . . Wafd asha'ir Al-Anbar ila Washintun lan yunaqish mas'alat al-fidiraliya" [The Iraqi Government Objects to Not Having Been Informed of the Invitation Which Bush Sent . . . The Delegation from the Tribes of Al-Anbar Heading to Washington Will Not Discuss Federalism], *Al-Hayat*, 19 October 2007, http://international.daralhayat.com/print/153205/archive.

13. Ibid.

14. Ibid.

15. "Ra'is asha'ir Al-Dulaym yutalib, min Al-Qahira, bi-waqf al-nufudh al-irani fi Al-Iraq" [The Head of the Dulaym Tribes Demands, from Cairo, an End to Iranian Influence in Iraq], *Al-Sabah Al-Jadid*, 11 May 2008, hereafter "Ra'is asha'ir Al-Dulaym," www.newsabah.com. The previous year, Shaykh Rad Al-Mashahadani, the secretary general of the council, while on a visit to Saudi Arabia, had called on the latter to play a major role in solving disputes within Iraq, something no doubt viewed as anathema by Shia politicians. Hazzam Al-Utaybi, "Al-Iraqiyyun ya'mulun fi dawa saudiya li-hall khilfathim" [The Iraqis Hope for a Saudi Appeal to Solve Their Differences], *Ukaz* (Jeddah, Saudi Arabia), 9 February 2007, www.okaz.com.sa/okaz/osf/20070209/PrinCon2007020985979.htm.

16. "Qissat al-muwajaha bayn Al-Qaida wa-Hay'at Ulama' Al-Muslimin fi'l-Iraq" [An Account of the Confrontation between Al-Qaida and the Association of Muslim Scholars in Iraq], *Al-Hadath*, 18 December 2006, www.al-hadath.com. A Qaida writer in Iraq—in a work carrying Mother Al-Qaida's imprimatur, as it was published by Mother Al-Qaida—later was to claim that Saudi Arabia had also played a key role in brokering deals with tribal shaykhs and insurgent groups leading to the formation of the Sahwa, Al-Masri, *Dawlat Al-Iraq*, 51, 65.

17. "Ra'is sahwat Al-Anbar: Han al-waqt li-yusbih Al-Iraq halif li'l-Wilayat Al-Muttahida" [The President of the Anbar Sahwa: The Time Has Come for Iraq to Become an Ally of the United States], *Aswat al-Iraq*, 17 November 2008, http://ar.aswataliraq.info.

18. Shawn Brimley and Colin Kahl, "Baghdad's Misguided Crackdown on the Sons of

Iraq," *Los Angeles Times*, 26 August 2008, www.latimes.com/news/nationworld/iraq/complete/la-oe-brimley26-2008aug26,0,1415439.story.

19. Sabah Jasim, "Majalis al-isnad fi Al-Iraq ma bayn al-masalih al-hizbiya wa'l-maslaha al-wataniya" [The Support Councils between Party Interests and National Interests], Shabakat Al-Naba' Al-Malumatiya, 16 October 2008, www.annabaa.org/nbanews/71/937.htm. In 2010, there were 242 support councils with 6480 tribal shaykhs and notables, and were sometimes referred to by critics as "Al-Maliki's militias." "Adad majalis al-isnad fi Al-Iraq balagh 242 majlis bi-adwiyat 6480 shaykh" [The Number of Support Councils in Iraq Reached 242, with 6480 Member Shaykhs], *Babil*, 10 June 2010, www.babil.info/printVersion.php?mid=26017.

20. "Al-Maliki yulin an ijra'at tamhidan li-ghalq milaff al-sahwat" [Al-Maliki announces Steps in Preparation for Closing Out the Sahwa File], *Al-Sabah*, 15 September 2008, www.alsabah.com/paper.php?source=akbar&mlf=copy&sid=69761.

21. "Fi khutbat salat al-id" [From the Sermon for the Id Prayers], Presidency of the Supreme Islamic Iraqi Council, 21 December 2007, www.almejlis.org/news_article_997.html.

22. Khulud Al-Amiri, "Damha amirikiyan dafa qadatha ila al-mutalaba bi-makasib idafiya ... qada amniyun yuhdhirun min majalis 'al-sahwa': tajawazat hududha" [American Support Impelled Leaders to Demand Greater Privileges ... Security Leaders Warn Against the "Sahwa" Councils: They Have Gone beyond the Bounds], *Al-Hayat*, 19 October 2007, http://international.daralhayat.com/print/196612/archive.

23. "Majlis inqadh Al-Anbar yaftatih markazan fi Baghdad li-jam al-malumat an Al-Qaida" [The Al-Anbar Salvation Council to Open a Center in Baghdad to Collect Information on Al-Qaida], *Al-Sabah Al-Jadid*, 3 November 2007, www.newsabah.com, hereafter "Majlis inqadh Al-Anbar."

24. According to Ali Hatim, shaykh of the Dulaym confederation, "The Al-Anbar tribes have a major role in fighting Al-Qaida and other extremists in the Baghdad area." "Asha'ir iraqiya." The Al-Anbar Sahwa, for example, also operated in Salah Al-Din. "Ma-

jlis inqadh Al-Anbar."

25. Abu Risha, "Min Al-Iraq."

26. Ibid.

27. Ibid.

28. "Asbab al-qatia bayn Al-Maliki wa-Abu Risha" [The Causes for the Rift between Al-Maliki and Abu Risha], *Babil*, 12 October 2009, hereafter "Asbab al-qatia," www.babil.info/printVersion.php?mid=21967.

29. "Al-Asha'ir al-iraqiya tughrib bi-tahdhib wa-tashih arafha allati tataarad ma al-islam wa-huquq al-insan wa'l-qawanin" [The Iraqi Tribes Want to Amend and Correct Their Customary Laws Which Conflict with Islam, Human Rights, and [Government] Laws], *Sumarriya News*, 9 October 2010, www.sumarianews.com/ar/12172/print-article.htm.

30. Umar Sattar, "Ata yarfud 'al-taharrukat ghayr al-nizhamiya' . . . Al-Hashimi yuhadhdhir min tahmish 'quwwat al-sahwa' wa'l-asha'ir tutalib bi-dimj kull anasirha fi al-ajhiza al-amniya" [Ata Bans All "Irregular Actions" . . . Al-Hashimi Warns against Marginalizing "Sahwa Forces" and the Tribes Demand That All Their Members Be Absorbed into the Security Apparatus], *Al-Hayat*, 24 December 2007, hereafter Sattar, "Ata yarfud," http://international.daralhayat.com/print/171761/archive.

31. Abd Allah Al-Anbari, "Radd ala maqal: Ra'is Jamiat Al-Anbar yatasallaq al-mansib bi-thawra musallaha" [Response to an Article: The President of Al-Anbar University Reaches His Position through an Armed Revolution], *Wikalat Al-Akhbar Al-Iraqiya* (Baghdad), 3 August 2008, www.iraq-ina.com/newactivities.php?tnid=30754.

32. As is the case in Al-Anbar, where, once they were secure, tribal shaykhs were said to have flaunted their power in traditional ways, such as by ignoring local building codes or by promoting their own personal interests and those of their clients. "Asha'ir Al-Anbar."

33. Al-Anbaki, "Shaykh ashira." At times, when a single shaykh would seek to dominate, this might cause friction with other shaykhs, as in the case when Shaykh Ahmad Abu

Risha arbitrarily sought to pick Al-Anbar's governor, Fadil al-Badrani. "Khilafat bayn al-sahwa wa-hazhr tajwal bi'l-Falluja" [Disputes within the Sahwa, and a Ban on Traffic in Falluja], *Al-Arab Al-Yawm*, 9 April 2009, http://alarabalyawm.net/print.php?news_id=154148.

34. Shaykh Ali Hatim Ali, "Al-Mashhad al-iraqi."

35. "Al-Hukuma azima ala hasr al-silah bi'l-ajhiza al-amniya al-shariya wa-dimj majalis al-sahwat wa-istiabihim fi quwa al-amn ala thalath marahil" [The Government Is Determined to Limit Weapons to the Legal Security Authority's Forces and to Integrate the Sahwa Councils into the Security Forces in Three Phases], *Al-Sabah Al-Jadid*, 10 September 2008, www.newsabah.com.

36. "Shuyukh asha'ir nahiyat Al-Siniya tuqarrir istibdal mudir al-shurta" [Tribal Chiefs in Al-Siniya Subdistrict Decide to Replace The Police Chief], *Mawtini*, 20 June 2008, www.mawtani.com/cocoon/iii/xhtml/ar/features/iii/features/2008/06/20/feature-04.

37. "Al-Maliki yadu asha'ir Al-Anbar ila adam al-tadakhkhul fi shu'un al-ajhiza al-amniya" [Al-Maliki Calls on the Tribes in Al-Anbar to Stop Interfering in the Security Establishment's Affairs], *Sumarriya News*, 2 October 2010, www.sumarianews.com/ar/11902/print-article.htm.

38. "Asha'ir Al-Anbar."

39. "Abu Risha yuhaddid bi-tashkil quwwat sahwa jadida li-munahadat mashru madd unbub al-ghaz al-irani ila Suriya" [Abu Risha Threatens to Raise Forces for a New Sahwa to Oppose the Project to Extend the Iranian Gas Pipeline to Syria], *Sumarriya News*, 29 September 2010, http://ww2.sumarianews.com/ar/11804/print-article.html.

40. "Al-Anbar tatarid ala al-tarakhis al-jadida: ladayna ru'yatna fi tatwir Akkas" [Al-Anbar Is Opposed to Granting New Licenses; We Have Our Own Views on the Development of Akkas], *Al-Mada*, 20 October 2010, http://almadapaper.net/popup.php?action=printnews&id=28690.

41. Interview with Abd Al-Nasir Al-Mahdawi, "Muhafizh Diyala: Al-Wizarat tuharibna

wa-tuamilna ka-muwatinin min al-daraja al-thaniya" [The Governor of Diyala: The Ministries Are Waging a War against Us and Treat Us Like Second-Class Citizens]. *Al-Alam*, 15 December 2010, www.alaalem.com/index.php?aa=new&id22=21855. That this interview reflected enduring political perceptions, rather than being a spur-of-the-moment venting of anger, is suggested by the fact that the interview was also posted subsequently on the Diyala province's official website. The situation is complicated by widespread corruption, such as that by senior bureaucrats in Diyala, who reportedly had siphoned off tens of millions of dollars of aid money intended for local projects. "Akbar amaliyat fasad tashadha al-muhafazha khilal al-awam al-khamas al-madiya" [The Biggest Corruption Operation Witnessed By the Province in the Last Five Years], Wikalat Al-Akhbar Al-Iraqiya, 11 March 2009, http://al-iraqnews.net.

42. "Majlis Diyala yarfud naql arba mahattat kahraba'iya ila Al-Basra" [The Diyala Council Refuses to Transfer Four Electric Power Stations to Basra], *Aswat al-Iraq*, 25 January 2011, http://ar.aswataliraq.info/printer.aspx?id=271120.

43. "Rasa'il adida li-tafjirat Baghdad tartabit bi-shakl aw akhar bi-mulahaqat al-sahwat" [Multiple Messages from the Explosions in Baghdad Linked in One Way or Another to the Crackdown on the Sahwa], *Al-Sabah Al-Jadid*, 6 April 2009, www.newsabah.com/tpl?IdLanguage=17&NrIssue=1394&NrSection=7&NrArticle=26025.

44. "Ra'is asha'ir Al-Dulaym."

45. Hatim, "Asha'ir iraqiya."

46. Interview with Major General Tahir Yusuf, "Ightiyal shuyukh al-asha'ir."

47. Dagher, "Tribal Rivalries."

48. "Shuyukh al-sahwa bayn mitraqat 'Al-Qaida' wa-sindan al-hukuma" [The Sahwa Shaykhs Are between the Hammer of "Al-Qaida" and the Anvil of the Government], *Al-Sharq Al-Awsat*, 25 January 2009, www.awsaat.com/print.asp?did=504253&issueno=11016.

49. Suad Jarus, "Shaykh mashayikh Shammar: Rafadna liqa' Al-Maliki fi Dimashq li-an-nahu yurid an yumli alayna ma yurid" [The Paramount Chief of the Shammar: We Refused to Meet with Al-Maliki in Damascus Because He Wants to Dictate to Us What He Wants], *Al-Sharq Al-Awsat*, 20 August 2009, www.awsaat.com/print.asp?did=532602&issueno=11223.

50. According to the director for Administrative and Financial Affairs of the Monitoring and Implementation of National Reconciliation Committee. "Al-Maliki yuiz bi-inha' milaff al-sahwat khilal thalath ashhur" [Al-Maliki Instructs That the Sahwa File Be Closed in Three Months], *Al-Sabah Al-Jadid*, 18 January 2009, www.newsabah.com.

51. Thamir Al-Tamimi, interview in "Istihdaf al-sahwat" [Targeting the Sahwa], *Baghdad Satellite TV* (Baghdad), 18 July 2010, hereafter Al-Tamimi, "Istihdaf al-sahwat," www.baghdadch.tv/news_special.php?id=1800&print=1.

52. According to Ahmad Al-Mujammai, leader of the Sahwa in Diyala, "Ratib 4500 muqatil bi-Diyala tadur fi halqa mufragha wasat dawat li-tasrihhim" [The Salary of 4500 Fighters in Diyala Is Caught in a Vicious Circle Amid Calls for Their Disbandment], *Aswat Al-Iraq*, 21 August 2010, http://ar.aswataliraq.info/wp-content/themes/aswat/print.php?p=241690.

53. "Tadhammur fi sufuf sahwat Diyala li-ta'akhkhur sarf rawatibhim" [Grumbling in the Ranks of the Diyala Sahwa Due to the Lateness of Paying Salaries], *Sumarriya News*, 30 April 2010, www.sumarianews.com/ar/6039/print-article.htm.

54. "Anasir al-sahwat yashkun qillat al-ihtimam al-hukumi bi-awdahim" [Sahwa Personnel Complain of Government Lack of Interest about Their Conditions], *Qanat Al-Furat Al-Fada'iya TV*, 27 July 2010, http://alforattv.net/index.php?show=news&action=print&id=47072.

55. Maggie O'Kane and Ian Black, "Sunni Militia Strike Could Derail US Strategy against Al-Qaida," *Guardian*, 21 March 2008, hereafter O'Kane and Black, "Sunni Militia," www.guardian.co.uk/world/2008/mar/21/iraq.alqaida.print.

56. "Insihab majmua min muntasibi al-sahwat al-yawm al-arbia' min wajibhim fi mintaqat Baladruz ihtijajan," [A Unit of Sahwa Personnel Pulls Back Today, Wednesday, from Their Duty Posts in the Baladruz Area in Protest], Wikalat Anba' Al-Mustaqbal, 9 February 2011, www.mustakbal.net/ArticlePrint.aspx?ID=1563.

57. "Ahali Al-Azhamiya li'l-*Sharq Al-Awsat*: Al-Qaida tatarakkaz fi Shari' Al-Akhtal... wa tastaghill al-atilin" [The Inhabitants of Al-Azhamiya to *Al-Sharq Al-Awsat*: Al-Qaida Is Concentrated in Al-Akhtal Street . . . and Is Taking Advantage of the Unemployed], *Al-Sharq Al-Awsat*, 1 August 2010, www.aawsat.com/print.asp?did=580572&issueno=11569.

58. "Akhir tasrih li-Adil Al-Mashhadani: Bukhl al-hukuma wa-karam Al-Qaida" [Adil Al-Mashhadani's Latest Statement: The Government's Stinginess and Al-Qaida's Generosity], *Al-Sabah Al-Jadid*, 29 March 2009, www.newsabah.com.

59. "Anasir al-sahwa yashurun bi'l-qalaq min ta'akhkhur rawatibhim wa-adam wuduh mustaqbalhim" [Al-Sahwa Elements Feel Concern about Their Late Salaries and Their Uncertain Future], *Al-Sabah Al-Jadid*, 16 August 2009, www.newsabah.com.

60. The Sahwa's representative, Thamir Al-Tamimi, for example, put the blame squarely on the immediate paymaster, the Iraqi army, which was allegedly carrying out a deliberate policy of harassment and pressure. Interview in Al-Tamimi, "Istihdaf al-sahwat."

61. Muhannad Abd Al-Wahhab, "Al-Majami al-irhabiya al-musallaha aghlabha iraqiya wa-laysat mustawrida min Qandahar wa-jibal Al-Yaman" [The Armed Terrorist Organizations Are in the Main Iraqi and Not Imported from Kandahar or from the Mountains of Yemen], *Al-Sabah*, 16 August 2010, hereafter Abd Al-Wahhab, "Al-Majami," www.alsabah.com/paper.php?source=akbar&mlf=copy&sid=107326.

62. "Mu'tamar li-tabdid shukuk al-sahwat hiyal al-hukuma" [A Conference to Allay the Sahwa Doubts Vis-a-Vis the Government], *Al-Sabah Al-Jadid*, 19 May 2009, www.newsabah.com.

63. "Qa'id sabiq li'l-sahwat yantaqid ihmal al-hukuma laha wa-mas'ul fi sahwat Al-Iraq

yushir ila tahawwulha li-kiyan siyasi" [A Former Commander of the Sahwa Criticizes the Government's Neglect of the Latter, While an Official of the Iraq Sahwa Indicates That It Has Been Transformed into a Political Body], *Aswat Al-Iraq*, 14 February 2010, http://ar.aswataliraq.info.

64. "Al-Sahwa takhsha al-hukuma al-muqbila: Masirna ghamid" [The Sahwa Fears the Next Government: Our Destiny Is Unclear], *Al-Sabah Al-Jadid*, 10 August 2009, hereafter "Al-Sahwa takhsha al-hukuma," www.newsabah.com.

65. "Al-Sahwa takhsha intiqam Al-Qaida bad insihab al-quwwat al-amirikiya" [The Sahwa Fears Al-Qaida's Revenge after the American Forces Withdraw], *Al-Hayat*, 22 August 2010, hereafter "Al-Sahwa takhsha intiqam," http://international.daralhayat.com/print/174456.

66. "'Muthallat al-mawt' dun sahwat ihtijajan ala adam tasallum al-rawatib" [The "Triangle of Death" Is without the Sahwa as a Protest about Not Receiving Pay], *Al-Sabah Al-Jadid*, 2 May 2009, www.newsabah.com.

67. Interview with Ali Ghalib Baban, Minister of Planning and Cooperation, "Al-Takhtit: Nisbat al-bitala tasaadat bi-shakl mukhif wa-tajawazat al-25% min nisbat al-quwa al-amila" [Ministry of Planning: The Unemployment Rate Increased in a Frightening Way and Has Surpassed 25% of the Work Force], *Al-Sumarriya News*, 23 October 2010, www.sumarianews.com/ar/12739/print-article.htm. The Deputy Minister of Planning, Mahdi Al-Allaq, put the unemployment rate at 15 percent, but added another 30 percent who are working only part time. Sarra' Hasan, "Al-Takhtit: Al-Wazha'if al-jadida ghayr kaffa wa'l-bitala 15 bi'l-mi'a" [Ministry of Planning: The New Jobs Are Not Sufficient Since Unemployment Is at 15 Percent], *Al-Zaman*, 17 January 2011, www.azzaman.com/index.asp?fname=2011\01\01-17\99.htm&storytitle=. Unofficial figures by the Committee of Iraqi Advisers were even worse, with poverty levels pegged at 55 percent and real unemployment at 50 percent. "Hay'at al-istishariyin tu'akkid ann 55% min al-iraqiyin yuanun min al-faqr wa'l-bitala" [The Committee of Advisers Confirms That 55% of Iraqis Are Suffering from Poverty and Unemployment], Radio Nawa, 28 February 2011, http://radionawa.com/ar/NewsDetailIN.aspx?id=53920&LinkID=155.

68. "Diyala tu'akkid inhiyar 80% min raka'iz al-qita al-khass al-mahalli" [Diyala Confirms the Collapse of 80% of the Mainstays of the Local Private Sector], *Sumarriya News*, 2 October 2010, www2.sumarianews.com/ar/11899/print-article.htm. In fact, in the same report, one Iraqi economic expert rued the lack of government support for the private sector "as was available in the 1990s."

69. According to Nizar Al-Wa'ili, a member of the Executive Council of the Iraqi Chamber of Industries, quoted in Nur Ibrahim, "80% min al-sinaa al-iraqiya muattala" [80% of Iraqi Industry Is Idle], Wikalat Al-Akhbar Al-Iraqiya, 10 November 2010, http://al-iraqnews.net.

70. Majid Shakir, "Khubara' li-*Babnyuz*: Taraju al-intaj al-zirai al-iraqi kamman wa-nawan" [Experts to *Babnyuz*: Decrease in the Iraqi Agricultural Production, Both in Quantity and Quality], *Babnyuz* (Najaf), 11 February 2011, www.babnews.com/inp/view_printer.asp?ID=34670&AUTHOR=.

71. Ali Baban, Iraq's minister of Planning, for example, complained that the country needed to invest ten times what it is now investing in its economy yearly. "Al-Takhtit: Al-Iraq yahtaj asharat adaf ma yatimm takhsishu min al-muwazana al-istithmariya sanawiyyan" [The Ministry of Planning: Iraq Needs Ten Times the Present Allocation in the Investment Budget Annually], Radio Nawa, 18 November 2010, http://radionawa.com/ar/NewsDetailIN.aspx?id=40991&LinkID=155.

72. Quoted in "Na'ib muhafizh Al-Anbar: Ihmal al-hukuma li'l-atilin yajalhum luqma sa'igha li'ljamaat al-musallaha" [The Deputy Governor of Al-Anbar: The Government's Neglect of the Unemployed Makes Them an Easy Prey for the Armed Groups], Ur News Agency, 19 January 2011, www.uragency.net/index.php?aa=news&id22=15964.

73. "Amir asha'ir Al-Dulaym li-Radio Sawa: Al-Insihab al-amiriki sayu'addi ila tamarrud fi shurtat Al-Anbar" [The Amir of the Dulaym to Radio Sawa: The American Withdrawal Will Lead to a Revolt of Al-Anbar's Police], Radio Sawa (Baghdad), 18 September 2007, www.radiosawa.com/article_print.aspx?id=1377051.

74. Jonathan Steele, "Iraq Special Report: 'American Soldiers Sacrificed a Lot. But We

Sacrificed More.'" *Guardian*, 27 August 2010, www.guardian.co.uk/world/2010/aug/27/iraq-was-us-special-report/print.

75. O'Kane and Black, "Sunni Militia."

76. Abu Azzam Thamir Al-Tamimi, interview by Abd Al-Azim Muhammad, "Al-Mashhad al-iraqi: Waqi wa-masir majalis al-sahwa" [The Iraqi Scene: The Status and Future of the Sahwa Councils], Al-Jazira TV, 3 September 2008, www.aljazeera.net.

77. Sattar, "Ata yarfud."

78. Hatim, "Min haraka iraqiyya."

79. "Sahwat Baghdad tashtaki: Jawazatna fi juyubna wa-nashur bi-qalaq hiyal al-mustaqbal" [The Baghdad Sahwa Complains: Our Passports Are in Our Pockets and We Are Uneasy about the Future], *Al-Sabah Al-Jadid*, 6 July 2009, hereafter "Sahwat Baghdad," www.newsabah.com.

80. According to Muhammad Al-Askari, the public relations adviser in the Iraqi Ministry of Defense, in Al-Shayib, "Ma wara' al-khabar."

81. For example, "Al-Sahwa takhsha al-hukuma."

82. Khulud Ramzi, "Al-Sahwat fi ahdan Al-Qaida" [The Sahwa in Al-Qaida's Embrace], *Al-Usbuiya*, 31 October 2010, www.alesbuyia.com/inp/view.asp?ID=19977.

83. "Qubul jami afrad al-sahwat fi al-mu'assasat al-hukumiya bi-Wasit" [All Members of the Sahwa in Wasit Accepted into Government Institutions], *Al-Sabah Al-Jadid*, 12 February 2010, www.newsabah.com.

84. "Al-Musalaha al-wataniya tu'akkid hajat bad al-muhafazhat ila khadamat Abna' Al-Iraq" [The National Conciliation Committee Confirms That Some Provinces Need to Provide Services for the Sons of Iraq], *Al-Wikala Al-Ikhbariya li'l-Anba'* (Baghdad), 1 December 2010, hereafter "Al-Musalaha al-wataniya," www.ikhnews.com/popup.php?action=printnews&id=4992.

85. Raghavan, "A New Breed."

86. Quoted in "Adil Abd Al-Mahdi: Ahyanan najiz an tamyiz harakat al-sahwa al-haqiqiya min al-za'ifa" [Adil Abd Al-Mahdi: Sometimes We Are Unable to Distinguish the Real Sahwa Movements from the False Ones], *Al-Sabah Al-Jadid*, 14 April 2009, www.newsabah.com.

87. Hadi Al-Anbaki, "Tahdhirat min taghalghul anasir Al-Qaida ka-addadin fi Diyala" [Alert to the Penetration of Al-Qaida Elements as Census Takers in Diyala], *Al-Sabah*, 1 October 2010, www.alsabah.com/paper.php?source=akbar&mlf=copy&sid=109350.

88. "Musallahu Al-Iraq yatanazalun an hayat al-tamarrud muqabil wazha'if hukumiya" [Iraqi Armed Elements Abandon Their Life of Rebellion in Return for Government Jobs], *Al-Sabah Al-Jadid*, 30 January 2010, hereafter "Musallahu Al-Iraq," www.newsabah.com.

89. According to Shaykh Khalid Al-Naimi, a Sahwa commander, "Tadhammur fi awsat al-sahwa bad amayn min tasallum Baghdad milaffihim" [Discontent Within the Ranks of Sahwa Two Years after Baghdad Assumed Responsibility], *Al-Arab Al-Yawm*, 2 October 2010, hereafter "Tadhammur fi awsat," www.arabstoday.net.

90. "Quwwat al-sahwa madi ghamid wa-mustaqbal akthar ghumudan" [The Sahwa Forces: Murky Past and Even More Murky Future], Shabakat Akhbar Al-Iraq, 28 August 2010, www.aliraqnews.com; and "Tadhammur fi awsat."

91. "Sahwat muadiya li'l-Qaida taud ila al-tamarrud fi shamal Baghdad" [Sahwas Hostile to Al-Qaida Returns to Dissidence in the North Baghdad Area], *Al-Sabah Al-Jadid*, 19 October 2010, hereafter "Sahwat muadiya," www.newsabah.com.

92. "Ahmad Abu Risha ra'is sahwat Al-Iraq: Muhafazhat Al-Anbar lam tadmuj siwa thamanin shakhs faqat fi al-ajhiza al-amniya" [Ahmad Abu Risha, Head of the Iraq Sahwa: Only Eighty Individuals from Al-Anbar Province Absorbed into the Security Services], Baghdad Satellite TV, 27 September 2010, www.baghdadch.tv/news_special.php?id=928&print=1.

93. "Muwatinun: Al-Khuruqat al-amniya bi'l-Anbar natija li-adam ittifaq al-kutal al-siyasiya wa-ihmal al-mas'ulin" [Citizens: The Security Lapses in Al-Anbar Are the Result of the Lack of an Agreement among the Political Blocs and the Neglect by Officials], *Aswat Al-Iraq*, 18 July 2010, hereafter "Muwatinun: Al-Khuruqat," http://ar.aswataliraq.info.

94. "Tadhammur fi awsat."

95. "Al-Sahwat yufaddilun al-amal al-amni" [The Sahwat Prefer Security Work], *Al-Sabah Al-Jadid*, 14 April 2009, www.newsabah.com/tpl?IdLanguage=17&NrIssue=1401&NrSection=21&NrArticle=26363.

96. "Anasir al-sahwat yashkun qillat al-ihtimam al-hukumi bi-awdahim" [Sahwa Members Complain of Government Lack of Interest about Their Conditions], Qanat Al-Furat Al-Fada'iya, 27 July 2010, http://alforattv.net/index.php?show=news&action=print&id=47072.

97. "Taqrir: Intizham al-rawatib aw al-dimj ahamm matalib sahwat Diyala" [Report: Regularizing Salaries or Integration Are the Most Important Demands by the Diyala Sahwa], *Wikalat Al-Iraq Baytna*, 16 June 2010, http://iraq-beituna.net//show.php?sho=18039.

98. "Al-Musalaha al-wataniya."

99. "Musallahu Al-Iraq." As "many Iraqis believe," one Sahwi noted that "the government will provide us a lifetime guarantee." Ibid.

100. According to Iraq's minister of Planning, even today 70 percent of the country's bureaucracy "do not have real jobs to do." Interview with Minister Ali Baban, "Wazir al-takhtit li'l-*Alam*: Al-Maliki mutahammis li'l-iqtisad lakinnahu mashghul bi-humum al-siyasa" [The Minister of Planning to *Al-Alam*: Al-Maliki Is Enthusiastic about the Economy, But He Is Preoccupied with Political Concerns], *Al-Alam*, 10 October 2010, 3.

101. "Asha'ir Al-Anbar."

102. "Sahwat muadiya." Other government sources placed the remaining number at 40,000. "Al-Musalaha Al-Wataniyya: Qariban ghalq malaff abna' Al-Iraq (al-sahwat)" [The National Reconciliation Committee: Closing the Sons of Iraq (the Sahwa) Account Soon], *Al-Wikala Al-Ikhbariya Li'l-Anba'*, 7 October 2010, hereafter "Al-Musalaha Al-Wataniyya," www.ikhnews.com/popup.php?action=printnews&id=2847.

103. "Shuyukh wa-mas'ulun fi Al-Anbar: Dimj al-sahwat khutwa jayyida ala an takun wafq aliya tamna ikhtiraqha" [Shaykhs and Officials in Al-Anbar: The Absorption of the Sahwa Is a Good Step Provided That It Happens in Accordance with a Mechanism Which Prevents Penetration], *Aswat Al-Iraq*, 8 August 2008, http://ar.aswataliraq.info/printer.aspx?id=160919.

104. Joshua Partlow and John Ward Anderson, "Tribal Coalition in Anbar Said to Be Crumbling," *Washington Post*, 11 June 2007, A11.

105. Interview with Colonel Said Muhammad Muad Al-Fahadawi in Montgomery and McWilliams, *Al-Anbar Awakening, Vol. 2*, 204.

106. "Ri'asat al-sahwat fi Diyala tuiz bi-sahb muqatiliha min niqat al-taftish" [The Diyala Sahwa Leaders Order the Fighters to Withdraw from the Checkpoints], *Aswat Al-Iraq*, 23 January 2010, http://ar.aswataliraq.info.

107. Abd Al-Wahhab, "Al-Majami."

108. Raghavan, "A New Breed."

109. "Asha'ir Al-Anbar."

110. "Sahwat Baghdad."

111. Ibid.

112. "Al-Musalaha Al-Wataniyya."

113. "Sahwat Diyala tu'akkid itiqal 300 min anasirha wa-tadu al-hukuma al-markaziya ila ijad al-hulul al-jadhriya li-mashakilha" [The Diyala Sahwa Confirms that 300 of Its

Members Were Arrested and Calls on the Central Government to Come Up with Effective Solutions to Its Problems], *Al-Sumarriya News*, 30 April 2011, www.sumarianews.com/ar/20996/print-article.html.

114. Umar Abd Al-Latif, "Alanat lajnat al-amn wa'l-difa fi majlis al-nuwwab inn al-marhala al-muqbila satashhad tashri qanun khass li-hasr al-silah bi-yad al-dawla" [Parliament's Security and Defense Committee in Announced That a New Law Will Be Crafted in the Next Session to Specifically Restrict the Possession of Weapons to the State], *Al-Sabah*, 8 May 2011, www.alsabaah.com/ArticlePrint.aspx?ID=7175.

115. Shaykh Ali Hatim, interview by Ili Nakuzi, "Ma Ali Al-Hatim al-qiyadi bi-sahwat Al-Anbar" [With Ali Al-Hatim, the Anbar Sahwa Leader], Al-Arabiya TV, 3 February 2008, www.alarabiya.net/save_print.php?print=1&cont_id=45115. Firearms are ingrained in tribal culture, as all important occasions are marked by shooting firearms into the air, and the authorities' plan to end this practice may prove difficult and will make disarming the tribes even less likely to succeed, "Mu'tamar li-asha'ir Karbala' yutalib bi-ilgha' bad al-adat wa'l-taqalid al-asha'iriya" [The Conference of the Karbala Tribes Requests the Suppression of Some Tribal Customs and Traditions], *Aswat Al-Iraq*, 12 December 2010, http://ar.aswataliraq.info.

116. "Ziyadat al-iqbal ala shira' al-silah ma iqtirab al-insihab al-amiriki" [A Greater Interest in Buying Arms with the Approach of the American Withdrawal], *Al-Mada*, 8 August 2010, http://almadapaper.net.

117. "Asha'ir janub Al-Iraq tarfud taslim tarsanatha min al-asliha" [The Tribes of Southern Iraq Refuse to Turn Over Their Weapons Arsenals], *Shabakat Akhbar Al-Iraq*, 24 July 2010, www.aliraqnews.com.

118. Shaykh Ali Hatim, interview by Ilyas Husam Al-Samuk, "Al-Sulayman yuhaddid bi-ilan al-iqlim: Al-Hukuma baat al-sahwat wa-ahmalat Al-Anbar" [Al-Sulayman Threatens to Declare Autonomy: The Government Sold Out the Sahwa and Has Neglected Al-Anbar], *Al-Mada*, 15 May 2011, http://almadapaper.net/popup.php?action=printnews&id=40618.

119. "Sahwat Diyala: Itiqal nahw 60 unsuran min quwwatna bi-daawi kaydiya" [The Diyala Sahwat: The Arrest of About 60 of Our Personnel Based on Revenge Charges], *Al-Sumarriya News*, 3 June 2010, www.sumarianews.com/ar/7379/print-article.htm.

120. "Sha'iat tanfiha al-sultat an mudhakkirat itiqal tu'addi ila ikhla' maqarr lil'l-sahwat fi Diyala" [Rumors Which the Authorities Deny of Arrest Warrants Lead to the Abandonment of Posts by the Sahwa in Diyala], *Al-Sabah Al-Jadid*, 9 May 2009, www.newsabah.com.

121. "Sudur 500 mudhakkira qada'iya li-itiqal muwazhzhafin hukumiyin fi Diyala" [The Issuing of 500 Court Warrants for the Arrest of Government Employees in Diyala], Radio Nawa, 9 November 2010, http://radionawa.com.

122. "Sahwat Baghdad."

123. Muhammad Abd Allah Muhammad, "Al-Sahwat wa'l-Qaida" [The Sahwa and Al-Qaida], *Al-Rafidayn*, 4 November 2010, www.alrafidayn.com.

124. Muhammad Al-Tamimi, "Diyala: Quwwa askariya min Baghdad tataqil zaim Majlis Al-Sahwa" [Diyala: A Military Force from Baghdad Arrests the Chief of the Sahwa Council], *Al-Hayat*, 16 July 2010, http://international.daralhayat.com/print/163279.

125. "Mudahamat manzil qa'id sahwat Diyala wa-itiqal ammih" [Raid on the Home of a Commander of the Diyala Sahwa and the Arrest of His Uncle], Shabakat Akhbar Al-Iraq, 26 September 2010, www.Shabakat Akhbar Al-Iraq.

126. "Quwwa amniya tataqil ahad shuyukh Al-Jibur wa-musaidah Shamali Babil" [A Security Force Arrests a Shaykh of the Jiburi and His Aide North of Babil], Qanat Al-Furat Al-Fada'iya TV, 1 October 2010, http://alforattv.net/index.php?show=news&action=print&id=48185.

127. "Ihtijaz zaim ashirat Saddam li-dimat majami irhabiya" [The Detention of the Chief of Saddam's Tribe for Supporting Terrorist Groups], Wikalat Al-Akhbar Al-Iraqiya, 10 November 2010, http://al-iraqnews.net.

128. Anthony Shadid, "An Iraqi Cleric's Swift Rise and Swift Fall," *Washington Post*, 14 May 2009, www.washingtonpost.com; and "Quwwa min maghawir al-dakhiliya tudahim manzil qa'id quwwat al-sahwa al-maduw Al-Mulla Nazhim Al-Jiburi fi Al-Duluiya" [Commando Force from the Ministry of the Interior Raids the House of the Sahwa Commander Known as Al-Mulla Nazhim Al-Jiburi in Duluiya], Wikalat Anba' Al-Buratha, 5 March 2010, www.burathanews.com.

129. "Quwwa amniya tudahim maqarr al-sahwa fi madinat Rawat fi Al-Anbar" [Security Force Raids the Sahwa's Headquarters in the City of Rawat, Al-Anbar], Ur News Agency, 6 February 2011, www.uragency.net/index.php?aa=news&id22=16499.

130. "Asha'ir Al-Anbar tuhammil ala al-ajhiza al-amniya fi qissat ikhtifa' al-shaykh Al-Jarbu wa-tutalib Al-Maliki bi'l-tadakhkhul" [The Tribes of Al-Anbar Blame the Security Forces in the Case of Shaykh Al-Jarbu's Disappearance and Demand That Al-Maliki Intervene], *Al-Sumarriya News*, 6 January 2011, www.sumarianews.com/ar/15627/print-article.htm.

131. "Ata yulin wujud 80 dawa qatl wa-irhab ala Ali Al-Mashadani" [Ata Announces There Are 80 Warrants for Murder and Terrorism against Ali Al-Mashadani], *Al-Sabah Al-Jadid*, 29 March 2009, www.newsabah.com.

132. "Itiqal 11 min qadatha wa-mushkilat al-rawatib tuhall al-usbu al-muqbil" [The Arrest of 11 of Its Leaders, While the Problem of Salaries Will Be Resolved Next Week], *Al-Sabah Al-Jadid*, 4 April 2009, www.newsabah.com.

133. "Ahali Al-Azhamiya li'l-*Sharq Al-Awsat*: Al-Qaida tatarakkaz fi Shari Al-Akhtal wa-tastaghill al-atilin" [The People of Al-Azhamiya to *Al-Sharq Al-Awsat*: Al-Qaida Is Concentrated on Al-Akhtal Street and Is Taking Advantage of the Unemployed], *Al-Sharq Al-Awsat*, 1 August 2010, www.aawsat.com/print.asp?did=580572&issueno=11569.

134. "Ri'asat al-sahwat fi Diyala tuiz bi-sahb muqatiliha min niqat al-taftish" [The Diyala Sahwa Leaders Order the Fighters to Withdraw from the Checkpoints], *Aswat Al-Iraq*, 23 January 2010, http://ar.aswataliraq.info.

135. "Al-Qaida tusdir fatawi tazwij aramil qatlaha min anasir al-sahwat" [Al-Qaida Issues Fatwas Promoting Marriage to the Widows of Its Members Who Had Been Part of the Sahwa], *Al-Sabah*, 19 June 2010, www.alsabah.com/tpl/print.tpl?IdLanguage=17&NrIssue=1745&NrSection=1&NrArticle=408880.

136. "Qiyadat fi al-sahwa tuhadhdhir min ta'thir fi sufufha ala nisbat irtidad al-musallahin min tanzhim Al-Qaida" [Leaders in the Sahwa Caution about the Impact in Its Ranks on the Rate of Reversion of Fighters to Al-Qaida], Qanat Al-Furat Al-Fada'iya TV, 9 May 2010, http://alforattv.net/index.php?show=news&action=print&id=45075.

137. "Shuyukh asha'ir tutalib bi'l-ifraj an mas'ul mahalli wa-qiyadi fi al-sahwa" [The Tribal Shaykhs Demand That a Local Official and a Sahwa Leader Be Set Free], *Al-Sabah Al-Jadid*, 19 May 2009, www.newsabah.com/tpl?IdLanguage=17&NrIssue=1431&NrSection=21&NrArticle=27890.

138. "Manshurat li'l-sahwa tutalib bi'l-insaf wa-tuhaddid bi'l-mazhahir fi Al-Duluiya" [Leaflets from the Sahwa Demanding Fairness and Threaten Demonstrations in Al-Duluiya], Radio Nawa, 18 September 2010, http://radionawa.com.ar/NewsDetailN.aspx?id=33011&LinkID=151.

139. "Intiqad istimrar al-itiqalat fi Salah al-Din" [Criticism of the Continuing Arrests in Salah Al-Din], Shabakat Akhbar Al-Iraq, 11 January 2011, www.Shabakat Akhbar Al-Iraq.

140. "Asha'ir Ninawa tastankir itiqal amin amm majlis shuyukh asha'ir al-muhafazha" [The Ninawa Tribes Condemn the Arrest of the Secretary General of the Council of Shaykhs of That Province], *Sumarriya News*, 15 August 2010, www.sumarianews.com/ar/10048/print-article.htm. Later in the year, the army arrested another senior shaykh and his son at their home south of Mosul, and there were complaints that the latter were beaten and insulted in the process. "Itiqal ra'is tajammu asha'ir Al-Hadba' janub Al-Mawsil" [The Arrest of a Tribal Grouping in Al-Hadba', South of Mosul], Wikalat Al-Akhbar Al-Iraqiya, 27 December 2010, http://al-iraqnews.info/

new/security-news/41028.html?print.

141. Rami Nuri, "Asharat al-mutaqalin fi Al-Mawsil baynhum tujjar wa-anasir fi al-shurta" [Dozens Arrested in Mosul, Including Merchants and Members of the Police], *Al-Hayat*, 12 October 2009, http://international.daralhayat.com/print/65041.

142. Qasim Al-Kabi, "Awdat 'Zarqawi al-shia' min Iran tuthir al-rub fi Baghdad" [The Return of the "Shia Zarqawi" from Iran Sparks Terror in Baghdad], *Al-Sharq Al-Awsat*, 21 August 2010, www.aawsat.com/print.asp?did=583349&issueno=11589.

143. Hisham Al-Rikabi, "Hamad Al-Hayis: sanuharib Al-Qaida idha hawalat al-awda ila Al-Anbar" [Hamad Al-Hayis: We Will Fight Al-Qaida If It Tries to Return to Al-Anbar], *Al-Mada*, 8 August 2010, http://almadapaper.net.

144. "Majlis Salah Al-Din yattahim quwwat hukumiya bi-qasd itiqal rijal amal wa-ayan li-ibtizazhim" [The Salah Al-Din Council Accuses Government Forces of Intending to Arrest Businessmen and Notables with the Intent of Extorting Money], *Al-Sumarriya News*, 9 January 2011, www.sumarianews.com/ar/15786/print-article.htm.

145. Sam Dagher, "Report Details Torture at Secret Baghdad Prison," *New York Times*, 27 April 2010, www.nytimes.com; and Jane Arraf, "Report: Secret Prison in Iraq Raises Fresh Concerns over Torture," *Christian Science Monitor*, 1 February 2011, .

146. "'Abriya' qadimun min wara' al-qudban; Al-Mutatarrifun al-judad yaduqqun nawaqis al-khatar fi Diyala" [The Innocent Coming Out from behind Bars; The New Extremists Setting Off Alarm Bells in Diyala], *Al-Sabah Al-Jadid*, 18 February 2011, www.newsabah.com.

147. As one local official noted sarcastically about a recently arrested Sahwa leader, "He forgot that the Americans are going to leave one day. It's like a fiancee and her groom. Before he marries her, he promises her a lot. After the marriage, he forgets everything. The Americans have pulled the carpet from under his feet." Shadid, "An Iraqi."

148. Ali Latif, "Al-Sahwat samita wa-majlis Al-Falluja yulin al-hidad ala al-qatla fi al-ghara al-amrikiya al-mushtaraka muhajamatan mabna muhafazhat Baghdad wa-masra 10

junud fi Al-Mawsil" [The Sahwa Is Silent, While the Baghdad Province Council Proclaims Mourning, and Ten Troops Die in Mosul], *Al-Zaman*, 15 September 2010, hereafter Latif, "Al-Sahwat samita," www.azzaman.com.

149. "Al-Sahwa takhsha intiqam." As of 2011, U.S. forces were still participating in some combined combat operations with Iraqi forces, such at the combined raid in Diyala to arrest Al-Qaida operatives. "Quwwa iraqiya-amrikiya tataqil athnayn min tanzhim Al-Qaida bi-inzal jawwi shimal Baquba" [An Iraqi-U.S. Force Arrests Two Al-Qaida [Members] in an Airborne Operation North of Baquba], *Al-Sumarriya News*, 31 January 2011, www.sumarianews.com/ar/16742/print-article.htm.

150. Shaykh Daydan Abd Allah quoted in "Qiyadi fi al-sahwa: Al-Jaysh al-amiriki akhla al-saha li'l-Qaida li-ta'khudh tha'rha min al-sahwa" [A Leader in the Sahwa: The American Army Cleared the Field for Al-Qaida to Take Its Revenge against the Sahwa], *Al-Jiwar*, 5 April 2010, www.aljewar.org/news-23213.aspx.

151. Ayman Al-Zawahiri, "Al-Azhar arin al-usud; Hiwar ma al-shaykh Ayman Al-Zawahiri 1429" [Al-Azhar Is a Den of Lions: An Interview with Shaykh Ayman Al-Zawahiri 1429], 1429/2008, www.tawhed.ws/pr?i=7828.

152. Quoted in "Al-Sahwat takhsha al-intiqam bad rahil al-quwwat al-amirikiya" [The Sahwa Fears Revenge after U.S. Forces Depart], *Al-Sharq Al-Awsat*, 22 August 2010, www.aawsat.com/print.asp?did=583411&issueno=11590.

153. "Al-Sahwa takhsha."

154. Khulud Al-Amiri, "Al-Sahwa' tutalib al-hukuma bi-iadat silahha" ["Al-Sahwa Requests the Government to Give Back Its Arms], *Al-Hayat*, 18 June 2010, http://international.daralhayat.com/print/153745.

155. According to internal orders that the Sahwa leaders had seen. "Talimat jadida tamna sahwat Diyala min tanfidh itiqalat wa-haml silah kharij niqatha al-amniya" [New Guidance Prohibits the Diyala Sahwa from Carrying Out Arrests and from Bearing Arms Outside Security Points], *Al-Rafidayn*, 29 July 2010, www.alrafidayn.com.

Al-Qaida, the Tribes, and the Government

156. According to Muhammad Al-Askari, the Public Relations Adviser in the Iraqi Ministry of Defense. Al-Shayib, "Ma wara' al-khabar."

157. According to Samir Al-Tamimi, general adviser to the Sahwa. Ibid.

158. "Quwwat al-sahwa fi muhafazhat Diyala tuhaddid bi'l-takhalli an mas'uliyatha al-amniya" [The Sahwa Forces in Diyala Province Threaten to Withdraw from Their Security Responsibilities] ,*Al-Rafidayn*, 6 June 2010, www.alrafidayn.com.

159. Ibid.

160. Muhammad Al-Sardani, "Azmat al-sahwat fi Al-Iraq . . . Sahwat Diyala tantazhir tajdid al-tarakhis" [The Sahwa Crisis in Iraq . . . The Diyala Sahwa Awaits the Renewal of the Permits], *Al-Usbuiya* (Baghdad), 8 June 2010, www.theiraqweekly.com/inp/view_printer.asp?ID=11062&AUTHOR.

161. "Ashirat Albu Alwan tutalib bi-fath tahqiq bi-maqtal ahad shuyukhha" [The Albu Alwan Tribe Demands That an Investigation Be Opened into the Death of One of Its Shaykhs], Shabakat Akhbar Al-Iraq, 20 September 2010, www.Shabakat Akhbar Al-Iraq.

162. "Sahwat Diyala tutalib bi-idam umara' Al-Qaida al-mutaqalin wa-muwatinun yadun li-tatbiq 'hukm Saddam'" [The Diyala Sahwa Demands the Execution of Imprisoned Al-Qaida Commanders and Citizens Call for the Application of Saddam's Law], *Al-Sumarriya News*, 16 September 2010, www.sumarianews.com/ar/11286/print-article.htm.

163. "Mustashar al-sahwat: hasalna ala muwafaqa ala ratib wa-himaya li-qadatna" [Sahwa Adviser: We Reached an Agreement on Salaries and Protection for Our Commanders], *Al-Sabah Al-Jadid*, 5 May 2010, www.newsabah.com.

CHAPTER 11: THE EVOLVING TRIBAL ENVIRONMENT

1. Typically, in the keynote address at the general conference of tribal shaykhs of Iraq, Shaykh Abbas Bayat Mahmud Al-Ubaydi noted his opposition to partition in tribal terms: "The partition of Iraq is a red line . . . it is not possible to leave this tribal tent, since it is of superior weaving and a tribal symphony." Likewise, the representative of the

tribes of the mostly Shia South, Shaykh Abbud Wahid Al-Isawi, linked the tribal and national concepts: "The tribal fabric is important and there must be consideration for the tribe, for the latter is the basis for national unity," "Shuyukh asha'ir yadun ila al-wahda al-wataniya wa-tahsin wad al-asha'ir" [Tribal Shaykhs Call for National Unity and for an Improvement in the Status of the Tribes], *Al-Adala*, 8 March 2009, www.aladalanews.net/index_lite.php?show=news&action=print&id=49123.

2. Quoted in Muhannad Muhammad Ali, "Sunnat Baghdad: Insha' iqlim khass bina hulm yajib tahqiquh … wa-haqq dusturi" [The Sunnis of Baghdad: The Creation of a Special Canton for Us Is a Dream Which Must Be Fulfilled … And It Is a Constitutional Right], Al-Wikala Al-Ikhbariya li'l-Anba', 13 December 2010, www.ikhnews.com/popup.php?action=printnews&id=5484.

3. Quoted in "Barlamaniyun yulawwihun bi-ilan iqlim Al-Anbar fi hal istamarrat al-hukuma bi-hamlat al-itiqalat al-ashwa'iya" [Parliamentarians Signal the Proclamation of an Al-Anbar Canton If the Government Continues Its Campaign of Arbitrary Arrests], Shabakat Akhbar Al-Iraq, 6 February 2011, www.Shabakat Akhbar Al-Iraq.

4. "Masadir: Tujjar iraqiyun yudirun min Amman tashkil iqlim sunni" [Sources: Iraqi Businessmen Set in Motion from Amman the Creation of a Sunni Canton], *Al-Rafidayn*, 29 January 2011, www.alrafidayn.com.

5. Hafizh Al-Jiburi quoted in "Shuyukh asha'ir tutalib bi'l-ifraj an mas'ul mahalli wa-qiyadi fi al-sahwa" [The Tribal Shaykhs Demand That a Local Official and a Sahwa Leader Be Set Free], *Al-Sabah Al-Jadid*, 19 May 2009, www.newsabah.com/tpl?IdLanguage=17&NrIssue=1431&NrSection=21&NrArticle=27890.

6. "Qabilat Zawba al-iraqiya tattahim hukumat Al-Maliki bi-intihak huquq al-insan wa-tathir irqi wa-ibada jamaiya" [The Iraqi Zawba Confederation Accuses the Maliki Government of Violating Human Rights and of Ethnic Cleansing and Mass Extermination], *Babil*, 19 December 2009, www.babil.info/printVersion.php?mid=23234.

7. "Abu Risha: Ala al-mutalibin bi'l-Nakhib al-mutalaba bi'l-aradi al-iraqiya allati istahwadhat alayha Iran" [Abu Risha: Those Who Are Demanding Al-Nakhib Must Demand

the Iraqi Lands Which Iran Seized], Ur News Agency, 27 November 2010, www.ura-gency.net/index.php?aa=news&id22=14319.

8. "Al-Watani wa'l-iraqiya yarfudan dawat Abu Risha ila insha' 'iqlim ghayr ta'ifi' yadumm Al-Anbar wa-Karbala'" [Al-Watani and Al-Iraqiyya [Parties] Reject Abu Risha's Call for the Creation of a "Nonsectarian Canton" Composed of Al-Anbar and Karbala], *Marsad Al-Iraq* (Baghdad), 26 January 2011, www.marsadiraq.com. One Iraqi journalist taxed such separatist proposals as originating from "their corrupt tribal mentality." Abd Allah Al-Anbari, "Busulat al-hara'iq al-qadima fi Al-Iraq" [The Compass toward the Impending Conflagrations in Iraq], Shabakat Akhbar Al-Iraq, 30 January 2011, www.Shabakat Akhbar Al-Iraq.

9. Hamza Mustafa, "Shuyukh fi Al-Anbar yuhaddidun bi-qat yad man yufakkir bi-iqamat iqlim" [Shaykhs in Al-Anbar Warn They Will Cut the Hand of Anyone Thinking about Setting Up a Canton], *Al-Sharq Al-Awsat*, 3 February 2011, www.aawsat.com/print.asp?did=606647&issueno=11755; and "Haraka siyasiya fi Ninawa tatabir mashari al-aqalim masrahiya hadafha taqsim Al-Iraq" [A Political Movement in Ninawa Considers Plans for Cantons a Charade Whose Goal is the Partitioning of Iraq], *Al-Sumarriya News*, 12 July 2011, www.alsumarianews.com/ar/24776/print-article.html.

10. Abu Hawra' Al-Tamimi, "Khutuwat al-farmata al-amniya" [Steps for Security Planning], part 1, Shabakat Akhbar Al-Iraq, 4 January 2011, www.Shabakat Akhbar Al-Iraq.

11. "Al-Falluja tushayyi Mushtaq wa'l-Hayis yadu li'l-hudu wa-yu'akkid 'Arkhas al-bashar ind al-hukuma ahl Al-Anbar'" [Falluja Buries Mushtaq and Al-Hayis Calls for Calm and Asserts That "For the Government, the Cheapest Lives Are Those of the People of Al-Anbar"], *Al-Rafidayn*, 20 May 2010, www.alrafidayn.com.

12. Interview of 12 October 2010. Information from my wife, Nidhal, who served for over two years as an interpreter and cultural affairs adviser in various parts of Iraq with the U.S. Army, hereafter interview with author's wife, 12 October 2010.

13. Khulud Al-Amiri, "Shaykh asha'ir Al-Dulaym yu'akkid taswiyat khilafatih ma qa'imat Al-Maliki" [The Shaykh of the Dulaym Tribes Confirms That His Differences with Al-

Maliki's Party Have Been Resolved], *Al-Hayat*, 28 November 2009, http://international.daralhayat.com/print/80855.

14. Ned Parker and Saif Rasheed, "In Anbar, Sunni Rivalries Surface," *Los Angeles Times*, 21 January 2008, hereafter Parker and Rasheed, "In Anbar," www.latimes.com/news/nationworld/world/la-fg-iraq21jan21,0,3570350,print.story.

15. Dagher, "Tribal Rivalries."

16. Michael Gisick, "U.S. Tries to Bridge Gap between Iraqi Rivals," *Stars and Stripes*, 19 February 2008, www.stripes.com/news/u-s-tries-to-bridge-gap-between-iraqi-rivals-1.75199.

17. "Qatla wa-jarha bi'l-asharat fi niza asha'iri bi-muhafazhat Al-Anbar gharb Al-Iraq" [Dozens of Dead and Wounded in a Tribal Dispute in Al-Anbar Province in Western Iraq], *Kuttab Min Ajl Al-Hurriya* (Baghdad), 20 April 2010, www.iwffo.org.

18. Ali Hatim yatahaddath hawl indimamih bi'l-Maliki wa-yaqul: Intikhabat Al-Iraq satakun asha'iriya hadhih al-marra" [Ali Hatim Discusses His Joining Al-Maliki and Says: The Iraqi Elections This Time Will Be Tribal], *Al-Jiwar*, 12 October 2009, www.aljewar.org/news.aspx?id=17766.

19. Khulud Al-Amiri, "Humma muharabat Al-Qaida tantaqil ila muhafazhat Karkuk" [The Focus of the Fight against Al-Qaida Shifts to the Province of Kirkuk], *Al-Hayat*, 22 June 2007, hereafter Al-Amiri, "Humma," http://international.daralhayat.com/print/164706/archive.

20. "Maqtal saba."

21. Al-Amiri, "Humma."

22. "Mu'tamar asha'iri li-munaqashat daf al-waqi al-khadami fi Al-Anbar" [Tribal Conference to Discuss the Inadequacy of Current Services in Al-Anbar], Wikalat al-Akhbar Al-Iraqiya (Baghdad), 22 June 2010, http://al-iraqnews.net/new/province-news/14017.hyml?print.

23. "Asbab al-qatia."

24. Sam Dagher, "Rift Threatens U.S. Antidote to Al Qaeda in Iraq," *Christian Science Monitor*, 13 February 2008, hereafter Dagher, "Rift," www.csmonitor.com/layout/set/print/content/view/print/220853.

25. According to the testimony of a former Al-Qaida fighter, Ala' Hasan, "Ishtibakat bayn ashiratayn fi Al-Qa'im tuqi asharat al-qatla wa'l-jarha" [Clashes between Two Tribes in Al-Qa'im Claim Dozens of Killed and Wounded], *Al-Watan*, 28 August 2005, www.alwatan.com.sa/daily/2005-08-28/first_page/first_page04.htm.

26. "Al-Sahwa: A'ilat anasir Al-Qaida tuqadina" [The Sahwa: The Families of Al-Qaida Members Are Taking Us to Court], *Al-Sharq Al-Awsat*, 20 May 2009, www.aawsat.com/print.asp?did=580572&issueno=11131. Similar concerns were voiced by shaykhs in other provinces. "Mu'tamar li-tabdid shukuk al-sahwat hiyal al-hukuma" [A Conference to Allay the Sahwa's Doubts Vis-a-Vis the Government], *Al-Sabah Al-Jadid*, 19 May 2009, www.newsabah.com.

27. "Al-Faqr wa'l-jahl."

28. "Muhafizh Ninawa yu'akkid: Al-Asha'ir hiya al-umq al-istiratiji li-bina' al-wad al-amni" [The Governor of Ninawa Emphasizes: The Tribes Are the Strategic Depth to Develop the Security Situation], *Al-Rafidayn*, 11 December 2006, www.alrafidayn.com,

29. Shaykh Ahmad Abu Risha, interview by Suhayr Al-Qaysi, "Min Al-Iraq: ma al-shaykh Ahmad Abu Risha" [From Iraq: With Shaykh Ahmad Abu Risha], Al-Arabiya TV, 23 November 2007, www.alarabiya.net/save_print.php?print=1&cont_id=42097.

30. Tahsin Sabbar, "Mu'tamar musalaha wataniya li-qaba'il wa-asha'ir muhafazhat Diyala tunazhzhimuh qiyadat shurtatha" [National Reconciliation Meeting for the Tribal Confederations and Tribes of Diyala Province Organized by the Police Leadership], Wikalat Al-Akhbar Al-Iraqiya, 20 October 2010, http://al-iraqnews.net/new/province-new/30953.html?print. The motto for the meeting, intended to appeal to the shaykhs' vanity, was "The shaykhs and leaders of the tribes are a basic element to bring about social re-

form and to secure the pillars of stability."

31. Ibid.

32. Brigadier General David G. Riest, interview in McWilliams and Wheeler, *Al-Anbar Awakening, Vol. 1*, 156-157.

33. Raghavan, "A New Breed."

34. Based on Colonel Sean MacFarland's experience. Jim Michaels, "Behind Success in Ramadi an Army Colonel's Gamble," *USA Today*, 1 May 2007, www.usatoday.com/cleanprint/?1291073743841. As one Marine liaison officer noted of one of these new shaykhs, the military was "supporting his leadership." Raghavan, "A New Breed."

35. Dagher, "Tribal Rivalries."

36. Major General John F. Kelly, interview in McWilliams and Wheeler, *Al-Anbar Awakening, Vol. 1*, 243.

37. Jim Michaels, "U.S. Gamble on Sheiks Is Paying Off—So Far; Military's Alliances with Tribes in Iraq Foster Peace," *USA Today*, 27 December 2007, A1.

38. Dagher, "Tribal Rivalries,"

39. Interview in "Dawr shuyukh al-asha'ir fi tahqiq al-istiqrar" [The Role of the Tribal Shaykhs in Creating Stability], Baghdad Satellite TV, 25 August 2009, www.baghdadch.tv/channel_series.php?id=271&print=1.

40. Ned Parker, "Al Qaeda in Iraq Rises Again," *Los Angeles Times*, 13 September 2010, www.latimes.com/news/nationworld/world/la-fg-iraq-qaeda-20100913,0,2035120.story.

41. Ibid.

42. Interview with author's wife, 12 October 2010

43. "Muntasibu sahwat Karbala' yuqadun mudirhum li-adam tasallumhim al-rawatib" [The Personnel of the Karbala Sahwa Sue Their Boss Because They Have Not Been Re-

ceiving Their Salaries], *Aswat Al-Iraq*, 25 March 2009, http://ar.aswataliraq.info.

44. "Taqrir: Intizham al-rawatib aw al-dimj ahamm matalib sahwat Diyala" [Report: Regularizing Salaries or Integration Are the Most Important Demands by the Diyala Sahwa], Wikalat Al-Iraq Baytna, 16 June 2010, http://iraq-beituna.net//show.php?sho=18039.

45. "Qa'id sabiq li'l-sahwat yantaqid ihmal al-hukuma laha wa-mas'ul fi sahwat Al-Iraq yushir ila tahawwulha li-kiyan siyasi" [A Former Commander of the Sahwa Criticizes the Government's Neglect of the Latter, While an Official of the Iraq Sahwa Indicates That It Has Been Transformed into a Political Body], *Aswat Al-Iraq*, 14 February 2010, http://ar.aswataliraq.info.

46. "Al-Qaida tutliq hamla li-iqna rijal al-sahwa al-mutadhammirin bi'l-awda ilayha" [Al-Qaida Launches a Campaign to Convince Disgruntled Members of the Sahwa to Rejoin It], *Al-Sharq Al-Awsat*, 7 August 2010, www.aawsat.com/print.asp?did=580572&issueno=11575.

47. "Al-Hukuma al-mahalliya fi Al-Rifai tatarid ala taklif shuyukh al-asha'ir bi-tayin hurras amniyyin li'l-sharikat al-naftiya" [The Local Government in Al-Rifai Balks at Authorizing Tribal Shaykhs to Appoint Security Guards for the Oil Companies], *Al-Muwatin*, 10 May 2010, www.almowatennews.com/news_view_9699.html. Tribes have considerable clout to extort such jobs, including the tactic of threatening to prevent the operation of foreign oil companies unless the latter hires unemployed workers from the tribes. "Ala khalfiyat mutalabat al-asha'ir bi-tawzhif abna'iha mushkila tuhaddid al-sharikat al-naftiya al-amila fi al-janub" [Behind the Tribes' Demands That Their People Be Hired Is the Problem of Threatening the Oil Companies Operating in the South], *Al-Sabah Al-Jadid*, 28 September 2010, www.newsabah.com. The oil police hires local tribesmen specifically in the hope that that will prevent tribal attacks. "Shurtat al-naft: La namlik ta'irat istikshaf wa-yanqusna 10 alaf rajul" [The Oil Police: We Do Not Have Observation Aircraft and We Are Short 10,000 Men], *Al-Alam*, 25 August 2010, www.alaalem.com/index.php?aa=new&id22=15748.

48. "Hard to Get Out: Foreign Oil Companies Are Still Finding Iraq a Tough Place to Do Business," *The Economist*, 19 August 2010, www.economist.com/node/16846742/print.

49. Ernesto London, "Iraq's Foreign Laborers: Disillusioned and Disliked," *Washington Post*, 15 June 2009, A08; and "Al-Imala al-wafida tuzahim al-iraqiyin ala furas al-amal fi khidamm al-bitala al-mutafashshiya" [Imported Labor Competes with Iraqis for Work Opportunities in the Midst of Rampant Unemployment], Shabakat Al-Naba' Al-Malumatiya, 10 September 2009, www.annabaa.org/nbanews/2009/09/074.htm.

50. Muhammad Hamid Al-Sawwaf, "Sunnat Al-Iraq wa-tumuh al-awda ila al-sulta; Al-Qawa'im al-alamaniya taktasih Al-Mawsil wa-Salah Al-Din wa'l-Anbar" [Iraq's Sunnis and Their Desire to Return to Power; The Secular Parties Sweep Mosul, Salah Al-Din, and Al-Anbar], Shabakat Al-Naba' Al-Malumatiya, 10 March 2010, www.annabaa.org/nbanews/2010/03/134.htm.

Chapter 12: Al-Qaida's Own Carrot-and-Stick Approach

1. In his speech "Imnauhum la taqtuluhum" [Restrain Them, Do Not Kill Them], 22 March 2010, www.shamikh1.net/vb/showthread.php?t=58348.

2. Even while he was still alive, Al-Zarqawi acknowledged that over 3000 foreign fighters had already been killed in Iraq, "Hiwar ma al-shaykh Abi Musab al-Zarqawi." Indicative of the change, when a number of senior Al-Qaida commanders were arrested in Al-Anbar in 2010, Shaykh Ahmad Abu Risha could claim that he knew most of them, their fathers, and their tribes. "Abu Risha: Tanzhim Al-Qaida intaha ka-fikr fi Al-Iraq" [Abu Risha: Al-Qaida as an Idea Is Finished in Iraq], *Aswat Al-Iraq*, 2 December 2010, hereafter "Abu Risha: Tanzhim Al-Qaida," http://ar.aswataliraq.info.

3. Martin Chulov, "Iraq Prison System Blamed for Big Rise in Al-Qaida Violence," *The Guardian*, 23 May 2010, www.guardian.co.uk/world/2010/may/23/iraq-prison-al-qaida-violence/print.

4. According to a former Al-Qaida commander and himself at one time a detainee in one

of the U.S.-run camps, Al-Mulla Nazhim Al-Jiburi, "Al-Mulla Al-Jiburi: Al-Qaida sanat qiyadat jadida fi Krubir" [Al-Mulla Al-Jiburi: Al-Qaida Developed New Leaders in Camp Cropper], *Al-Mada*, 10 February 2011, http://almadapaper.net.

5. Al-Masri, *Dawlat Al-Iraq*, 141.

6. "Tanzhim Al-Qaida bi'l-Iraq yumaththil tahdidan akbar bad tahawwulha ila tanzhim mahalli" [The Al-Qaida Organization in Iraq Represents a Greater Threat after Its Transformation into a Local Organization], *Al-Usbuiya*, 27 October 2010, www.alesbuyia.com/inp/view_printer.asp?ID=19990&AUTHOR=. Of course, there are still some foreign commanders present, such as the Tunisian arrested in January 2011 who was in charge of operations against government employees in Baghdad. "Itiqal tunisi yudir amaliyat ightiyal muwazhzhafi al-dawla" [The Arrest of a Tunisian Directing the Assassination Operations against Government Employees], *Al-Sabah*, 8 January 2011, www.alsabaah.com/ArticlePrint.aspx?ID=606.

7. Abd Al-Wahhab, "Al-Majami."

8. "Al-Qaida bi-Diyala"; and "Al-Qaida tusdir fatawi tazwij aramil qatlaha min anasir al-sahwat" [Al-Qaida Issues Fatwas Promoting Marriage to the Widows of Its Members Who Had Been Part of the Sahwa], *Al-Sabah*, 19 June 2010, www.alsabah.com/tpl/print.tpl?IdLanguage=17&NrIssue=1745&NrSection=1&NrArticle=408880.

9. "Al-Faqr wa'l-jahl."

10. Thus a local interpreter working with U.S. forces was killed by his own son and nephew on the orders of an Al-Qaida-affiliated group in Samarra. "Maqtal mutarjim iraqi amal ma al-quwwat al-amrikiya ala yad ibnih wa-ibn akhih" [Iraqi Interpreter Working with U.S. Forces Killed by His Son and His Nephew], *Al-Rafidayn*, 18 June 2010, www.alrafidayn.com. On the other hand, a father from the Al-Anbaki tribe killed his young daughter when he learned that she was planning to conduct a suicide attack on behalf of Al-Qaida. "Al-Tafjirat wa'l-hajamat ma zalat tahduth bi-shakl yawmi fi Al-Iraq" [Explosions and Attacks Are Still Occurring on a Daily Basis in Iraq], *Babil*, 25 December 2010, www.babil.info/printVersion.php?mid=29270. In another case, a Sahwa fighter

was killed by his cousin in Al-Anbar. Parker and Rasheed, "In Anbar."

11. See *Hakadha intahat*, 9.

12. "Sira ala al-nufudh bayn Al-Sadr wa'l-munshaqqin anhu wa Al-Qaida tuhawil istiqtab Al-Jaysh al-islami" [Struggle for Power between Al-Sadr and the Dissidents, and Al-Qaida Tries to Recruit Al-Jaysh Al-Islami], *Al-Hayat*, 22 August 2010, hereafter "Sira ala al-nufudh," http://international.daralhayat.com/print/174471/archive. Usama Bin Ladin himself had suggested that such groups in Iraq "oust their hypocritical leaders and join the true mujahidin." Bin Ladin, "Al-Sabil li-ihbat."

13. "Qiyadat fi Al-Qaida tanjah fi shaqq Al-Jaysh al-islami" [Al-Qaida's Leaders Succeed in Splitting the Islamic Army], *Al-Hayat*, 8 September 2010, http://international.daralhayat.com/print/179899/archive; and Sahib, "Tanzhim Al-Qaida." For example, the Islamic Army had negotiated a deal with the U.S. in 2006-07; subsequently, a rift had developed between the Islamic Army's top leadership living abroad, who were accused of having embezzled money, and the younger cadres. Sahib, "Tanzhim Al-Qaida." Likewise, a communique from the Islamic State of Iraq of 26 April 2010, announced that "most of the members" of another resistance group, the Jaysh Abu Bakr, had joined the Islamic State of Iraq. "Dawlat Al-Iraq Al-Islamiya tulin an indimam Jaysh Abu Bakr Al-Siddiq al-salafi ila Dawlat Al-Islam" [The Islamic State of Iraq Announces That Salafi Jaysh Abu Bakr the Veracious One Has Joined the Islamic State], http://216.95.249.110/~leyothin/vb/showthread.php?t=21902.

14. Abu Hamza Al-Muhajir.

15. "Al-Hashimi yaltaqi wujaha' wa-shuyukh qaba'il talaban li-damhim fi muwajahat al-hukuma" [Al-Hashimi Meets with the Tribal Notables and Shaykhs Seeking Their Support in Confronting the Government], *Al-Hayat*, 25 September 2007, http://international.daralhayat.com/print/168237/archive.

16. Ibid.

17. Dagher, "Rift." Muqtada al-Sadr's Shia militia has also long operated in the province.

Richard A. Oppel, "Sectarian Rifts Foretell Pitfall of Iraqi Troops' Taking Control," *New York Times*, 12 November 2006, www.nytimes.com.

18. "Mas'ulun mahalliyun yuhdhirun min tafashshi al-asabat al-mintaqa wa-istighlal Al-Qaida li-mawarid al-naft fi Diyala" [Local Officials Warn against the Spread of Gangs in the Area and Al-Qaida's Exploitation of Oil Resources in Diyala], Ur News Agency, 29 July 2010, www.uragency.net/index.php?aa=news&id22=9847.

19. Al-Anbaki, "Shaykh ashira."

20. "Arab Karkuk yarfudun nashr quwwat amniya tadumm al-bishmarka" [The Arabs of Karkuk Reject the Deployment of Security Forces Which Include the Peshmerga], *Al-Sabah Al-Jadid*, 5 September 2009, www.newsabah.com.

21. "Asha'ir wa-wujaha' muhafazhat Ninawa yutalibun al-hukuma bi-mawqif hazim didd irhab al-milishiyat al-kurdiya" [The Tribes and Notables of Ninawa Province Demand the Government Take a Resolute Stand against the Terrorism by the Kurdish Militias], Wikalat Al-Akhbar Al-Iraqiya, 21 February 2010, www.iraq-ina.com/newactivities.php?tnid=47447.

22. For example, Abu Hamza Al-Muhajir. When Abu Umar Al-Baghdadi addressed the Iraqis, he said, " My people and my brothers, we are the Sunnis of Iraq." Al-Baghdadi, "Jarimat al-intikhabat."

23. Abu Hamza Al-Muhajir, "Tafrigh al-liqa'."

24. Al-Baghdadi, "Fa-Amma al-zabadu."

25. Nazhim Al-Jiburi, "Al-Mulla Nazhim min Al-Qaida."

26. "Qiyadi fi Al-Qaida: Qumt ma afrad majmuati bi-qatl wa-tahjir al-kathir wa'l-tamthil bi-juthathihim wa-kan yusajjal ala CD wa-nursilha ila umara' al-tanzhim li-nayl ridahum" [An Al-Qaida Leader: I and the Companions in My Unit Carried Out Killings, Expulsions, and the Mutilation of Bodies Against Many People and This Was Recorded on CDs Which We Would Send to the Organization's Commanders in Order to Get Their

Approval], Qanat Al-Furat Al-Fada'iya TV, 2 August 2010, http://alforattv.net/index.php?show=news&action=print&id=47254.

27. "Al-Dakhiliya: Al-Maliki yuid al-nazhar bi-malaff al-sahwat" [Ministry of the Interior: Al-Maliki to Review the Sahwa Account], *Al-Mada*, 23 January 2011, http://almadapaper.net/popup.php?action=printnews&id=33855.

28. According to an Iraqi defense expert, Ali Al-Haydari, "Munshaqq an Al-Qaida yakshif an indimam shia li'l-tanzhim wa-khabir yatabir tahalufah al-jadid akhtar min sabiqih" [Al-Qaida Dissident Reveals Shia Joining the Organization and an Expert Considers the New Alliance More Dangerous Than the Previous One], *Al-Sumarriya News*, 14 August 2010, www.alsumarianews.com/ar/9978/print-article.html.

29. Abu Hamza Al-Muhajir.

30. Ibid. Earlier, Al-Qaida in Iraq had sought to deflect accusations of killing innocent people by arguing that there was no proof, blaming agents who had infiltrated Al-Qaida, by casting doubt on whether such killers were actually from Al-Qaida, or labeling such killings as unauthorized individual acts, as in Abu Fahd, "Shubuhat," 36.

31. Abu Umar Al-Baghdadi, broadcast posthumously, "Ghazwat al-asir 2" [The Prisoner Raid 2], Ramadan 1431/September 2010, hereafter Al-Baghdadi, "Ghazwat al-asir 2," http://216.95.249.110/`leyothin/vb/showthread.php?p=54032.

32. Abu Hamza Al-Muhajir.

33. Al-Baghdadi, "Ghazwat al-asir 2."

34. Al-Jaza'iri, "Ma yajri fi Al-Jaza'ir."

35. Al-Jaza'iri, "Ma yajri fi Al-Jaza'ir."; "al-intarnit bi-hadaf adam istighlalha li-nashr al-afkar al-mutatarrifa" [The Diyala Council Calls for Monitoring Internet Cafes with the Intent of Preventing Their Misuse to Spread Extremist Ideas], *Al-Sumarriya News*, 1 April 2011, www.alsumarianews.com/ar/19536/print-article.html.

36. "Istinfar amni janubi Al-Mawsil wa-kitabat fi al-shawari tu'ayyid ma yusamma bi-

Dawlat Al-Iraq Al-Islamiya" [Security Alerts South of Mosul and Graffiti in the Streets in Support of the So-Called Islamic State of Iraq], *Al-Rafidayn*, 10 January 2011, www.alrafidayn.com.

37. "Liqa' sawti ma wazir al-harb bi-Dawlat Al-Iraq Al-Islamiya Abi Hamza Al-Muhajir" [Verbal Interview with Abu Hamza Al-Muhajir, Minister of War of the Islamic State of Iraq], *Qadaya Jihadiya*, Dhu al-qada 1429/November 2008, 25.

38. "Al-Qaida tutliq hamla li-iqna rijal al-sahwa al-mutadhammirin bi'l-awda ilayha" [Al-Qaida Launches a Campaign to Convince Disgruntled Members of the Sahwa to Rejoin It], *Al-Sharq Al-Awsat*, 7 August 2010, www.aawsat.com/print.asp?did=580572&issueno=11575.

39. Ibid.

40. Hadi Al-Anbaki, "Tashkil khalaya istikhbariya fi Diyala li-ifshal khutat Al-Qaida bi-shira' al-dhimam" [Creation of Intelligence Cells in Diyala to Abort Al-Qaida's Plans to Buy People], *Al-Sabah*, 7 August 2010, hereafter Al-Anbaki, "Tashkil khalaya," www.alsabah.com/paper.php?source=akbar&mlf=interpage&sid=106797.

41. "Sahwat muadiya."

42. Ibid.

43. Al-Anbaki, "Tashkil khalaya."

44. "Al-Qaida tabtazz ashab al-amal fi Al-Mawsil . . . wa'l-kull yadfa 'dun niqash'" [Al-Qaida Extorting Businessmen in Mosul . . . and Everyone Pays Up "Without Discussion"], *Al-Sharq Al-Awsat*, 8 September 2010, www.aawsat.com/print.asp?did=585808&issueno=11607; and "Mas'ul hukumi: Khamsa malayin dular shahriyan qimat ibtizaz tanzhim Al-Qaida li-ahali Al-Mawsil" [A Government Official: Five Million Dollars a Month Is in Extortion by Al-Qaida from the People of Mosul], *Al-Sabah*, 15 August 2010, www.alsabah.com/paper.php?source=akbar&mlf=copy&sid=107268. Other Iraqi press sources, on the other hand, reported that the majority of Al-Qaida funding in neighboring Diyala came from abroad. "Al-

Mas'ul al-mali li'l-Qaida fi Diyala yahrib bi 3 malayin dular" [Al-Qaida's Financial Officer in Diyala Absconds with 3 Million Dollars], *Al-Sabah Al-Jadid*, 7 September 2010, www.newsabah.com.

45. "Mas'ulun mahalliyun," and Wisam Al-Mulla, "Mudir amm shurtat al-naft: Masfa Bayji kan yushakkil tamwil kabir li-tanzhim Al-Qaida" [The General Director of the Oil Police: The Bayji Refinery Was a Major Source of Financing for Al-Qaida], *Mawsuat Al-Nahrayn* (Baghdad), 14 March 2010, http://nahrain.com/d/news/10/03/100313cb.htm.

46. "Majlis Diyala yu'akkid ann mahattat al-wuqud al-ahliya ahad masadir tamwil Al-Qaida" [The Diyala Council Confirms That the Public Gas Stations Are a Source of Al-Qaida's Financing], *Al-Sumarriya News*, 29 September 2010, www.alsumarianews.com/ar/11792/print-article.html. It is not possible to verify Al-Qaida's claims that it receives contributions from sympathizers in the army and security in Diyala, but that cannot be excluded. Ismail Alwan Al-Tamimi, "Ihbat mashru al-inqilab al-ahmar fi muhafazhat Diyala, nuqtat tahawwul fi al-ada' al-amni [Prevention of the Violent Coup Plot In Diyala Province; Turning Point in Security Performance], Wikalat Al-Iraq Baytna, 12 October 2010, http://iraq-beituna.net//show.php?sho=25141.

47. "Al-Qaida tatahawwal ila sharikat muqawalat fi al-Mawsil" [Al-Qaida Transforms Itself into Contracting Companies in Mosul], *Al-Mada*, 1 May 2011, http://almadapaper.net/popup.php?action=printnews&id=39801. Al-Qaida front companies reportedly even garnered the construction contracts for Mosul University. Ibid.

48. Ibid.

49. Nizar Hatim, "Qaba'il Al-Dulaym taksir al-hajiz al-ta'ifi wa-tahtakim li-hall nizaatha fi Al-Kufa" [The Dulaym Tribes Break the Sectarian Barrier and Seek a Legal Decision in Kufa to Solve Their Disputes], Ur News Agency, 19 December 2010, www.uragency.net/index.php?aa=news&id22=14989.

50. "Dabit amni kabir: Al-Qaida khattatat li-istiqtab al-sahwat bad inhiyar al-qawaid al-lati tastanid alayha" [A Senior Security Officer: Al-Qaida Plans to Recruit the Sahwa after the Foundations for Its Own Support Collapsed], Wikalat Al-Anba' Al-An (Bagh-

dad), 14 July 2010, http://alanews.org/news.php?action=view&id=921. At times, Al-Qaida sought to exploit family ties, as in the case of one shaykh who found his cousin, a member of Al-Qaida, asking him to rejoin the insurgency. Timothy Williams and Duraid Adnan, "Sunnis in Iraq Allied with U.S. Quitting to Rejoin Rebels," *New York Times*, 16 October 2010, www.nytimes.com.

51. "Al-Qaida tutliq hamla li-iqna rijal al-sahwa al-mutadhammirin bi'l-awda ilayha" [Al-Qaida Launches a Campaign to Convince Disgruntled Members of the Sahwa to Rejoin It], *Al-Sharq Al-Awsat*, 7 August 2010, www.aawsat.com/print.asp?did=580572&issueno=11575.

52. Interview with author's wife, 12 October 2010

53. Muhammad Al-Tamimi, "Sahwat Diyala tatawad Al-Qaida tha'r wa-tutalib al-hukuma bi'l-silah" [The Sahwa of Diyala Threatens Al-Qaida with Revenge and Requests Arms from the Government], *Al-Hayat*, 29 August 2010, http://international.daralhayat.com/print/176634.

54. "Al-Qaida tatawaad."

55. "Manshurat fi Diyala tuharrid ala qatl al-sahwat" [Leaflets in Diyala Incite the Killing of Sahwa Personnel], Ur News Agency, 15 July 2010, www.uragency.net/index.php?aa=news&id22=9380.

56. "Musallahun majhulun yuhaddidun al-madaniyyin bi-mughadarat manazilhim fi Al-Yusufiya" [Unidentified Armed Men Threaten Civilians with Expulsion from Their Homes in Al-Yusufiya], Wikalat Anba' Al-Ilam Al-Iraqi (Baghdad), 14 October 2010, http://al-iraqnews.info/new/security-news/30009.html?print.

57. Interview with Abu Bakr Al-Qurayshi Al-Baghdadi, "Liqa' khass ma mujahidi wilayat Ninawa bi'l-dawla al-islamiya" [Special Interview with the Mujahidin of Ninawa Province in the Islamic State], *Sada Al-Jihad*, Safar 1429/February-March 2008, 15.

58. Abu Hamza Al-Muhajir.

59. "Mughadara jamaiya li-qiyadiyin fi sahwat Abu Ghurayyib ithr sahb silah himayathim wa-tahdidat Al-Qaida" [The Mass Departure of Commanders from the Abu Ghraib Sahwa in the Wake of the Withdrawal of their Bodyguards' Weapons and the Threats from Al-Qaida], *Al-Sumarriya News*, 22 November 2010, hereafter "Mughadara jamaiya," www.sumarianews.com/ar/13898/print-article.htm.

60. "Al-Iraq: asha'ir Diyala tatahhad bi-tathir al-muhafazha min al-bua'r al-irhabiya" [Iraq: The Tribes of Diyala Commit Themselves to Clear the Province of the Terrorist Centers], *Al-Sabah*, 19 September 2010, www.alsabah.com/paper.php?source=akbar&mlf=interpage&sid=108659.

61. "Al-Qaida bi-Diyala."

62. Al-Fayha' TV (Baghdad), 16 December 2010, www.alfayhaa.tv/news/govnews/47527.html.

63. *Khutta istiratijiya*, 36-37.

64. According to a 2011 Ministry of the Interior report commissioned by Prime Minister Al-Maliki, in fact, the majority of recent attacks in Baghdad had targeted senior interrogators in the ministry. "Al-Dakhiliya tu'akkid ann aghlab amaliyat al-ightiyal fi Baghdad tastahdif dubbat al-tahqiq al-kibar" [The Ministry of the Interior Confirms That Most of the Assassination Operations in Baghdad Target Senior Interrogators], Radio Nawa, 9 January 2011, http://radionawa.com/Ar/NewsDetailIN.aspx?id=47673&Link ID=151. Some 240 Ministry of the Interior intelligence personnel alone have been killed in this manner. "Maqtal 240 dabit wa-muntasib li-istikhbarat al-dakhiliya bi-kawatim" [The Killing of 240 Officers and Personnel from the Ministry of Interior Intelligence by Silencers], Ur News Agency, 11 January 2011, www.uragency.net/index.php?aa=news&id22=15717.

65. "Marsad huquqi: 4561 qatil wa-12749 jarih bi-amal unf khilal 2010" [Human Rights Group: 4561 Dead and 12749 Wounded As a Result of Violence in 2010], *Aswat Al-Iraq*, 1 January 2011, http://ar.aswataliraq.info/wp-content/themes/aswat/print.php?p=268193. These figures compare favorably with the worst year, 2006, when an estimated 24,000

Iraqis died, *Iraq Body Count Project*, *Iraq Body Count Project*, www.iraqbodycount.org/database.

66. "Masadir amniya: Tanzhim Al-Qaida aad hukumat ma yuraf bi-Dawlat Al-Iraq Al-Islamiya bad maqtal Al-Baghdadi wa'l-Masri" [Security Sources: Al-Qaida Reorganizes the Government of What Is Known as the Islamic State of Iraq Following the Death of Al-Baghdadi and Al-Masri], Qanat Al-Furat Al-Fada'iya TV, 28 April 2010, http://alforattv.net/index.php?show=news&action=print&id=44792. These numbers are probably inflated. U.S. estimates are lower, and Leon Panetta in his confirmation hearings for secretary of defense offered a figure of 1500. "Panetta: Iraq Will Ask for Some US Troops to Stay," MSNBC, 9 June 2011, www.msnbc.com/id/43339609/ns/politics. However, the latter total may be low, given the high number of arrests on almost a daily basis reported by the Iraqi media, which would mean an almost complete depletion of Al-Qaida operatives within a short time if the 1500 figure were accurate.

67. "Abu Risha: Tanzhim Al-Qaida."

68. Abd Al-Karim quoted in "Al-Halqa al-thalitha" [The Third Episode], Baghdad Satellite TV, 10 April 2010, www.baghdadch.tv/channel_series.php?id=1648. The anchor and callers into the program raised numerous instances of similar grievances against the Iraqi army elsewhere, but Abd Al-Karim instead blamed such incidents on the tribes themselves. Ibid.

69. "Ahali Al-Azhamiya li'l-*Sharq Al-Awsat*: Al-Qaida tatarakkaz fi Shari' Al-Akhtal... wa tastaghill al-atilin" [The Inhabitants of Al-Azamiya to *Al-Sharq Al-Awsat*: Al-Qaida Is Concentrated in Al-Akhtal Street... and Is Taking Advantage of the Unemployed], *Al-Sharq Al-Awsat*, 1 August 2010, www.aawsat.com/print.asp?did=580572&issueno=11569.

70. Sahib, "Tanzhim Al-Qaida." Shaykh al-Tamimi, in fact, claimed that, thanks to its ability to develop local intelligence, a Sahwa company was more effective than an army brigade. Ibid.

71. Interview with Staff Major General Abd Al-Husayn Al-Shammari by Da'ud Al-

Saidi, "Qa'id shurtat Diyala al-liwa' al-rukn Abd Al-Husayn Al-Shammari: Majlis muhafazhat Diyala dahiyat siraat siyasiya" [Diyala's Police Chief Staff Major General Abd Al-Husayn Al-Shammari: The Diyala Provincial Council Is the Victim of Political Struggles], Wikalat Al-Akhbar Al-Iraqiya, 2010 (no exact date provided), http://al-iraqnews.net/new/specific-palaver/30823.html?print.

72. "Barlamani: Tafjirat Baghdad tu'akkid daf al-juhd al-istikhbarati wa-ikhtiraq al-mu'assasat" [A Member of Parliament: The Baghdad Bombings Confirm the Ineffectiveness of the Intelligence Effort and That the Institutions Are Penetrated], *Aswat Al-Iraq*, 2 November 2009, http://ar.aswataliraq.info/printer.aspx?id=179155.

73. "Mas'ul anbari: Al-Jihaz al-amni mukhtaraq wa-infijarat al-yawm risalat tahdhir" [Al-Anbar Official: The Security Apparatus Is Penetrated and Today's Bombing Is a Warning], Ur News Agency, 27 December 2010, www.uragency.net/index.php?aa=news&id22=15250.

74. Latif, "Al-Sahwat samita."

75. "Al-Maliki yarfud matlab ahali Al-Falluja bi-sahb al-quwwat al-hukumiya min al-madina" [Al-Maliki Refuses the Demand by the People of Falluja to Withdraw Government Forces from the City], *Al-Rafidayn*, 1 March 2011, www.alrafidain.tv/SingleNews.aspx?6.

76. "Muwatinun: Al-Khuruqat." The Ministry of the Interior, in fact, has consolidated central control over the security apparatus in the provinces, as is illustrated by the fact that—according to a senior police officer in Salah Al-Din Province—the local police had to wait for orders from Baghdad before reacting when Al-Qaida seized the Provincial Council building, with the delay leading to loss of life. "Amaliyat Salah Al-Din intazharat muwafaqat al-dakhiliya ala iqtiham majlis al-muhafaza li-saa wa-nisf" [Salah Al-Din's Security Waited for the Ministry of the Interior's Approval for One and a Half Hour before Storming the Provincial Council], Radio Nawa, 2 April 2011, http://ar.radionawa.com/Detail.aspx?id=1804&LinkID=63&AspxAutoDetectCookieSupport=1.

77. "Al-Qaida tatahawwal."

78. Major General Qasim Ata quoted in "Ata: Amaliyat al-ightiyal al-akhira sababha ikhtiraq al-ajhiza al-amniya min qibal al-majami al-musallaha" [Ata: The Latest Assassination Operations Are Caused by the Penetration of the Security Establishment by the Armed Groups], *Al-Sumarriya News*, 2 January 2011, www.alsumarianews.com/ar/15895/print-article.html. Significantly, according to Adnan Al-Asadi, principal deputy minister of the Interior, many of these killings have also involved the use by Al-Qaida of police and military vehicles, weapons, and IDs. "Al-Asadi: Al-Ightiyalat al-akhira tatimm bi-wasitat istikhdam huwiyat wa-sayyarat wa-asliha tabia li-wizaratay al-dakhiliya wa-l'-difa [Al-Asadi: The Recent Assassinations Have Been Carried Out with Vehicles, Weapons, and IDs Belonging to the Ministries of the Interior and of Defense], Wikalat Khabar li'l-Anba', 9 January 2011, www.khabar.com/popup.php?action+printnews&id=12990.

79. Figures provided by Deputy Minister of the Interior for Police Affairs, Lieutenant General Aydan Khalid, in "Al-Dakhiliya al-iraqiya takshif mukhattan li'l-Qaida li-tafkhikh falatir al-sayyarat wa-ustiwanat al-ghaz [The Iraqi Ministry of the Interior Reveals an Al-Qaida Plot to Boobytrap Car Filters and Propane Gas Containers with Explosives], *Al-Arab Al-Yawm*, 7 February 2011, www.arabstoday.net/index.php?option=com_content&view=article&id=68606&catid=314&Itemid=111.

80. "Sahwat muadiya."

81. Nazhim Al-Jiburi by Majid Hamid, "Al-Mulla Nazhim min Al-Qaida."

82. Jawdat Kazhim and Yasin Muhammad Sidqi, "Qa'id fasil musallah yattahim jamaat tamil bi'ghita' asha'iri bi-tawatu' ma Al-Qaida" [The Commander of an Armed Unit Accuses Some Groups of Working under Tribal Cover in Collusion with Al-Qaida], *Al-Hayat*, 1 October 2007, http://international.daralhayat.com/print/168508/archive.

83. "Sahwat muadiya."

84. "Itiqal 14 shaykhs baynhum 8 min anasir al-sahwat shamal sharq Baquba" [The Arrest Northeast of Baquba of 14 Individuals, 8 of Whom Are Members of the Sahwa], *Al-Sumarriya News*, 19 April 2010, www.sumarianews.com/ar/5573/print-article.html.

85. Al-Anbaki, "Tashkil khalaya."

86. Al-Anbaki, "Itirafat amir." In some cases, Al-Qaida members are still in the organizations, as is said to be the case in Diyala. "Qal mas'ul majalis al-sahwat fi Diyala, Husayn Al-Mujammai, inn tashkilat al-sahwat fi Diyala la zalat ghayr mutahhara min anasir Al-Qaida wa-mukhtaraqa min qibal anasir amalat ma tanzhim Al-Qaida fi al-sabiq" [Husayn Al-Mujammai, an Official of the Sahwa Councils in Diyala Said That the Diyala Sahwa Units Are Still Not Cleansed of Al-Qaida Elements and That They Are Penetrated by Elements Who Worked with Al-Qaida in the Past], Wikalat Al-Iraq Baytna, 19 June 2010, http://iraq-beituna.net/show.php?sho=18336.

87. "Al-Qabd ala 12 matlub min tanzhim Al-Qaida baynhum qa'idan li'l-sahwa fi Al-Suwira" [The Arrest of 12 Wanted Men from the Al-Qaida Organization, Including Two Commanders of the Sahwa in Al-Suwira], *Al-Sabah*, 15 May 2009, www.alsabah.com/paper.php?source=akbar&mlf=interpage&sid=82850.

88. "Quwwa min al-jaysh tataqil qa'id sahwat Gharb Baghdad bi-tuhmat al-irhab" [An Army Force Arrests the Commander of the West Baghdad Sahwa on Charges of Terrorism], *Al-Rafidayn*, 31 March 2010, www.alrafidayn.com.

89. "Liwa' al-radd al-sari yataqil qa'id sahwat Jurf Al-Sakhr al-muntami li'l-Jaysh Al-Islami" [The Quick Reaction Brigade Arrests the Commander of the Jurf Al-Sakhr Sahwa as a Member of Al-Jaysh Al-Islami], Al-Fayha' TV, 12 January 2011, www.alfayhaa.tv/news/iraq/49496.html.

90. "Mughadara jamaiya."

91. Al-Anbaki, "Tashkil khalaya."

92. "Sira ala al-nufudh."

93. Timothy Williams and Duraid Adnan, "Sunnis in Iraq Allied with U.S. Quitting to Rejoin Rebels," *New York Times*, 16 October 2010, www.nytimes.com.

94. Interview with author's wife, 12 October 2010.

95. According to Shaykh Sad Al-Mazhar, "Ratib 4500 muqatil bi-Diyala tadur fi halqa mufragha wasat dawat li-tasrihhim" [The Salary of 4500 Fighters in Diyala Is Caught in a Vicious Circle Amid Calls for Their Disbandment], *Aswat Al-Iraq*, 21 August 2010, http://ar.aswataliraq.info/wp-content/themes/aswat/print.php?p=241690; and Al-Anbaki, "Tashkil khalaya."

96. "Al-Qaida fi Diyala."

97. "Ihbat 'inqilab ahmar' fi Diyala yastahdif al-muhafizh wa'l-qada al-amniyin wa-itaqal dubbat wahid al-mustasharin" [Thwarting of a Bloody Coup Which Targeted the Governor and Security Commanders, and the Arrest of One Adviser's Officers], *Al-Sumarriya News*, 4 October 2010, www.alsumarianews.com/ar/11970/print-article.html; and "Itiqal nahw 70% min mukhattiti 'al-inqilab al-ahmar' fi Diyala" [The Arrest of about 70% of the Plotters of the "Bloody Coup" in Diyala], *Al-Sumarriya News*, 6 October 2010, www.alsumarianews.com/ar/12061/print-article.html.

98. Husayn Al-Baqubi, "Dabt hizamayn nasifayn dakhil al-muhafazha qubayl ijtima hukumi; Ifshal inqilab ahmar yastahdif kibar qadat Diyala" [Two Explosive Belts Seized inside the Province Center Just Before a Government Meeting: The Foiling of a Bloody Coup Attempt Targeting Diyala's Leaders], *Al-Zaman*, 5 October 2010, www.azzaman.com.

99. "Al-Maliki yadu asha'ir Al-Anbar ila adam al-tadakhkhul fi shu'un al-ajhiza al-amniya" [Al-Maliki Calls on the Tribes of Al-Anbar Not to Interfere in the Affairs of the Security Apparatus], *Al-Sumarriya News*, 2 October 2010, http://ww2.sumarianews.com/ar/11902/print-article.html.

100. "Insihab 8 nuwwab min al-iraqiya wa-tashkil al-kutla al-bayda' bi-ri'asat Al-Alawi" [The Withdrawal of Eight Parliamentarians from Al-Iraqiya and the Formation of the

White Bloc Headed by Al-Alawi], *Al-Dustur*, 7 March 2011, www.daraddustour.com.

101. Qutayba Al-Juburi, "Sanusahhih akhta' al-akharin alladhin hamalu al-mashru al-watani ka-shiarat za'ifa" [We Will Correct the Errors by the Others Who Promoted the National Program Only as False Slogans], Al-Ikhbariya, 31 March 2011, www.ikhnews.com/popup.php?action=printnews&id=10931.

102. "Al-Btikh yutalib bi-manh al-asha'ir dawr akbar fi al-malaff al-amni" [Al-Btikh Demands a Greater Role for the Tribes in the Security Sphere], *Nina* (Baghdad), 27 February 2011, www.ninanews.com/arabic/News_Print.asp?ar95_VQ=FFILHG; and Haydar Al-Hajj, "Jamal Al-Btikh: Al-Ghazw al-ajnabi qawwad al-dawla al-madaniya fi Al-Iraq" [Jamal Al-Btikh: The Foreign Invasion Smashed the Civil State in Iraq], *Al-Ra'y* (Kuwait), 22 May 2011, http://alraimedia.com/Alrai/Article.aspx?id=276832&searchText.

103. "Wizarat al-dawla li-shu'un al-asha'ir tuhdhir min muhawalat li-mundasin li-ishaat al-fawda khilal al-tazahurat" [The Ministry of State for Tribal Affairs Warns of Attempts by Discredited Elements to Spread Chaos by Means of the Demonstrations], Al-Fayha' TV, 23 February 2011, www.alfayhaa.tv/news/iraq/52568.html?print.

104. "Wazir al-dawla li-shu'un al-asha'ir yanfi naba' istiqaltih" [The Minister of State for Tribal Affairs Denies the News That He Is Resigning], Wikalat Anba' Al-Buratha, 26 February 2011, www.burathanews.com; and Jamal Al-Btikh, interview by Zayna Kazhim, "Jamal Al-Btikh: Namal li-iadat haykalat al-'asha'ir" [Jamal Al-Btikh: We Are Working to Rebuild the Tribal Structure], *Al-Usbuiya*, 26 June 2011, hereafter "Jamal Al-Btikh: Namal," www.alesbuyia.com/inp/view_printer.asp?ID=28772&AUTHOR=.

105. "Jamal Al-Btikh: Namal."

106. "Shuyukh Al-Anbar yattahimun qa'id amaliyat Al-Anbar bi-annahu halif li'l-Qaida" [The Shaykhs of Al-Anbar Accuse the Chief of Operations in Al-Anbar of Being an Al-Qaida Ally], Wikalat Anba' Baghdad Al-Dawliya, 8 June 2011, www.baghdadiabian.com/popup.php?action=printnews&id=6891.

107. "Hazhr li'l-tajawwul fi Al-Anbar wa-hamlat itiqalat wasia fi Al-Falluja' [Traffic Banned in Al-Anbar and a Campaign of Widespread Arrests in Falluja]; and "Asha'ir Al-Dulaym fi Al-Anbar: Ala Al-Maliki ikhraj quwwat al-jaysh min al-muhafazha" [The Dulaym Tribes in Al-Anbar: Al-Maliki Must Withdraw the Army from the Province], *Radio Dijla* (Baghdad), 28 February 2011, www.radiodijla.com.

108. For example, "Asha'ir Ninawa fi al-dhikra al-thamina li'l-ghazw al-amriki tarfud tamdid baqa'ihi" [On the Eighth Anniversary of the American Invasion, the Tribes of Ninawa Refuse Any Extension of Its Presence], *Aswat Al-Iraq*, 13 April 2011, http://ar.aswataliraq.info/printer.aspx?id=276154; "Shuyukh asha'ir Tikrit yunazhzhimun tazhahurat li'l-mutalaba bu-khuruj al-ihtilal wa-itlaq sarah al-abriya'" [The Tribal Shaykhs of Tikrit Organize a Demonstration to Demand the End of the Occupation and the Liberation of Those Who Are Innocent], Wikalat Anba' Baghdad Al-Dawliya (Baghdad), 23 April 2011, www.baghdadiaan.com/popup.php?action=printnews&id=5486; and "Al-Tazhahurat taumm Al-Anbar bad Al-Mawsil mutalibatan bi-rahil quwwat al-ihtilal wa'l-mufsidin" [Demonstrations Spread Throughout Al-Anbar Following Those in Mosul, Demanding That the Occupation Forces and the Corrupt Ones Leave], Ur News Agency, 29 April 2011, www.uragency.net/index.php?aa=news&id=1000.

109. "Tabligh ru'asa' al-asha'ir bi-shakl rasmi bi-iqaf sarf mabaligh al-isnad li-ayy shaykh ashira yusharik abna' ashiratih fi al-tazhahurat" [Informing Officially the Tribal Leaders That Support Money Would Be Cut Off to Any Shaykh Whose Fellow Tribesmen Participate in the Demonstrations], *Babil*, 8 March 2011, www.babil.info/printVersion.php?mid=30591.

110. "Quwwat khassa tataqil sitta min shuyukh asha'ir Ninawa" [Special Forces Arrest Six of Ninawa's Tribal Shaykhs], AK News (Kirkuk), 30 April 2011, www.aknews.com/ar/aknews/3/235882/?tpl=print.tpl; and "Al-Jaysh al-iraqi yahtajiz 30 min shuyukh asha'ir Salah Al-Din wa'l-Najaf" [The Iraqi Army Detains 30 Tribal Shaykhs from Salah Al-Din and Najaf], Al-Baghdadiya TV (Baghdad), 24 April 2011, www.albaghdadia.com. The shaykhs from Najaf had come to express solidarity with protesters in Mosul.

111. "Al-Asha'ir tubligh Al-Maliki: Ihanat al-shuyukh khatt ahmar" [The Tribes Let Al-Maliki Know: Insulting the Shaykhs Is a Red Line], Ur News Agency, 27 April 2011, www.uragency.net/index.php?aa=news&id22=926.

112. Staff Lieutenant General Hasan Karim Khadir press conference, "Qa'id amaliyat Al-Mawsil: Tujad jihat mashbuha bi-tawjihatha al-muadiya li'l-Iraq tuhawil harf masirat al-tazhahurat" [The Operations Commander in Mosul: There Are Suspicious Actors Hostile to Iraq Who Are Seeking to Pervert the Course of the Demonstrations], Al-Fayha' TV, 28 April 2011, www.alfayhaa.tv/news/iraq/56614.html.

Conclusions and Prospects

1. According to Sayf Al-Adl's handwritten memoirs, reproduced in Fu'ad Husayn, *Al-Zarqawi: Al-Jil al-thani li'l-Qaida* [*Al-Zarqawi: Al-Qaida's Second Generation*] (Beirut: Dar al-Khayyal, 2005), 123, 124.

2. One intellectual who was skeptical of the effect of tribalism on the prospects for democracy even blamed the United States for having reinvigorated tribalism as part of its counterinsurgency strategy. Hasan Nazhim, "Ijtithath al-asha'iriya" [Detribalization], *Al-Alam* (Baghdad), 24 January 2010, www.alaalem.com/index.php?aa=news&id22=1187.

3. Khalid Al-Qara Ghuli, "Al-Iqtaiya taud li-muhafazhat Al-Anbar min jadid" [Feudalism Returns Once Again to Al-Anbar Province], Sharikat Akhbar Al-Iraq, 12 March 2011, www.aliraqnews.com.

4. "Al-Sadriyun yatatallaun ila al-ajhiza al-amniya" [The Sadrists Are Eying the Security Establishment], *Al-Usbuiya*, 9 November 2010, www.alesbuyia.com/inp/view_printer.asp?ID=20318&AUTHOR=; and "Ali Al-Tamimi: Al-Tayyar al-sadri yarghrab bi-istlam al-sihha wa'l-tarbiya wa'l-iskan wa'l-naql" [Ali Al-Tamimi: The Sadri Movement Wants the Ministries of Health, Education, Housing, and Transportation], Wikalat Al-Anba' Al-An, 24 November 2010, http://alanews.org/news.php?action=view&id=2638. Iraqi press reports suggested that Al-Maliki had agreed to accept a significant number of fighters from the Shia militias

into the police. "Al-Maliki ya'mur bi-idkhal adad kabira min Jaysh Al-Mahdi wa-asa'ib Ahl Al-Haqq fi al-shurta" [Al-Maliki Orders the Inclusions of Large Numbers from the Jaysh Al-Mahdi and the Ahl Al-Haqq Gangs into the Police], Shabakat Akhbar Al-Iraq, 30April 2011, www.aliraqnews.com.

About the Author

Norman Cigar is director of regional studies and a Minerva Research Chair holder at the Marine Corps University, Quantico, Virginia. Before retiring, he was on the staff of the Marine Corps Command and Staff College and the Marine Corps School of Advanced Warfighting, where he taught military theory, strategy and policy, military history, and regional studies. Previously, he was a senior political-military analyst in the Pentagon, where he was responsible for the Middle East in the Office of the Army's Deputy Chief of Staff for Intelligence and supported the Secretary of the Army, the Chief of Staff of the Army, and Congress with intelligence. He also represented the Army on national-level intelligence issues with the interagency intelligence community. During the Gulf War, he was the Army's senior political-military intelligence staff officer on the Desert Shield/Desert Storm Task Force.

He is the author of numerous works on politics and security issues dealing with the Middle East and the Balkans, and has been a consultant at the International Criminal Tribunal for the former Yugoslavia at the Hague. He has also taught at the National Defense Intelligence College; was a visiting fellow at the Institute for Conflict Analysis & Resolution, George Mason University; and was a senior associate with the Public International Law and Policy Group. He is now focusing on the strategic and military aspects of radical Islamic movements and on proliferation issues.

Dr. Cigar holds a D. Phil. from Oxford (St. Antony's College) in Middle East History and Arabic; a Master of International Affairs degree from the School of International and Public Affairs, and a Certificate from the Middle East Institute, Columbia University; and a Master of Science of Strategic Intelligence degree from the National Defense Intelligence College. He has studied and traveled widely in the Middle East.

www.ingramcontent.com/pod-product-compliance
Lightning Source LLC
Chambersburg PA
CBHW080638170426
43200CB00015B/2877